DRESS, FASHION, AND TECHNOLOGY

Dress, Body, Culture

Series Editor: Joanne B. Eicher, *Regents' Professor, University of Minnesota*

Advisory Board:
Djurdja Bartlett, *London College of Fashion, University of the Arts*
Pamela Church-Gibson, *London College of Fashion, University of the Arts*
James Hall, *University of Illinois at Chicago*
Vicki Karaminas, *University of Technology, Sydney*
Gwen O'Neal, *University of North Carolina at Greensboro*
Ted Polhemus, *Curator, "Street Style" Exhibition, Victoria and Albert Museum*
Valerie Steele, *The Museum at the Fashion Institute of Technology*
Lou Taylor, *University of Brighton*
Karen Tranberg Hansen, *Northwestern University*
Ruth Barnes, *Ashmolean Museum, University of Oxford*

Books in this provocative series seek to articulate the connections between culture and dress which is defined here in its broadest possible sense as any modification or supplement to the body. Interdisciplinary in approach, the series highlights the dialogue between identity and dress, cosmetics, coiffure, and body alternations as manifested in practices as varied as plastic surgery, tattooing, and ritual scarification. The series aims, in particular, to analyze the meaning of dress in relation to popular culture and gender issues and will include works grounded in anthropology, sociology, history, art history, literature, and folklore.

ISSN: 1360-466X

Previously published in the Series

DRESS, FASHION, AND TECHNOLOGY

From Prehistory to the Present

PHYLLIS G. TORTORA

Bloomsbury Academic
An imprint of Bloomsbury Publishing Plc

B L O O M S B U R Y
LONDON • NEW DELHI • NEW YORK • SYDNEY

Bloomsbury Academic

An imprint of Bloomsbury Publishing Plc

50 Bedford Square	1385 Broadway
London	New York
WC1B 3DP	NY 10018
UK	USA

www.bloomsbury.com

BLOOMSBURY and the Diana logo are trademarks of Bloomsbury Publishing Plc

First published 2015

British Library Cataloguing-in-Publication Data

A catalogue record for this book is available from the British Library.

ISBN:	HB:	978-0-8578-5190-1
	PB:	978-0-8578-5191-8
	ePDF:	978-0-8578-5192-5
	ePub:	978-0-8578-5193-2

Library of Congress Cataloging-in-Publication Data

Tortora, Phyllis G.
Dress, fashion, and technology: from prehistory to the present/Phyllis G. Tortora.
Pages cm – (Dress, body, culture)
Includes bibliographical references and index.
ISBN 978-0-85785-190-1 (hardback) – ISBN 978-0-85785-191-8 (paperback) –
ISBN 978-0-85785-192-5 (epdf)   1. Fashion design–History.
2. Clothing and dress–History.   3. Tailoring–History.   I. Title.
TT504.T67 2015
746. 9'2–dc23
2014036563

Series: Dress, Body, Culture, ISSN: 1360-466X

Typeset by RefineCatch Limited, Bungay, Suffolk

CONTENTS

LIST OF ILLUSTRATIONS

ACKNOWLEDGMENTS

I want to dedicate this book to Joanne Eicher in gratitude for her encouragement throughout the several years required to get from a short article on Technology and Fashion in the electronic additions to the *Berg Encyclopedia of World Dress and Fashion* to this book. Joanne, mentor and friend, Thank you.

The Berg staff (when I began), many of whom morphed into Bloomsbury staff (by the time I finished), especially Hannah Crump and Anna Wright and Emily Ardizzone, were always willing to answer my questions promptly and cheerfully, even when I should already have known the answers. My understanding family, son Chris and daughter-in-law Vicki in Hawaii and daughter Giulia and partner Randy in Alaska, provided places to work even when my time with them was really supposed to be a holiday. Computer assistance from my grandsons Nicholas Tortora and Daniel Wiest and also from their parents was available as needed. Thanks to Daniel for being willing to pose in his hockey gear, to his parents for taking the photos, and to his Dad, Randy Wiest, for providing the nitty-gritty details of what all that gear was. The best outcome of that was the relief I felt after learning how well-protected these young athletes are!

A number of colleagues were willing to spend time reading chapters and providing feedback and Internet items they thought would be helpful – they always were! For this I want to acknowledge especially the generosity of Joanne Eicher, Carol Anne Dickson, and Nan Mutnick. Various libraries in various places proved to have a wealth of useful material. Nearby were The Westchester County New York Library System, especially Shelly Glick of the Briarcliff Manor library and the library of the Westchester Community College, and the Hawaii Public libraries in Honolulu, Aiea, and Pearl City, as well as the Fashion Institute of Technology and a number of other libraries and museums in New York City.

The willingness of Bloomsbury to increase the number of illustrations that were allocated for the book was important, and the assistance that I received from many individuals in locating the desired material made the search easier and even fun. Appreciation to Fairchild Books for granting permission to reproduce images from some of their books; the willingness of Dover to permit the use of a number of illustrations from the outstanding resources that serve those who study historic dress is most appreciated, as is the help from the image banks acknowledged in the illustration captions. Thanks to Lorinda and George at Photo Works in Pleasantville, NY, for helping to meet a deadline for scanning of images I own. Among the sources of images I must thank Professor Anita Racine and Kristen Morris of Cornell University for help in obtaining photographs of some of the exciting work being done there.

Finally, thanks to the many friends who put up with my absence from events I should have attended over the months preceding completion of the work. Their understanding and encouragement was essential to completing the work.

Phyllis Tortora

1
CONNECTING TECHNOLOGY, DRESS, AND FASHION

Technology has been intimately involved with dress and fashion throughout human history. Interrelationships among dress, fashion, and technologies may arise from a number of factors. In the pages that follow I will explore those relationships. Processes used in the creation of dress include tools that range in complexity from the eyed needle, known since prehistory and powered by human hands, to advanced textile production machines powered by electricity, such as the air jet looms of the twentieth century. Channels of communication about dress and fashion have benefited from innovations in printing techniques and the invention of motion pictures and computers. Technology may also lead to situations in which dress styles must change as a result of some new technology. Once automobiles became the basic mode of transportation for many, long skirts for women drivers largely disappeared. Space travel required rethinking the functions and form of dress. The results of technological innovations may make new fashions possible. Fashion may stimulate the development of new technology with dress serving as the medium.

Readers about the history of dress and fashion are not likely to look at books that deal with technology. And those interested in technical change rarely see the technologies behind changes in dress and fashion. And, yet, the three are intimately related. To begin to see those relationships requires understanding of these three words: technology, dress, and fashion.

The importance of terminology

Technology at its most basic is the use and understanding of tools, techniques, and processes that use these tools, a definition confirmed by a look at any current

English language dictionary. Technology that relates to dress can range from the simplest devices, such as an awl used to punch holes in skins so that they can be held together by lacings, to the creation of solar collectors that can be mounted on garments to generate enough electricity to recharge cellular telephones. The manufacturing processes for the production of textiles used in fashionable dress are a major aspect of technology and helped to jump-start the Industrial Revolution.

Dress is a word that has developed multiple meanings. But at its most inclusive, and as it is used in this book, it applies to anything that defines or modifies the human body. Anthropologist Joanne Eicher and dress scholar Mary Ellen Roach-Higgins (Eicher and Roach-Higgins, 1992) developed this definition for those who study dress. Dress includes not only undergarments and outer garments, headwear, and footwear, but also items suspended from the body – handbags, types of jewelry, and a host of other things suspended from various regions of the anatomy, often from holes created by body piercing. Body modifications can take place either through garments that push in one part of the anatomy and push out another or by cosmetic surgery that adds to or subtracts from or alters the body. Cosmetics temporarily applied to the body or permanent decorations such as tattoos, as well as perfumes that create pleasant odors or deodorants that prevent odors, are all part of dress.

Fashion is another word with multiple definitions and can be a synonym for dress. Eicher *et al.* (2010) provide a useful summary of the gradual evolution of scholarly thought about dress and fashion terminology as it is presented in seminal publications. These range from scholarly works by historians, sociologists, and psychologists to contemporary comments by those participating in fashion behavior.

Social scientists refer to fashion as a type of human behavior in which a large number of individuals accept the same form of behavior for a short period of time and then change that behavior. Women are often assumed to be the primary participants in "fashion" as they choose "the latest" among the options in their closets or the marketplace. From this stereotype comes the use of the word "fashions" as a synonym for women's dress. But active following of fashion is not just a female trait. Men's clothing depicted in portraits of European kings, dukes, and princes of the periods before the French Revolution proves that men can be just as fashion-conscious as women in their dress. Nor is fashion limited to dress. In fact, fashions defined as a taste shared by many for a short period of time can be seen in automobiles, furniture, architecture, food fads, and in a multitude of other areas. Therefore, in this book, I consider fashionable dress to be dress that has the characteristics of both acceptance and change.

Fashion always present in dress?

Scholars disagree about whether fashion is present in all cultures and at all times. For many years dress historians tended to see fashion only in the Western world and only since some time during or after the Middle Ages. This view is changing and today some scholars argue that unless one is intimately familiar with a culture it is not always possible to see the presence of fashion, therefore one cannot rule out its presence. Cannon (1998) sees fashion as a universal process, but cautions that the ways the fashion process operates can be radically different from one society to another. Craik (1944) argues that what is fashionable is related to culture rather than time period. Acceptance and relatively frequent change are the simplest and most visible aspects of fashion in Euro-American history. Scholarly study of fashion as a social phenomenon has looked not only at how and where and when fashion occurs but, as Japanese sociologist Kawamura (2005) notes, also engages in debate about whether it is a behavior that belongs to sociology, psychology, aesthetics, or economics. In my view it has elements of all these areas and even more. This complexity complicates the question of the identification of fashion in times and places where evidence about dress is limited. The question I will address is where and how technology has in some way impacted dress in general and fashionable dress when those influences can be identified. The evidence I will use to support conclusions about those impacts is to be found in visible representations, historical accounts, and other written records. Although my major focus will be on developments in the Western world, I will include some brief explorations of material outside my own culture.

It is not unreasonable to suggest that the human need to show group affiliation and one's place in his or her society is probably universal, as is the need for self-expression. Participating in fashion can satisfy both needs. Anspach (1967) described a cycle of adoption in which early adopters choose a new behavior. The cycle continues with a new group whose members adopt the behavior initiated by the earliest adopters; the peak of adoption is reached and on the downhill side of the cycle later adopters participate, and finally a group of very late adopters complete the cycle, participating either before or after the cycle begins again with something new. In this way fashion, with its constantly changing current styles, provides an opportunity to show that the participant is a part of the group, while at the same time being a mechanism that permits those adopting new behaviors to add unique aspects to their dress that make them stand out at least temporarily until the rest of the population follows the fashion leaders and adopts the newer behavior.

Those early adopters can vary with the culture. In earlier periods in Europe and North America, for example, they were often royalty or the upper, more affluent classes. In more recent times they have sometimes been individuals who are visibly present in the various media that depict what is being worn currently. Or they may be members of sub-cultural groups who want to show that they belong to a unique group that differs from others within the culture. The mechanisms of the fashion cycle are not the focus of this book, but wherever fashion is present, so too is change. And I would argue that the constant developments in technology throughout history and in modern life have had and still have a major impact on dress and on fashion in dress when fashion is evident.

Other themes that will appear

Although my major focus will be on developments in the Euro-American world, I will include some explorations of material outside my own culture. Furthermore, it is not possible to discuss fashion, dress, and technology in almost any period of civilization without including elements that move from one part of the world to another. This book, however, is more heavily weighted toward the English-speaking Euro-American world, as the literature I have drawn upon is written or translated into English.

Gender is another aspect of dress, fashion, and technology that will emerge throughout this history. Gender-related aspects appear in the production of components of dress such as textiles and in both the consumption of dress and in fashionable behavior. While these are not the primary focus, they are consistently present.

The organization of this book

I have chosen to begin this exploration of technology and dress in prehistory, and have divided the book into four sections. Chapters are arranged in approximately chronological order. Part One, *Before the Revolution*, takes its title from the central place of the Industrial Revolution in the history of technology and also because it was the textile industry that provided the raw materials from which dress was most often made, which was the initial focus of the Industrial Revolution. Chapter 2 begins with a look at the technology and dress of prehistory. It is not possible to identify fashions in prehistoric dress with certainty, because sources of information and visual representations are limited. Chapters 3 through 5 take the reader to some early civilizations, in particular to ancient Egypt, Mesopotamia, Greece, Rome, China, and India, and chronologically to the eighteenth century and precursors to the Industrial Revolution, with a detour outside the Western world in Chapter 5.

In Part Two, titled *The Industrial Revolution and First Steps toward the Fashion Industry,* I include developments in the eighteenth to the twentieth centuries, with its major focus being on the nineteenth century. Chapters 6 and 7 look at the central role of dress and fashion in the Industrial Revolution, while Chapter 8 identifies social changes resulting from industrialization and their impact on dress and fashion. The data that underlies this discussion relates to changes in Great

Britain. In North America these changes are reflected, but softened because the English-speaking, North American states did not evolve from feudal states as did the European countries, and therefore had, in some unspecified respects, an easier path to industrialization. Part Two concludes with Chapter 9 focusing on nineteenth-century technologies that served as midwives to the fashion industry in the United States and to certain fashionable styles of dress.

Chapter 10 in Part Three, *The Fashion Industry is Born*, begins as new technological tools for the fashion industry appear. Chapters 11 through 13 show how some aspects of life and technology in the nineteenth to the twenty-first centuries (transportation, communication, sports) can have reciprocal impacts on dress and fashion. Part Four, *High Tech Enters* begins with Chapter 14, which looks at twentieth and twenty-first century developments in chapters on technology in the fashion industry and resulting changes, relating some of this technology to globalization. A somewhat different subject is the focus of Chapter 15, which looks at technologies that require new kinds of dress and environments that call for new technologies. The book concludes with Chapter 16 providing a look at ways in which the fashion world is using technology as a spur to creativity and giving some hints of possible developments predicted to come to fashions and dress through technology.

As a means of providing concrete examples of the interactions among technology, dress, and fashion, each chapter will include illustrations that depict individuals who lived at that time period wearing various elements of dress. Depictions of past styles of dress may be difficult to understand. For this reason, the text that accompanies each illustration begins with a description of the dress shown. This introduction to dress of a specific period provides information about those elements of dress that are depicted, what they are made from, how constructed, and any special purposes. The accompanying text identifies the technologies needed to create the elements of depicted aspects of the dress of the person. When fashion is or may be a factor, reasons for seeing fashionable behavior will be given. If fashion cannot be readily identified, reasons will be offered that may explain this absence. Examples are chosen from different time periods, different geographical regions, and depict men, women, or items of dress. Through these illustrations the reader may find concrete examples of the interactions of technology, dress, and fashion.

PART ONE
BEFORE THE REVOLUTION

2

DRESS AND THE TECHNOLOGIES OF PREHISTORY

(Upper Paleolithic to the Neolithic period)

An office or school room with computers on every desk, a factory full of sewing machines stitching together T-shirts that will be shipped around the world, rockets headed for a space station, and high-speed trains connecting one city to another. Twenty-first century individuals would identify all these as examples of technology, but showing that same person a pair of knitting needles or scissors and describing these objects as technology might elicit a puzzled look. But to the anthropologist, technology is the knowledge used in "fashioning implements, practicing manual arts and skills, and extracting or collecting materials" (*American Heritage Dictionary,* 1992). In other words, technology is the development and use of tools, and has been a part of hominid life since prehistory. Knitting needles, scissors, even a needle and thread, are a part of the modern technology used to make body enclosures, one type of human dress. Early humans clearly had their own versions of tools and technologies that were essential for creating dress.

To be curious is to be attracted to the unknown, to mysteries. Perhaps this is the underlying reason for the interest in human beginnings that many scholars bring to exploring the past. Who were the first people? How did they live? How much were they like us? What could they do? What did they do? How did they dress? And what does what we learn about them tell us about ourselves?

"They" were *Homo Sapiens*, the species category assigned to anatomically modern humans; the only survivors of a long line of hominid species that originated in what is now called Africa. The history of *Homo Sapiens* constantly undergoes revision as anthropologists, archeologists, and paleontologists make new discoveries. Based on current knowledge, the Human Origins Program of the Smithsonian Museum of Natural History assigns c. 200,000 years ago as the

Table 2.1 *Terminology used to identify archeological periods*

Name given to period	Defined as	Comments
Prehistory	Time before the development of writing	Differs in different parts of the world
Paleolithic	Period beginning with the emergence of humans, beginning about 1.75 million years ago	Generally divided into lower, middle and upper Paleolithic Periods
Lower Paleolithic	Earliest hominids appear. Use of pebbles made into tools, hand axes, and choppers	
Middle Paleolithic	Neanderthals, considered by some a human species, *homo sapiens neanderthalensis*, and by others a separate species *homo neanderthalensis* appear. They used flake tools	
Upper Paleolithic	Neanderthals and genetically modern humans co-exist. Cave art appears, tools include blades and burins	Neanderthals no longer appear in the fossil record after about 25,000 years ago. The New World and Australia are colonized.
Mesolithic	Period between Paleolithic and Neolithic after the end of geologic ice age (c. 8300 BCE), hunting and gathering societies predominate	In areas farther away from glacial regions some evidence of the beginnings of agriculture
Neolithic	Period when *homo sapiens,* now the only remaining hominid species, cultivate crops and domesticate animals. Stone tools and weapons in use	
Three Stage System in which periods are based on technologies in use		
Stone Age	Stone, wood, bone, and antlers used for tools; metals unknown	Dates vary by region. Some cultures have Stone Age technologies until the recent past
Copper Age	Period when copper comes into use for tools and weapons	Quite variable, as copper deposits are not found in all parts of the world

Bronze Age	An alloy of copper and tin that becomes the main material for tools and weapons	The need to trade for materials for bronze starts trade routes, helps to spread technology, and increases cultural exchanges. Bronze is not used in America. Types of writing begin in Asia
Iron Age	Largely replaces bronze for use in tools and weapons. Hittites first to use iron c. 1500 BCE; Europe c. 1100 BCE	Regional differences substantial: Africa: spread of iron technology so rapid, there was no bronze age America: iron arrived only with the Europeans

time that this species evolved in Africa and about 100,000 years ago as the time when *Homo Sapiens* began to spread beyond Africa. The major evidence for the earliest hominids consists of fossil skeleton remains and some tools. Evidence about dress is scant and is largely inferred from durable materials. Durable tools, the servants of prehistoric technology, do provide some clues.

Needing ways to organize their writing about both ancient and more recent hominids, anthropologists have given names to various periods that they relate to technological developments. Table 2.1 presents a summary of generally accepted names for these divisions, which will be mentioned in this and the following chapters together with their definitions. The dates assigned to these named periods are not the same in all parts of the world. For example, a population that lives in an isolated area without iron deposits would not enter the "Iron Age" until they are able to obtain the raw material from other regions that possess iron. For this reason, specific dates are not given in the table.

The broad term "prehistory" is frequently assigned to the earliest of these periods. Prehistory refers to periods when no written records exist to provide information about human life. Written history in Eurasia generally begins after the so-called Agricultural or Neolithic Revolution, a time when many humans gradually abandoned a lifestyle that had required mobility to hunt for animals for food and to gather plant materials. In this transition, communities in which agriculture and herding became permanent settlements of considerable size gradually replaced the hunter-gatherer system. These settlements began to develop written languages around 3900 BCE, probably as a means of record-keeping for commerce (Scarre, 1993: 91). This chapter begins with dress in prehistory and explores what we know about dress before urban civilizations and writing.

Visual representations of dress

Dress history books are full of depictions of dress. Regrettably, prehistory provides relatively little visual evidence on which to base conclusions about dress. Many scholars have been attracted to the study of Europe after the end of what is called the Post Ice Age or the Upper Paleolithic Period, c. 35,000 to 12,000 years ago. Although interested amateurs had found ancient artifacts and human remains earlier, the discovery of cave art in the mid-nineteenth century stimulated interest in the prehistory of Europe among antiquarians, art historians, archeologists, and anthropologists and this interest continues. It seems reasonable to expect that the art found in European caves would be a prime source of information about dress. What does exist is not clear enough to be conclusive. Representations from c. 32,000 to 10,000 years ago are found as sculpture including statuettes, incised figures on bone, horn, and antler, and incised and painted art in caves or on rocks. Descriptions of these figures by scholars use terms such as "stylized," "probable," "schematic" and acknowledge the lack of clarity about what is being shown. Obviously there would not have been worldwide styles. Nor have all parts of the earth had the same level of attention from archeologists. The art of Europe is represented in the literature in English to a far greater extent than other regions. This disparity makes it more productive to focus on European evidence to determine to what extent art provides evidence about connections between technology and dress in the prehistoric period in Europe (Bandi *et al.*, 1961).

Henri Breuil, a French Catholic Priest and early archaeologist, counted 116 horses, 37 bison, 19 bears, 14 reindeer, 13 mammoths, 9 ibex, 7 head of cattle, 5 stags, 3 hinds, 5 lions, 4 wolves, 1 fox, and 39 figures of human beings in an analysis of the pictures in the French cave Combarelles. Given the masterful depictions of animals in these paintings, one would expect that this would provide plenty of information about the appearance of the humans. But the human figures are described as "always represented in an unskilled way." Even so, some conclusions can be drawn from these "unskilled" pictures. For example, the humans often seem to be wearing masks that are generally interpreted as ceremonial dress, possibly having religious or shamanistic significance. The level of detail used in representing humans varies from place to place and time period to time period. One painting from Cogul in Spain, known as Dancing Women that has been depicted in Anawalt (2007: 80), has been interpreted as women wearing fur skirts. Other figures in the group might be wearing skin skirts. Another Spanish painting that includes one figure shown in silhouette is described as "wearing knee breeches" (Bandi, 1961).

Sculpture provides additional information. Many of the sculpted statuettes (c. 25,000 BP) are unclothed, some are corpulent, and most of them are women. These are generally called Venus figures. One early speculation about these figures is that they might be fertility symbols; however, many archeologists do not agree with this hypothesis. Their function remains uncertain. But what is particularly interesting in regard to their dress is that some of them appear to be wearing elements of dress that were most likely made from fibers. These include what could be hairnets, cap-like headgear, string skirts, and bands above and below the breast and around the back. Where these representations exist, they are sometimes quite clear. From close examination of the carvings, Soffer *et al.* (2000) concluded that one type of head covering was a "spirally or radially hand-woven item." They viewed the head covering as a coiled construction made in much the same way that a basket might be made. They describe it as consisting of two elements, as in weaving where one element is placed horizontally and the other vertically. The horizontal or crosswise materials served as the foundation and the vertical elements are wrapped around several of the crosswise sections. From the other depictions they concluded that a grid-like covering shown over long hair was probably a hair net that was made by knotting and that the string skirt was made by tying cords made from twisted plant fibers with loose or frayed ends to another cord that formed a belt. The bandeaux appeared to be made by twining and its parts were probably sewn together at the points where they intersected (Soffer *et al.*, 2000).

From this kind of visual and artifact evidence, the only certain conclusions that can be drawn are that anatomically modern humans in Europe in the Late Ice Age probably wore body enclosures made from fur, skins, and fibrous materials that were held together in some type of textile construction. Probably some of this dress was ceremonial in nature.

Artifacts related to technology for making dress

Garments must have been needed to protect against the cold of the early post-glacial period. From one perspective it might be accurate to say that one of the artifacts most often found in association with human remains, the projectile point, may have been the earliest example of a technology that makes dress possible. Hunters or those scavenging for dead animals obtained the skins and fur from which their dress was made. The need for food, not the need for dress, was probably the most important motivation for securing these resources, but soon hunters must have recognized that these and other byproducts of hunting could be important for the comfort of the community.

Without some treatment, hides would have been less than satisfactory to use for dress. Organic material left clinging to the skins after butchering would have to be removed before they putrefied. Rock scrapers are among the stone tools found during excavations at prehistoric sites, but Mithen (1994) points out that the ability to scrape the skins to clean them would not have been sufficient to create a flexible skin or fur. Additional processing using natural materials with the appropriate chemical composition would have made hides or furs soft and flexible enough to wrap them around the body. Precisely how this was done is not clear; however, the relatively few examples of leather that have been found are supple and flexible and could have been worked into garments. Some type of technological process, comparable to what is called tanning today, produced a more useful material (Waateringe *et al.*, 1999).

According to Mellars (1994) writing on the history of prehistoric Europe, some kind of device to hold the skins or furs in place would have allowed freedom to use the arms. Before the use of metals, pins would have been made from bone. Very sharp awls of bone have been found that could have been used to punch holes in leather. Strips of hide or animal sinews cut with sharp stone tools probably laced the pieces together.

The dress of indigenous people, such as the Inuits who live in the Arctic, probably provides some insight into the kinds of garments that might have been worn by people of the post-glacial periods in Europe. In fact, in Paleolithic art there is an incised image that some archeologists interpret as a pregnant woman wearing an anorak, the hooded jacket that originates in the Arctic regions (White, 1986). Dress scholars tend to divide body enclosures into those that are draped (wrapped around the body) and those that are tailored (cut and sewn to fit the body closely). Tailored garments provide much greater warmth than draped clothing. Inuit people of the Arctic region wear tailored dress, cutting and sewing fur or skins into shapes that conform to the shape of the body. The people of the upper Paleolithic period probably did something similar. The tools they left behind point to that conclusion.

For millennia hominids had shaped stone into cutting tools. Some were probably used to cut meat; others are identified as scrapers. To make fitted garments, tailors use shears to cut the fabric. To make fitted fur garments, Paleolithic "tailors" of the Stone Age probably used stone cutting tools. A wide variety of flint and other stone tools could have been used for this purpose; a few have been analyzed to determine the kind of substances on which they were used and some were apparently used on hides, although it is not possible to tell whether the hides were cut for use as clothing. Cut pieces had to be held together in some way. The artifacts found from this period include the aforementioned bone awls and sharp, pointed stone flakes; both could have been used to make holes in skins or furs. Initially sinew, gut, or animal tendons could have been used to join pieces of leather or fur, but once people had learned to make cord this could have been used.

White (2007) states that the eyed needle of bone or antler made its appearance at least 20,000 years ago. As an alternative to lacing, this tool could be used to sew garment segments together. These tools, together with processes that support the technologies of tanning, cutting, punching holes, and sewing, could create dress made from animal skins to enclose the body.

Fiber use

But what of the items of dress depicted in prehistoric art that appear to be made from fibers? The technical definition of fiber is a unit of matter at least 100 times as long as its width. Fibers are the base materials from which most textile fabrics are made and can be joined together in a variety of ways. The simplest structure in which fibers can be united is in a mass of fibers joined together into a flexible web. One such web is bark cloth, a fabric made from the outer bark of trees in which the bark contains a high proportion of fibers. The layer of bark containing the fibers is removed from the tree and soaked to soften it, then placed on a flat surface and pounded, thereby making the fibers interlace, which gives the resulting material strength and structure. Another web fabric is made from wool fibers taken from the fleece of sheep. When these fibers, which have microscopic scales on the fiber surface, are subjected to heat, moisture, and pressure, the fibers shrink, the scales cling together, and so form a durable fiber web called felt. Collier *et al.* (2009: 358), while acknowledging that evidence is scanty, report that some textile historians believe that felt was probably the first textile material to be made in prehistoric times.

Fibers that are suitable for use in textile materials can be obtained from some types of plants and from the fleece of certain animals. The domestication of both plants and animals does not occur until well after dates around 25,000 BP that are assigned to the aforementioned Venus figures. The conclusion, then, is that the textile fibers used for the garments on these statuettes must have come from wild plants. Most probably these would have been bast fibers, the name given to fibers obtained from the stems of plants. Most of the earliest fiber remains are bast fibers and they most likely came from wild flax or a type of nettle, both of which are native to Eurasia. Archeologists continually move the fiber record farther into the past. In 2009, archeologists working in the country of Georgia found flax fibers that they dated to 30,000 years ago. The fibers show evidence of having been twisted, indicating to the archeologists that the fibers had been spun (Harris, 2011).

Additional excavations by Soffer *et al.* (2000) present evidence of textile weaving in the form of textile imprints on unfired and fired clay fragments. Dated at between 29,000 and 24,000 years ago, the archeologists reported that the textile imprints exhibited variations in the size of inter-lacings and in the weaves used. This led them to speculate about possible end uses, including woven garments. These imprints were found in association with eyed needles, some of which they believe are too small to use on hides and argue that "this likely reflects working on woven textiles and/or embroidering rather than conjoining animal hides" (Soffer *et al.*, 2000).

Other confirmation and evidence of these early dates is lacking. Future excavations and further evidence may well provide what is needed to build a complete picture. But what other evidence would be required? In order to create a textile fabric from the kind of short fibers that come from plants, those fibers must be twisted together to make a long yarn. Twisting is essential in order to make a yarn that will be strong enough and will not simply separate into its constituent fibers. Later devices made specifically for the task of spinning fibers into yarns by hand incorporated worked stone, ivory, metal, or bone weights called spindle whorls. Stone spindle whorls appear in the archeological record as early as 9250 to 9000 BP, but this still post-dates the Venus statuettes and the Czech textile imprints by several thousand years.

Barber (1991) describes a process of spinning using a stick or a stone that had not been modified in any way. Such aids could be discarded after use. Archeologists could not have identified such objects as tools even if such artifacts had survived. It is also possible to twist fibers together by rolling a strand of fibers against the thigh. Therefore, it is possible that yarns could be created without leaving evidence of tools. It is also possible that artifacts found in excavations

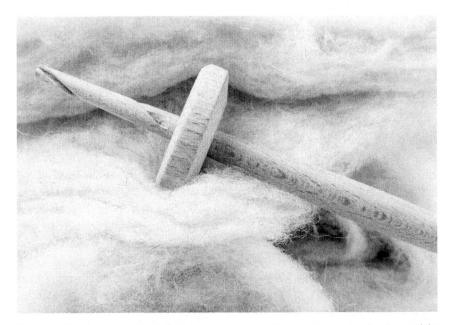

Figure 2.1 Spindle and whorl. Whorls can be made of stone, bone, or any other weight that stabilizes the spindle as the spinner drops it to the ground to spin the yarn (source: Shutterstock/Sergi Lopez Roig)

may not have been recognized as part of textile technology. Soffer and colleagues suggest that objects that have been used as spindle whorls, combs for aligning grass fiber, net spacers, or loom weights, may have been interpreted incorrectly.

Beyond body enclosing garments

There is little more to say about textiles and the technologies that make them such an important part of dress until the effects of the Neolithic Revolution appear and the evidence for weaving becomes incontrovertible. This evidence and the related processes follow this consideration of even older technology related to other aspects of dress from prehistory.

Body modifications are another facet of dress. Evidence of body modifications is generally found or seen on the human body. Occasionally modifications such as the shaping of heads can be observed in skulls recovered from archeological sites. Where mummies are preserved, they may show evidence of tattooing. But relatively few mummies are preserved, and therefore such remains make certainty about these ephemeral examples of body modifications impossible. Burial sites and excavation sites often include evidence of ochre, an iron oxide compound that seems to have been used as a red pigment in art and, perhaps, to color the skin. It may have had some ritual significance for burials. Without other supporting material, it is only possible to speculate about the significance of such finds.

Items suspended from the body were made from durable materials such as antler, bone, shell, or stone. Beads are possibly the most plentiful examples of adornment from early periods.

One European stone pendant has been dated to c. 35,000 years ago (Scarre, 1993: 1–4). Proof of the presence of body and garment ornaments appears in great quantity and variety and can be found almost everywhere that human presence is detected. Some who write about dress have argued that the most primary motivation for dress is the desire to decorate the body. Certainly ornaments – some would call it jewelry – have to be the earliest form of dress for which there is tangible evidence. According to Dubin (2009), the oldest beads are those found in Sikul Cave in Israel on Mount Carmel. These beads have been dated to 108,000 BCE. They were made of shells. The variety of materials used to make objects described as beads include natural materials such as stones with naturally-occurring holes, a variety of shells of marine animals, ostrich shell, animal teeth, ivory, animal bones, and antler.

By c. 36,000 to 28,000 BCE grinding, shaping, and polishing allowed Neolithic "jewelers" to produce beads in the shape of female breasts and torsos, while others benefited from advances in ceramic technology and created miniature clay-fired animal figurines that they mounted on cords. Archeologists often find beads in burial sites of the Upper Paleolithic and Neolithic Periods. From these

Figure 2.2 Prehistoric necklace made of shells (source: Ashmolean Museum/The Art Archive at Art Resource, New York)

remains several things become clear. Beads were often strung in quantity on something like cord or animal sinew. From the location of the beads on skeletons, long after the garments on which they were placed had disappeared, it was possible to tell that they were often sewn on garments. And from the locations of the beads, it was often possible to get a fairly good idea of how the garments had been constructed. One such photograph reported by Mellars (1994: 66) of the burial of a man near Moscow, Russia, shows many carved ivory beads. A head covering, now gone, had a broad band of beads at least three or four inches wide placed across the head above the eyes, strands of beads placed horizontally across the upper body, others circling the arms at the elbow, and what appear to be bracelets around both wrists. More beads lie on the lower torso below the waist. From this evidence, Fagen (2010) concluded that this man was probably wearing a cap and a tunic that ended below the hips. The quantity of beads on the body indicated he was probably of high status.

Studies of these bead artifacts provide not only information about how they were made, but White's analysis of deposits of beads made from animal teeth in several different Upper Paleolithic sites in France led to this conclusion: the teeth did not come from animals that were used for food. The animals providing teeth used for display were separate from those that were eaten. White (2007: 287–302) concluded: "This implies that the animals behind the parts transformed into ornaments are construed in terms that are largely of the collective symbolic imagination." He sees this use of ornamentation as evidence of abstract thinking and the ability to attach complex meaning about relationships to concrete objects.

A second conclusion that is contrary to what one might expect is that the materials used to make beads and pendants were not only those readily available in the immediate vicinity of the sites where they were found but must have been obtained either through travel to the sources or by trade with distant locations. After cataloging the resources (ivory, amber, lignite, mother of pearl, dental enamel, and soapstone), White noted that all of these materials share similar visual and tactile qualities, and concluded that these characteristics must have been valued within the culture.

Many of these beads and those from other parts of the world required fairly advanced human-driven technology for their creation. Specialized tools would have been required to shape and carve materials such as ivory, antler, and bone. Dubin (2009) points out the development of the burin, which had a beveled edge or point that was especially useful. She goes on to identify related technologies including "metal abrasives . . . in use for the demi-rotational drilling of . . . hard materials" and hollow bone bow drills filled with sand or stone abrasive. By analyzing the steps needed to make the object, White used ivory raw materials to create a bead and found that not only did it require three hours to produce a single bead but that in addition it was necessary to use metal abrasives to produce a comparable luster on the bead surface. Comparing the debris from different sites he determined that there were some locations in which beads were manufactured in "massive" quantities, others that indicated a lower or "maintenance" level of production, and a "no production whatsoever" site. Use of raw materials such as marine shells, or colorful mineral deposits that originated far from the archeological sites where they were found, testifies to the early development of trade routes used to obtain prized materials for jewelry.

Exploration of what is known about human dress during early human prehistory may not allow us to describe with certainty exactly what people wore or how they obtained it. But it does show clearly how dependent humans were on technology. As human social organizations and the dress that designated status grew more complex, the technologies used to create dress also gained in complexity and sophistication.

The importance of the Neolithic Revolution in Eurasia

Heretofore humans survived by migrating to take advantage of known food sources that could be obtained by hunting, fishing, and gathering. The gradual change to a sedentary lifestyle at locations where food was obtained by domestication and raising of plants and animals known as the Neolithic or Agricultural Revolution, is generally dated as c. 7000 to 3000 BCE (Whittle, 1994). These changes did not take place in all locales at the same time. While the Middle East and the Mediterranean regions and areas of Asia were the earliest to benefit from the advantages of settled life and to move toward urbanization (experiences that will be explored in Chapter 3), areas such as northern and central Europe were settling into farming communities by c. 3500 BCE. The plants that made agriculture possible, barley and wheat, were not native to Europe, but moved into Europe from the East, as did animals such as sheep and goats.

Even without the ability to present a detailed chronology of where and when the skills needed for weaving fabric developed, it is clear that by the time humans were settling into village life and cultivating plants and animals that provided both food and fibers, they were engaged in the production of textiles. They had learned to spin those fibers into yarns and to weave the yarns into cloth. Clues to advances in textile technology can be found in the remains of some of these early European communities and in the archeological sites through which historians have come to know these communities.

Fibers are the basic building blocks of textiles. Barber (1991) easily convinces her readers that flax, which is the source of linen fiber, was the first plant cultivated for fiber. In all likelihood flax was originally gathered and later planted for its edible seeds. The discovery of flax in a cave in Russia, which was dated to 34,000 years ago, buttresses her case. Some have argued that wool from sheep's fleece must have been the first fiber used by humans, but from Barber's investigations it is clear that wool in the fleeces of the earliest sheep species did not have fibers that could be spun. Linen fiber appears most often in the oldest textile remains. Furthermore, linen offers other advantages. It washes easily, is absorbent, can be made into fabric with a soft handle and is therefore comfortable to wear, and it is lustrous and attractive.

But simply having the plant does not mean the fiber is ready to use. A technological process is required to obtain the fibers, called bast fibers. These fibers are an integral part of the stems of flax. The stem must be rotted sufficiently to separate the fiber. Laying the stems of the flax plant in a moist environment until the stems decompose enough to at least partially free the fibers is the first step. This first step is known as retting. Next the stems are dried and then beaten to break them up. This step is known as scutching. Finally the remainder of the stem is removed with a comb-like device in a process called hackling. During the hackling process short, tangled fibers are separated from long, parallel smoother fibers. The latter are used for the best-quality yarns and the former for lower-quality yarn.

In order to appreciate what they were able to do, it is important to understand the technologies needed to make fiber into cloth. Some information about the equipment used can be gained through lake villages in Switzerland that were occupied from the late Neolithic Period to the early Bronze Age. These settlements on lakesides have been a source of artifacts that testify to the skill of Neolithic people in processing flax. Beating tools made of wood, hackling devices made from wood with imbedded thorns, and others of bone have been found. This equipment was used to remove linen fibers from the flax stems. Other fibers can be obtained from other bast plants. Examples include hemp from a cannabis plant that is a relative of marijuana, and another that is a species of nettle. In the Western Hemisphere, Native Americans obtained fibers from dogbane, also known as "Indian Hemp" and in Asia ramie, a linen-like fiber, can be taken from stems of a plant in the nettle family.

Wool was widely used only after 7000 BCE. By this time, species of sheep had evolved and been domesticated that had wool that was readily spun. Just as linen required pre-processing before it was ready for use, wool had to first be removed from the sheep. Evidence relating to wool use raises a number of questions, some of which will be discussed in Chapter 3 in relation to the urban centers of Mesopotamia. The problems that arise with wool processing include how to obtain the wool. It may well have been used initially much as skins were used by earlier people, with the wool being attached to the skin and the skin tanned to make it flexible. Probably the first method of obtaining the fiber without the skin attached would have been to pull off the fiber during the molting season. Devices that could remove wool from the living sheep efficiently had to await improvements in metallurgy. But whether the wool was attached to the skin or in tufts pulled from a shedding sheep, it was full of debris from grazing and had a coating of grease called lanolin on the fibers. Both of these had to be removed. Both linen and wool will occupy center stage in Chapter 3, as urban life encourages textile manufacture and trade.

Once fibers have been obtained they must be made into yarns. The fibers available in Europe and the Near East were, unlike the silk from China that was not yet available in the West, relatively short, although linen could be as long as the flax stem from which it had been removed. Nevertheless, the fibers had to be twisted together prior to weaving. By the Bronze Age people had learned that it was possible to form a long thread or yarn by twisting the fibers together. They had also learned that the tighter they were twisted, the stronger the yarn would be. While it was possible to twist these fibers together by hand, people had also learned that this task was far easier with some technological help from a spindle (Figure 2.1). That device, at its most basic, consisted of a stick on which was mounted a spindle whorl. A hole in its center allowed the spindle to be passed through the whorl. When the spindle is dropped to the ground in a twisting motion, the whorl acts as a fly wheel that maintains the motion for a longer time. The spinner must feed fiber to the stick continuously as it is dropped and spun, while the spindle inserts twist into the fiber and the weight of the whorl makes the process more efficient. A skilled spinner can feed the fiber smoothly and efficiently and create a very long, smooth, and strong yarn. Barber (1991) reports the presence in archeological sites of spindle whorls ranging from plain stone or baked clay disks with a hole in the center to spindle whorls made from valuable materials such as ivory, copper, or bronze, which testify to how ubiquitous these tools were and how women of all social classes were skilled at spinning. Sometimes spindles and whorls were made of metal, even of gold.

Once sufficient quantities of yarn were spun, the next step was making the yarn into a fabric. Schoeser (2003: 16–20) describes a number of fabric construction techniques that do not require a complex device. These may have preceded the weaving of cloth. Netting, in which the threads are knotted, and plaiting (similar to braiding) and sprang, described as plaiting with stretched threads, all require little or no equipment. Weaving fabric requires some type of loom. The basic process of weaving used in the Bronze Age can be compared to the process used for weaving in the twenty-first century. The requirements are a set of yarns that are held vertically, called warp yarns, and a second set of yarns that are horizontal, called weft yarns. These two sets of yarns interlace to form the fabric.

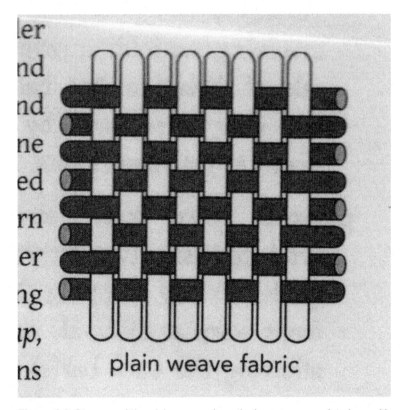

plain weave fabric

Figure 2.3 Diagram of the plain weave. Lengthwise warp yarns interlace with crosswise weft yarns traveling over one warp and under the next across the loom to form the fabric (courtesy of Fairchild Books)

The most basic pattern is one in which the crosswise yarn in the first row goes over one vertical yarn, under the next, over the next, and so on across the width of the fabric. In the next row the crosswise yarn goes under the first vertical yarn, over the second, under the third, etc. across the width of the warp yarns. The pattern of the first row is repeated in the third row, and the second row is repeated in the fourth row. This simple pattern is called a plain weave.

By varying the pattern of interlacing it is possible to change the pattern, texture, and appearance of the fabric. While it sounds very simple, there are technical problems to overcome that were solved by the development of looms. A loom is a device that allows lengthwise yarns to be stretched under tension so that the crosswise yarns can be inserted. Without that tension the lengthwise yarns would move out of place and any attempt to insert a crosswise yarn would be all but impossible. One type of loom in use today, in some parts of the world where weaving is done by hand by skilled weavers, can offer some clues about how this may have been done when weaving was a process in its infancy. The key requirement is that tension must be placed on the warp yarns so it is possible to insert the filling yarns. A back strap loom requires only something to which the weaver can fasten one end of the warp yarns, for example they could be tied to a tree or a constructed device, as in Figure 2.4. The other ends of the warp yarns can be wrapped around the back of the weaver, and by leaning forward or farther back the weaver can increase or decrease the tension on the lengthwise yarn as needed. This type of loom has some limitations in regard to the size of the fabric that can be made. But it may well have been the ancestor of the more complex looms that will be discussed in subsequent chapters.

What conclusions can be drawn from this exploration of prehistoric dress? In some parts of the world early humans needed dress to keep warm. That dress came from the animal skins that they found in their environment, but some forms of technology (tools) were required to obtain those materials and make them useful for garments. They also valued some items of dress as markers of status or as ornamentation. And for creating these, other technologies were required. When humans began to create textiles from fibers found in their environment, an even more complex technology developed. Technology was essential for the creation of even the earliest examples of human dress.

Relating technology and dress: The Ice Man

The foregoing survey has taken the reader from the time of *Homo sapiens* hunter-gatherers to the beginnings of the Neolithic or Agricultural Revolution when small communities began to sustain themselves in one place. The overview in this chapter is largely of developments in one region of the world, Western Europe. If the archeological record is adequate and published research available, it would most likely be possible to construct similar histories for other parts of the world.

It may be that the type of dress classified as body enclosures became necessary as humans encountered colder climates. But many of the items classified as body supplements pre-date the climate changes that required warmer dress. It is possible beads may have offered some type of spiritual protection. But whatever the motivation for dress, the evidence remaining generally implies the requirement of tools and technological processes for producing dress. The history behind the visible elements of dress leads inevitably to some aspect of technology. One way to gain a heightened sense of these relationships is to look at illustrations

Figure 2.4 This example of a backstrap loom was used in Peru. These ancient looms are still in use for hand weaving in many parts of the world. The necessary tension on the warp yarns is provided by the belt around the weaver's waist (source: Shutterstock/Kobby Dagan)

depicting specific examples of dress where the viewer can look for clues to the technology used in their creation. Fashion as a social phenomenon in which large numbers of people subscribe to styles for a short period of time cannot always be identified. One major reason, that is true in this chapter, is that the remains from prehistory are too few and too geographically scattered. And there are no memoirs, legal proclamations about dress, or fashion plates to consult. It is not possible to know precisely what the men and women of the Upper Paleolithic Period wore, but by accident we can close this chapter with a clear view of how one man of the Neolithic Period, c. 5,300 years ago, was dressed on the day of his death.

The drawing in Figure 2.5 is a reconstruction of some features of the ice man's dress displayed in the SudTyrol museum in Bolzano, Italy where his remains and related objects are held. The descriptions that follow are based on the information in books by Spindler (1994) and Fowler (2000), and some web sites cited in the references at the end of this book.

The ice man's dress

The dress of the prehistoric period rarely lends itself to careful analysis. Art showing humans of the period is rarely detailed enough to provide more than a vague idea of dress. But the accidental discovery of a mummified man in the Alps, close to the border of Italy and Austria in September 1991, provided a rare view of how a man of c. 5,300 years ago dressed. This view might be compared to having an archeologist from 7,300 years from now report on finding a mummy of a twenty-first century man dressed for the conditions he might find when headed into the mountains for hunting or when going on a trek in Autumn. Archeologists were surprised about the composition of his garments for two reasons. He did not wear or carry any woven textiles, even though weaving was known by this period and there are linen textile remains found in the Alpine regions. In more northern regions wool has been found. What he did wear was mostly leather and fur, materials that are rarely preserved from this early period. He was thought to have been either a hunter or herder. Opinions of scholars differ about his probable occupation. Most agree he lived in or was in contact with a farming community, because of the grains found in his clothing that were cultivated at that period in the sub-Alpine regions. From his dress the technology required for its creation is reasonably clear. But on fashion the remains are silent.

The dress of the ice man, as he has come to be called, includes several layers of body enclosures, some body modifications, and items suspended from the body. In addition to his dress, he carried a number of weapons and tools. He had a bow-stave and a quiver and arrows, an ax, two birch bark boxes, and a dagger with a scabbard. Interestingly, the scabbard is constructed using textile-like processes. The fiber is identified as bast fibers probably from a lime tree (called linden or basswood in North America) that are plaited into a small mat that is folded in half and plaited together with thread twisted from grass. The result is an oblong case coming to a point that was probably attached to a belt. He also carried an implement for making or sharpening flint tools and items that might be medicinal or food, and also a net that researchers theorize might have been used for catching birds for food.

From this collection it is clear that textile-making skills of knotting to create the net and plaiting (braiding) to make the scabbard for the knife were well known. It is also obvious that metal-working skills were fairly advanced as the ax of copper is skillfully made.

Some of the items found on or with the ice man might be called tools or equipment rather than dress, but by the definition of dress as body enclosures, body supplements, and body modifications, they would be considered to be part of his dress. The garment worn closest to the body was a loin cloth of which only the front flap remains. It was made of long strips of thin, soft leather that are sewn together with thread made from twisted fibers of animal sinew. Although the full loin cloth no longer exists, Konrad Spindler, an Austrian archeologist closely involved with the recovery and analysis of the ice man and his possessions, suggests in his book *The Man in the Ice* that probably the missing back, like the remaining front, was pulled up and over a belt (Spindler, 1994). Spindler also says that to make leather so soft and thin it could have been cut in layers (called splitting) or scraped thin. This provides at least some indication of contemporary leather processing technology.

The belt over which the loin cloth was pulled had a small pouch attached. The closest modern equivalent would be what is called a "fanny pack" or a "bum bag." This pouch was worn at the front over the abdomen and the ends of the belt were wrapped to the back, to circle the body and then pulled forward over the hips to knot behind the pouch with the ends dangling. Analysis showed the belt and the pouch to be made of calf's skin. Open at the top, it could have been closed with a narrow strip of leather. Inside the pouch were five items, three of which may have been used in making dress or as part of dress: a bone awl, a flint implement, and a stone bead attached to a tassel made of twisted fur strips. The awl with a very sharp bone point could have been used to punch holes in leather or furs or possibly used as a tattooing needle. The flint implement might have been used to make the holes in hard materials such as the stone bead or the stiff material used in a quiver that he carried. The bead of "brilliant white marble," archeologists theorize, might have been an ornament or have been thought to have magical powers.

Although the ice man's garments were remarkably well-preserved, some had undergone considerable degradation in the thousands of years that he had been

Figure 2.5 Ice man (source: South Tyrol Museum of Archaeology/Sara Welponer, www.iceman.it)

frozen in his glacial tomb. Some of this damage occurred during the recovery of the body. The garment that covered the upper part of his body was made of fur. It seems to have been either cloak- or cape-like, as it did not have set-in sleeves but was open under the arms. Made by sewing together small, square pieces of fur arranged to create a striped pattern, it reached from shoulder to knee, opening down the front. It probably closed, but the type of closure was not determined. Or it may have had a belt that tied around it. Once again, the fur had to have been tanned and the archeologists found evidence of scraping and of the use of vegetable matter for tanning.

He wore separate brown fur leggings on the lower part of his body. These covered the thigh and calf, and were fitted loosely enough to allow him to bend his knees easily. At the bottom was a fur tongue that could be pushed into a shoe or boot so that it would remain in place even when trekking through deep snow. A fur strip attached these leggings to the belt.

Each shoe was made from an oval piece of leather larger than the foot. The edges could therefore be turned up and were fastened with straps of leather. A net attached to the straps held grass that served to insulate the feet. Uppers, described as "probably fur," and as continuing up the leg "roughly in the form of a boot" protected the upper side of the foot and were tied around the ankle and held in place with grass cords.

His head covering was somewhat distorted, but appeared to be shaped like a blunted cone. Like the upper body garment, it was made of cut pieces of fur sewn together and had two leather straps attached.

Over all, he wore a cloak made of grass. The grasses measured more than one meter in length. The grass was plaited together at the top and fell loosely below the plaited area. As a result it would not have confined the movement of the legs and the water would have run down off the grass. This garment would have been water repellent, practical, and light in weight.

Two other items of dress were noted. One in very fragmentary condition was the equivalent of a backpack, and is called a "back pannier" by the archeologists. This type of carrying device is still used in the mountain regions of the area where the ice man was found. It consisted of a wooden horseshoe-shaped frame and some other wooden pieces that were separated from the pack but that fitted into notches in the frame. A number of cords made by twisting two twisted strands of grasses together were recovered near the frame. At its end, one cord fanned out in a tassel. The second item was another piece of ibex bone that was worked at both ends and looks like a small box. Its purpose was unclear, but it was suggested that it might have been an amulet.

The preservation of the body made it possible to see that the mummy had a number of tattoos. Some were in the form of three groups of vertical tattoos in the lumbar region. Others were at the knee and ankle joints. The suggestion that the tattoos were decorative, a form of ornamentation was thought unlikely as the tattoos would have been covered by his clothing. X-ray examination of the body revealed that the ice man had arthritis in the areas of the tattoos, and it has been hypothesized that given the placement of the tattoos in these areas, they could have been a form of medical treatment of the period.

No body or facial hair remained on the mummy, though some dark brown hairs were found with the remains. From this the technicians who recreated the clothes on a manikin guessed that the ice man would have been bearded and would have had long hair. This seems to be a reasonable conclusion because shaving implements even as late at the Roman era were dull and shaving something of an ordeal.

Technology

Some familiar tools are present or implied by the ice man's dress. The bone awl has continued to be part of the prehistoric tailor's or seamstress's tool kit and was likely used to punch holes in skin and fur. And though the ice man carried no needle, it is present by implication because the leather garments were sewn together. The animal skins and furs used included domesticated goat skin in the loincloth and the upper garment, the headwear and shoe soles were made of bearskin, and the uppers of the shoes and some straps were made from deerskin. The arrows in his quiver could have been used to obtain the bear and deer hides. The domesticated goat was probably killed for both food and skin to use in dress or in the home.

The skin would have been tanned. Plant substances used for tanning remained on the skins. And the skins showed markings indicating they had been scraped. Scraping the hide to make it thinner or cutting it into thin layers made the leather in the loincloth soft and flexible. Stone scrapers had been used for thousands of years, but the presence of a copper knife in the ice man's pack testifies to advances in the production of metal implements as well. Metal sickles could have been used to cut the grass that made up his cloak.

The flint implement in the pack could have made the hole in the white marble bead. The suggestion that the over fifty tattoos in the form of lines and crosses on the body might have been made using the awl does not appear to be accurate. Research reported from his museum home indicates that they were created by cutting fine incisions into which charcoal was rubbed.

Fashion

As noted previously, there is no way to know whether people engaged in any form of fashionable behavior at this time. One might be tempted to see the striping in the upper garment as a touch of fashion. Could it have been the latest style in fur jackets? Perhaps, but without other ice men of his and subsequent generations to compare with "Otzi" (the nickname given to him by the press based on the region where he was found, the Otztal Alps) we will never know. The words "style" and "fashion" are often used interchangeably, but they are not exactly the same. Fashion is short-term and changeable and style is how something appears. It can continue in use for an indefinite period of time (a tradition) or for a short time (a fashion), but the essential characteristic of fashion is change. It is known that in the twenty-first century both back panniers and garments such as the grass cape are still worn by agriculturists in the alpine regions. From this, one might speculate that in the dress of the prehistoric world, tradition might have been a stronger influence than fashion.

3

TECHNOLOGIES AND DRESS IN TOWNS, CITIES, AND EMPIRES
(Neolithic period to c. 500 CE)

Trading a lifestyle of hunting and gathering for farming and living in settled communities gradually led to the development of cities with large populations. At the same time social and political structures united larger areas beyond one city. As writing began to be used as a way of keeping records or became a way of recording history, the story of technological developments and their relationship to dress is increasingly set within those towns and cities where progress was also made in the arts, sciences, and extensive use of writing (*The American Heritage Dictionary*, 1992: 349).

The archeological record shows that *Homo sapiens* were not the first hominids to arrive in Europe and Asia, but they eventually became the only surviving hominid species. The earliest modern human remains in Europe and in Asia appear to date from about 100,000 years ago (Feder, 2010: 195). Probably in other regions the ability to make fibers into yarns and yarns into fabrics proceeded along a path similar to that described for Europe in Chapter 2.

Eureka moments seem less responsible for progress in making fabrics than the gradual accumulation of experience, knowledge, and skill. It is likely that making baskets from grasses and other plant stems could have served as an incubator for ideas about combining at least moderately flexible materials into mats, bags, or baskets. But the journey humans took between creating string, yarn, or thread (all names given to groups of fibers combined into a long continuous strand sturdy enough for many uses) remains a mystery, given the perishable nature of the materials used in textiles. I will use the word "yarn" to describe these structures, string being more often applied to use for wrapping or fastening and "thread" to such a strand used for sewing.

Human settlement and fiber use

Elizabeth Barber's overview of textile fibers and their production and use in *Prehistoric Textiles* (1991) and in *Women's Work* (1994) provides a broad overview useful in understanding early textile history. The steps and technological processes and tools needed to turn fibers into yarn and yarn into cloth have already been described in Chapter 2 for flax, the source of fibers used to make linen fabrics in Europe and the Middle East. Ancient Egypt became a major center for linen production. Flax is a widely distributed plant, available and used in both Europe and Asia, leading to the presumption that linen fibers from flax were the first fibers used in Eurasia. However, bast fibers growing in other regions were also important. Hemp apparently originated in Asia and was used extensively in China. Its cultivation spread into the Western world where it was used particularly for ropes, cords, and sails for boats as well as for utilitarian clothing. The botanical name is *Cannabis sativa* and it is a relative of marijuana, but it lacks the strong psychotropic qualities that cause marijuana to be classed as a drug. The fiber is obtained in a process like that for flax. In Europe, textile fibers were also obtained from nettle stems. A different nettle plant species in Asia was the source of ramie, which to this day is also known as China Grass.

Four population centers (Mesopotamia, Egypt, India, and China) serve to demonstrate the impact of different fiber species on the development of technologies that made possible the production of fabrics used for dress. Scholars generally agree that the first urban centers and civilizations arose in the Middle East in the area called Mesopotamia in the period from 5000 to 3000 BCE. At much the same time civilizations were developing in Egypt in the Nile Valley, in areas now part of China, and on the Indian sub-continent in the Indus River Valley. Fibers from the flax plant, hemp, cotton, various types of wools, and silk were, and still are, the most widely used natural fibers. Other natural fibers have been used in areas where the aforementioned fibers are not available, but the particular suitability of these five fibers for making cloth has given them the greatest appeal and value. Just as linen required retting, scutching, and hackling, the fibers from other plant and animal species required specialized processing.

All the evidence points to silk manufacture as beginning in the region occupied today by the Chinese. This fiber comes from the cocoon spun by the silkworm caterpillar that hatches from eggs laid by the *Bombex Mori* moth. Cultivated silk is the only natural filament fiber. Filament fibers are those measured in hundreds of meters or yards. In addition to cultivated silk there are a number of other silkworm species that spin cocoons; however, wild silk moths emerge from the cocoon by breaking through this outer enclosure, which means the fibers are cut and can only be used in what is called "staple" or short lengths. Also, these wild silks, which are also used to make fabrics, usually have brown or tan coloring and are somewhat coarser than cultivated silk. The species selected for cultivation undoubtedly was chosen for its white, fine fiber.

The legend of silk's origin reflects the almost mystical aura that surrounds this fiber. According to this story, silk fibers were discovered by Princess Hsi Ling-Shi c. 2640 BCE when a silkworm cocoon fell into a cup of hot tea and softened enough that the Princess could unwind the strands of silk from the cocoon. The reality is that silkworms were probably first cultivated as food (Feltwell, 1990). Furthermore, tea was not used in China until long after the time of this supposed accident (Steele and Major, 2000: 20). Other early evidence is cited by Vainker (2004). She notes that silk appears in an incised representation of a silkworm that has been dated to c. 4900 BCE and that the Chinese appear to have maintained a monopoly on the production of cultivated silk for at least 2,500 years.

All fibers have the characteristic of length, but the distance from fiber beginning to end can vary a great deal. The staple fibers of cotton, flax, hemp, nettles, and wool have a relatively short length, ranging from only a few millimeters or inches to a meter or a yard or more and must be twisted together to make a yarn. By comparison, cultivated silk fibers can be up to thousands of meters or yards in length and need not, though they can, be twisted when making yarns. Silk was the only filament fiber available for fabrics until the late nineteenth and early twentieth century when the first manufactured fibers were created. Of course, silk is also found in short, staple lengths if the silkworm moth makes an opening in the cocoon and in doing so breaks the fibers. But once the Chinese learned how to cultivate silkworms, a process called sericulture, they intentionally produced long continuous fibers.

Authorities generally agree that cotton was first cultivated on the Indian sub-continent at some time in the third millennium BCE. It was an important product of the ancient lands of the Indus Valley. And at much the same period of time, it appears to have come into use for textiles in South America. The species native to India is not the same as that in South America, indicating that cotton was an independent development in each area. Cotton staple is shorter than bast fiber staple, and therefore required different equipment for spinning. It was prized for the delicate fabrics into which it was made and for its excellent dyeing and color retention, characteristics that linen lacked (Yafa, 2006: 21).

The various parts of the world in which civilizations were developing also had access to hair fibers. In the Western Hemisphere these were animals in the camelid family, such as llamas, alpacas, and vicunas, and in some areas goat species, whereas in Eurasia sheep and goats were domesticated and their wool used. Wool from camels in the Middle East and the Far East was collected as it was shed. Gradual changes in the coats and the characteristics of the fibers of domesticated sheep fleece were evident to the people living close to these animals, and by the third and fourth millennia wool with "woolly" qualities was available. Mesopotamia became a major manufacturer and trader of wool fabrics as well as linen. Both fibers were used in their dress (Barber, 1991: 20–30).

Looms increase in complexity and variety

Given the fragility of textiles, sources of information about the hand-powered devices used to produce fabrics, the kind of textiles they produced, and how they differed from place to place are incomplete. Fortunately, Ancient Egyptian burial practices in combination with the hot dry climate of Egypt preserved a wealth of information, especially about textiles made for royalty and the upper classes. There are no other early civilizations that yield similar quantities of actual textiles. Then, too, in Egypt there are written records and tomb paintings that provide additional information about many aspects of dress. The Egyptian belief that the dead are expected to have a full afterlife resulted in provision of tomb

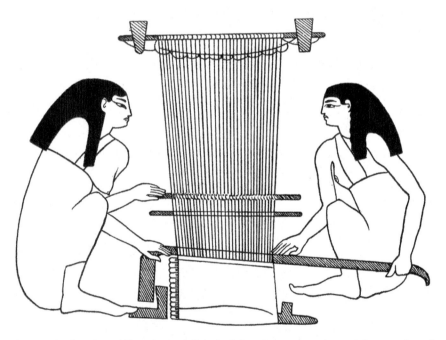

Figure 3.1 Drawing of Egyptian painting depicting women carrying out the weaving of linen fabric. Workers weave fabric on a two-bar loom that is parallel to the floor and has small feet at either end to raise the working area above floor level. Lengthwise yarns are fastened to the beams at each end of the loom. Kneeling weavers insert the crosswise (weft) yarns to create a closely woven square fabric (The Metropolitan Museum of Art. Image source: The Art Archive at Art Resource, New York)

contents that paralleled the activities of daily life. Small models of laborers carrying out daily activities were entombed along with other necessities, including textiles and actual items of dress.

Both models and paintings of textile workrooms illustrate the production of fabric from spinning through weaving. Drawing on these sources, we know that although wool was worn, linen was the major fiber used for Egyptian dress. Its premier status was due to the characteristics of its comfort in a hot climate and the ease of its care. Also, written records and accounts by travelers comment on Egyptian religious practice. Wool was considered unclean, and therefore not to be worn in temples and for religious rites (Tortora and Eubank, 2010: 35).

The relatively simple back strap loom of the hunter-gatherers was ideal for people who did not want to be burdened with having to carry large equipment from place to place. But in settled communities, such as those in Egypt and Mesopotamia, more complex looms could speed up weaving and facilitate creation of larger and more intricate fabric structures. To make the process practical it was necessary to find a way of placing tension on the warp yarns. Looms of the Neolithic period provided that tension in one of two ways. Both could have evolved from more primitive back strap looms. In ancient Egypt and in Mesopotamia, horizontal ground looms were used. Two beams were placed at ground level, slightly elevated so that there was room for the action of weaving. The warp yarns were fastened to one beam and then extended and fastened to the second beam. Some device, possibly a stick, carried the weft yarns. In order to avoid having to laboriously raise and lower two sets of yarns each time a row of weft yarns was inserted, one set of warps was placed over a rod called a shed rod and the second set of yarns was placed below. When the shed rod was raised, an area called the shed was opened sufficiently that the crosswise (weft) yarns could be inserted. This did not solve the problem of how to get the lower set of yarns above the upper set in order to vary the interlacing. Holding each yarn in a device called a heddle that was in turn fastened to a heddle bar solved this problem. Probably each heddle was a loop of yarn tied to the heddle bar through which the warp yarns could be threaded. When lifted, the heddle bar raised this second set of yarns above the first, allowing the yarns to be inserted so that they interlaced in a different pattern. The time required to set up the loom before weaving was well-spent, as it made the weaving progress far more rapid. One additional device and step was required. When first inserted into the fabric, weft yarns were not taut nor did they lie flat. A sword-like device made of wood, called a batten, was used to beat the weft yarns into place.

Another type of loom different from the horizontal flat loom solved the vital problem of placing tension on the lengthwise yarns by creating an upright vertical loom in which the warp yarns were fastened to a crosswise beam, a step comparable to fastening yarns around the warp beam of the horizontal ground loom.

Figure 3.2 Weaving in Athens, Greece (560 BCE). Painting that encircles a vase depicts the production of wool cloth. Figures at the far left are spinning the wool into yarn. Those at the far right have wound the wool yarn into balls that can be used in preparing the loom. The vertical loom at the center has warp yarns attached to a beam at the top. Groups of warp yarns are tied to weights at the bottom in order to provide tension on warp. The weaver on the right inserts a shuttle carrying weft yarns across the loom and interlaces these with the warps. The woman on the left beats the newly inserted weft against the formed fabric that is then folded at the top of the loom (source: HIP/The Art Archive at Art Resource, New York)

Tension was provided to the warp yarns by fastening weights to the ends of groups of warp yarns. This loom is called a warp-weighted loom and was used in areas to the north of the Mediterranean Sea. For early versions of this loom, often the only evidence are the weights used, which were usually made of clay or stone and shaped in ways that made it easy to fasten the yarns to the weights. Shed rods, heddles, and battens were also used in this loom and a Greek vase painting illustrates clearly the steps in weaving as they were done in Greece, c. 560 BCE. In China, further adaptations were made as a result of the special needs of silk weaving, and in order to create the very complex fabrics that characterized dress in China.

Dress materials and trade

In any consideration of the relationship between dress and technology, the tendency is to look only at the hand or power machines that are used to make textiles. This fails to get to some of the types of technology that underlie the ability to produce dress. As in Chapter 2, I suggested that the earliest technology for obtaining dress was the projectile point used as it was to kill animals, the pelts of which almost certainly were the earliest materials used to make body enclosures for humans. I would argue that the importance of boats and ships is generally overlooked when looking at the materials that are made into dress in later periods, whether they are textiles, body ornaments, or attachments. Small boats and larger ships must be acknowledged as a major means of transporting the raw materials of dress over the faster river and sea routes, thereby becoming major contributors to expanding options for dress beyond the locality where they were made.

Economic theorist Bernstein (2008), in a study of world trade, identified trade of copper for grain as beginning sometime around 3000 BCE. Not only was copper useful in making durable tools of many kinds, it was an attractive metal from which decorative objects worn on the human body could be and were made. Copper was also added to soldiers' armor, a utilitarian form of dress, to provide a layer of protection. Some unidentifiable ancient metallurgists discovered that if copper was alloyed with tin in certain proportions, it became the metal called bronze. This stronger metal replaced copper, and the Middle East and Europe moved into the Bronze Age about 2900 BCE. Scarce and valuable, tin was not found everywhere, thereby becoming another important trade commodity. There is no absolute certainty what trade routes were used to carry tin from Northern Europe to the Middle Eastern and the Mediterranean lands. It is clear, thanks to the written cuneiform records on clay seals from Mesopotamia, that by 3000 BCE, ships in the Persian Gulf were carrying trade goods. Other maritime routes were added that included the Red Sea and the Indian Ocean. And tin may have spent part of its journey in boats on European rivers.

The Atlantic Ocean was much more of a challenge to seafaring traders than local rivers and the more placid Mediterranean Sea. Winchester (2009) credits tin, obtained from Spain and farther away in Brittany and Cornwall, as the stimulus leading the seafaring Phoenician traders to brave the storm-tossed waters of the Atlantic. But by the seventh century BCE and after, dress motivated these sailors to explore the Atlantic Ocean as they hunted for murex snails south of the Straits of Gibraltar. The Minoans, 700 years earlier had discovered that through complex processing, they could extract a beautiful, durable, and costly, purple dye from these mollusks. Known as Tyrian purple (named after the Phoenician city Tyre) or royal purple, its scarcity and cost made textiles dyed purple a status symbol, particularly for the Roman ruling classes. Roman senators had a visible band of purple fabric sewn on their tunics that communicated the office they held to all who saw them. This dyestuff was worth its weight in silver, was a major status symbol, and sailors found the resulting profits worth risking the perils of the turbulent Atlantic.

Not all parts of the world are endowed with navigable rivers or seas and for long, overland trips some other conveyance had to be used. For desert areas, the camel with its physiological ability to conserve water was the solution. The dromedary camel, with a single hump on its back, presented loading difficulties. Once again, technology came to the rescue. Sometime between 1300 and 100 BCE, North African nomads developed a saddle that distributed the weight on the camel's back in such a way that the animal could carry up to 500 pounds and some stronger camels carried as much as 1,000 pounds of silk or other products on these packs (Bernstein, 2008: 56).

The durable materials used to make beads were most likely the first items related to dress to be traded over long distances. Diamanti (N.D) in *A Bead Timeline* provides this information. Marine shell beads occur such long distances from the sea that they had to have been obtained though trade (Diamanti, 2003). Coral beads, a product of the Mediterranean Sea, have been discovered in Central Europe and have been assigned dates as early as 30,000 years ago.

Jewelry has been found in all of the early civilizations. It is not always possible to know exactly what role the precious metals, gemstones, and jewelry played. They were likely used to designate status, to serve as a means of preserving wealth, or were simply ornamentation. They are always present and are made from both valued local materials and trade goods.

Gold and silver, two of the metals much used in jewelry, are distributed widely around the world. To capture gold carried away from where it was held in the soil in streams, the ancient equivalents of American "forty-niners" panned for the precious metal. This process takes advantage of the heavy weight of gold that causes it to sink to the bottom of the gold pan, while other debris is washed away. Another method may have given rise to the myth of Jason and the golden fleece. Prospectors would immerse a sheepskin in gold-bearing streams and the gold would catch in the wool. Drying and then shaking the pelt released the gold. Later, techniques developed for removing gold from deposits in rocks and still later gold was mined from human-made tunnel walls. Goldsmiths used a number of procedures to turn the precious metal into jewelry. The earliest uses were the simplest. Gold is malleable, relatively soft, and easily worked. Over time, more complex technologies were applied (Phillips, 1996).

Silver is only rarely found in the pure state, and more often in ores and alloys with other metals, including gold. Silver, which came into use later than gold, usually had to be separated from the ore or alloyed state through heating processes. Like gold it was valued for jewelry and also widely used for coins.

Precious metals and gems required specialized technologies for their production. Rather than pay the costs of shipping large quantities of materials containing waste discarded after making the final product, cities and ports on the trade routes developed technologies for making at least minimal improvements in the precious and semi-precious materials they were shipping. Workers developed a sophisticated repertory of tools and skills for making beads and jewelry. Gold crafts had developed all around the Mediterranean and artifacts created by the Egyptians, Mesopotamians, Minoans, Greeks, Etruscans, and Romans required a variety of techniques. Granulation made it possible to cover the surface with a multitude of small gold balls. Artisans created lacy patterns of filigree work by applying gold wires and beads. Punching holes in thin sheets of gold could make open tracery patterns. Gems were set in golden mounts or combined with enameled motifs, a process that has been used from Egyptian times on (d'Orange Mastai 1981: 26).

The silk of China and cotton of India were unique and highly desirable textiles that were pivotal in establishing trade with other regions. But long before the trade routes carried silk to ancient Egypt, Greece, and Rome, the aforementioned durable kinds of materials used for additional elements of dress had been moving around the world. Trade between the Far East and Europe in the period from the second century BCE to about the fourteenth century CE utilized the so-called Silk Road. Even though wild silk was apparently used in the Indus Valley and on the Greek Island of Cos, these fabrics did not compare with the luxurious silk fabrics that gave China a product with no parallel in the Middle East and the West. The Chinese closely guarded their secrets of sericulture and the technological skill needed for its creation. The origins of the Silk Road are obscure. By the second century BCE, China was trading with the peoples that occupied the territory to the west (Boulnois, 2004). Climatic, political, and territorial changes altered the specific routes over which goods and ideas passed between east and west. On its way west, silk found a welcome in the communities through which it passed. In the Indian sub-continent, cotton cultivation and its spinning and weaving progressed to the point that it too moved not only west to Mesopotamia, Egypt, Greece, and Rome but also east to China, where it was also prized. China maintained its hold on the technology for producing silk and the methods of spinning and weaving silk fabrics. The long journey of silk raised its price astronomically. Both the Greeks and Romans are reported to have unraveled silk fabrics to remove the silk threads and make them go farther by blending them with cotton or other fibers; however, there is no hard evidence to support this conjecture. By the time this luxury fabric passed from merchant to merchant, finally reaching Rome, it was quite literally worth its weight in gold.

Fibers and technology shape dress

The textile fabrics discussed above are, of course, some of the raw materials from which garments are made. And styles of dress made from those textiles can vary widely. However, fibers and the fabrics from which they are made often place limitations on the styles of dress that can be created. This topic will be addressed in the chapter summary in relation to some specific examples of dress of Egyptians and Romans. But it is worth noting some of the ways in which fibers can and have limited the development of styles of dress.

Textile scientists speak about the properties of different textiles. Although the yarns and fabrics made from these fibers can modify these qualities to some extent, the inherent fiber characteristics will always play a role. Linen, hemp, cotton and other bast fibers are primarily cellulose. Wool and silk, both animal products, are proteins. Cellulosic fibers tend to conduct heat away from the body, therefore they are cooler to wear. They tend to be fairly absorbent, another quality that makes them comfortable in a warm climate and they allow the evaporation of moisture. By contrast, protein fibers, especially wool, tend to be poor conductors of heat, and also less absorbent. As a result, they do have good insulation qualities, making them more comfortable in a cooler climate where they prevent the loss of body heat. When given certain kinds of finishes such as fulling, which shrinks and condenses tightly woven cloth, wool tends to shed rain. The Greeks used such fabrics for cloaks worn by travelers that provided warmth and some degree of water repellency. The fulling process was an important contributor to the usefulness of wool fabrics, and is an important textile technology, but is it only possible because of the characteristics of wool fibers. Cellulosic fibers are flammable; protein fibers will burn but the flame tends to go out fairly quickly. They are described as not supporting combustion. Both cellulosic and protein fibers can be dyed, but protein fibers tend to retain color better. Cellulosic fibers can be laundered easily, whereas protein fibers are damaged by alkaline materials that are present in laundry products such as soap. Individual fibers may have special characteristics that make them especially good or unsuitable for some specific uses. For example, sheep's wool is characterized by a microscopic cell structure that causes those fibers to cling together, and facilitates the production of felt and assists in fulling. Cotton is quite receptive to a wide variety of dyes, and has been valued for the colorful effects achieved.

Just as the fibers play an important role in styles, the technologies used to weave textile fabrics also have an impact on the styles of dress. The looms already described are essentially rectangular, and will produce rectangular fabrics. The quality of cutting tools during the time period under discussion was poor, because the technology did not exist for producing metals that could be made into sharp shears needed to cut fabrics into different shapes. As a result, much of the clothing worn in the ancient world is draped or has minimal cutting and sewing. In this sense, the loom can be a technological limitation on the type of dress that can be created most efficiently.

Production and consumption of textiles in the ancient world

One of the challenges of a culture or civilization is to produce enough raw materials to dress their populations. With smaller populations in which the labors of men and women are differentiated, it is often the women who do the textile production, although men may be responsible for harvesting plant materials or obtaining fibers from fleece. The tasks required in spinning and weaving could easily be interrupted to care for children and could be done within the home or by groups of women working together (Barber, 1994). Textile production in ancient Greece was most often done at home and the housewife was expected to produce fabric for the household. Greek dress was made from the rectangles or squares of woven cloth, essentially as they came from the loom. Wool or linen cloth was wrapped around the body, fastened at the shoulders, often with a type of decorative pin called a fibula, was usually hand sewn at the open side and belted. Color and ornamentation could be added by using more complex weaves, or by dyeing, painting, or embroidering.

Mesopotamian, Ancient Egyptian, and Ancient Roman civilizations show a mix of domestic and proto-industrial production. Scarre's timeline for the Smithsonian states that writing began in the fourth millennium BCE in Mesopotamia (Scarre, 1993). It consisted of incising markings on clay tablets. Wild (2003), writing about Mesopotamia in the Bronze Age, reports that the earliest Mesopotamian records were kept about businesses: the size of herds of sheep and production rates of textiles. Over time, what was written became more personal. The tablets are letters from which insights can be gained ranging from domestic relations between parents and children to the organization of textile production. For example, factories were so large that one tablet records 165 women working in one of them. Others record output targets, identify the types of wool being used and details about technical operations performed including dyeing and finishing. Scholars are unable to translate some of these technical terms. As the civilizations of the Middle East entered the Iron Age (c. 1000–500 BCE), the availability of iron made an important technological contribution to the production of wool: the development of sheep shears that could neatly and evenly cut off the sheep's fleece.

Egypt is sometimes called "the land of linen," because of its role in provision of linen fabrics. Until the New Kingdom (c. 1550 to 1070), women did the spinning and weaving. In the New Kingdom period, evidence indicates that there were variations introduced in the types of looms, that men worked as weavers, and cloth production was a cottage industry as well as being done in workshops in the harems of royal palaces, in temples, and in country estates. The fabric being woven was the simplest of weaves, the plain or tabby weave (Allgrove-McDowell, 2003).

Herlihy (1990), who writes about women and work, notes that Roman matriarchs, like those of Greece, were expected to know how to weave. To symbolize their mastery of this skill, brides carried a spindle and distaff. In the early years of Roman history, cloth production was done in the home, but by the time of the Roman Empire, female slaves on large estates produced many fabrics in a work area called a *gynaeceum*. These were factory-like business operations that employed as many as fifty or one hundred men and women. Given the broad expanse of the Roman Empire, manufacturing was done all over the Roman world and the products imported to Rome. Men skilled in the technologies for making specialized textiles carried out these separate operations: bleaching, fulling, or dyeing. Towns had active markets where fabrics or even ready-made garments could be bought. Additional items of dress such as footwear, head coverings, jewelry, make-up, and perfumes each had unique technologies (Tortora and Eubank, 2010: 82).

Evidences of fashion and limits of knowledge

While the role of technology in enabling the styles of dress in Ancient Egypt is relatively clear, identifying fashion, specifically styles that persisted for a short period of time that were widely adopted, is difficult. Egyptian civilization from the Old Kingdom to the New Kingdom lasted some 3,000 years. Even with the many artifacts found in tombs and depictions of Egyptian life, it is not possible to trace year-by-year style changes or even century-by-century changes. It is clear that some styles persisted from the earliest periods until the end of what is identified as the New Kingdom. New elements enter the repertory of dress from time to time. Often they are associated with interactions with populations outside of Egypt, but once adopted, these forms of dress persisted. What seems to be the static nature of Egyptian dress is generally considered to be the result of the relative isolation of the region compared to other regions and to be reflective of the conservative nature of Egyptian society. If fashion existed among the upper classes, it is hard to identify.

Chapter 2, with its limited resources for the study of dress and fashion and related technologies, is followed in this chapter by a look at a world in which technologies are becoming more sophisticated, and the information about our subject more plentiful. The development of systems for writing adds to the knowledge base from which conclusions are drawn when looking at dress and its components. In this chapter, one can see how, as in Chapter 2, there is a tendency to overlook technologies essential to dress that are not part of its production, but rather aid in its acquisition. While the changes in weaving technology that produce considerable differences in the dress made from fabrics of the time are important, the transport of textiles and other elements of dress cannot be ignored. Nor can one ignore advances in the technology for making the tools used to produce elements of dress. Examples include tools to cut fleeces, metal-working, and fabrication of jewelry, and as we will see when looking at the illustrations that follow, in methods of altering the human appearance and body.

The importance of gender in use of technology also appears in this chapter. Expectations for women of skill in using textile production tools that allow them to work in the home can be contrasted with the assignment of tasks requiring greater strength that are assigned to men. And in virtually all cultures, there is a difference in the dress assigned to men and women and in the relationship of dress to status.

Looking at relationships through illustrations

Egypt

The people in this reproduction of an Egyptian wall painting are dressed for a formal social occasion. This is made clear to the viewer by the small, pointed objects on their heads. The perfumed, inverted wax cones were intended to melt gradually during the evening and release perfume. This and other invisible fragrances are a part of the dress of upper-class men and women in the New Kingdom in Egypt. Other body modifications can also be observed in this painting. Both men and women outlined their eyes with paint, polished their finger and toenails, and colored their lips and cheeks. Eyebrows and eyelashes were colored and eyes outlined with kohl in the New Kingdom period. Kohl was made from galena, a mineral form of lead sulfate mixed with soot. Galena had to

Figure 3.3 Egyptian wall painting depicting formal dress. Image: The Metropolitan Museum of Art (source: The Art Archive at Art Resource, New York)

be obtained by mining deposits found in the desert. Henna, obtained from dried leaves and roots of a tree-like plant, was used to color nails and hair. Ground into a paste and mixed with water as needed, it yielded reds, purples, oranges, and browns. Lips and cheeks might be colored with ochre, a pigment obtained from clays tinted red by iron oxide. Before applying it to the body, the clay had to be cleansed of impurities such as sand, and mixed with oils or animal fats.

All of these cosmetics had to undergo manufacturing before they were useful, requiring a variety of supporting technological processes including mining, grinding, purification, and mixing that preceded their use. These same products have been used in other historical periods. For example, henna is used in much of the world in the twenty-first century.

Textile technologies

The garments worn by men and women had many similarities. Both were made of linen, which may have been woven on a horizontal ground loom, although some time in the Early New Kingdom a vertical loom with two beams seems to have also come into use. Women did the spinning by hand using spindles. The natural color of linen is gray to brown, and the upper class Egyptians preferred a whiter cloth, so once woven, male workers bleached the fabrics. The cloth was whitened by applying natron or potash (both natural detergents that facilitated bleaching), beating, and rinsing in running water, and then bleaching in the sun. Few fabrics for clothing were dyed. This is thought to be at least in part because the Egyptian lands had relatively few plants from which dyestuffs could be made (Allgrove-McDowell, 2003: 30–6).

Fabrics for dress were not cut and sewn, but wrapped and draped, often combining several pieces of fabric into layers that appear to be a single garment. Careful examination of the garment worn by the man depicted in the painting (Figure 3.3) shows that he is wearing a skirt and a separate cape, which together make a full outer garment. Fringes, visible in the depiction, remained when fabrics were taken from the loom. They form a decorative element.

Pleating added additional aesthetic effects to Egyptian dress. Devices identified as "pleating boards" are held by several museums; however, archeologists argue that the function of these boards is not clear and the pleating could have been done by hand using some form of starch. Metallurgy had not yet developed to the point where an ironing device could be used.

Other elements of Egyptian dress

Men did not allow beards to grow, but were clean-shaven. Occasionally, depictions of servants will show stubble. The hairstyles depicted on upper-class men and women are wigs. Most wigs, like those in this painting, were black. The highest-quality wigs were made of human hair and men's were usually shorter and women's longer. Some were quite complex in structure. Less costly wigs might be made of wool, flax, palm fiber, or felt.

In the depiction above, only the men wear sandals, which were the main footwear for upper-class individuals. They were made of rushes woven or twisted together.

White being the usual color of garments, beadwork and other jewels in vivid colors provided the major decorative elements of Egyptian dress in the New Kingdom. Beaded and jeweled collars and beaded headdresses are augmented by earrings for women (they were rarely worn by men) and bracelets. Much of Egyptian jewelry had religious or mystical significance. To create these elaborate items of dress, both international trade and development of an extensive technology were necessary. In larger cities and towns, specialists who had mastered specific skills were available. Shaping and drilling holes in stones was one of the most basic steps in making Egyptian jewelry. Most of the preferred stones were available locally; however, the highly prized lapis lazuli had to be imported from Afghanistan. The blue of this stone was valued for its aesthetic qualities and for its symbolism (it was considered to symbolize the night sky) (Phillips, 1996: 12). The materials used served not only as status symbols, but also had amuletic value, protecting the wearer from evil.

The Mesopotamians and Egyptians appear to have been the earliest to develop glass-making processes. The Egyptians used colored glass or faience as a less costly substitute for precious or semi-precious stones. Wall paintings also show depictions of artisans preparing jewelry by drilling and threading beads on cords and beside them, workers in metal. Faience beads were created by dyeing clay various colors. The colored clay was wrapped around a reed so that a tube was formed. Tubes were cut into the required lengths and dried in the sun, the reed removed, and the beads were baked.

Fashion

While the role of technology in enabling the styles of dress in Ancient Egypt is relatively clear, identifying fashion, specifically styles that persisted for a short period of time that were widely adopted, is difficult. Egyptian civilization from the Old Kingdom to the New Kingdom lasted some 3000 years. Even with the many artifacts found in tombs and depictions of Egyptian life, it is not possible to trace year-by-year style changes or even century-by-century changes. It is clear that some styles persisted from the earliest periods until the end of what is identified as the New Kingdom. New elements enter the repertory of dress depicted from time to time, and often they are associated with interaction with populations outside of Egypt, but once adopted, these forms of dress persisted. What seems to be the static nature of Egyptian dress is generally considered to be the result of the relative isolation of the region compared to other regions and to be reflective of the conservative nature of Egyptian society. If fashion existed among the upper classes, it would be hard to identify. It may be that a careful study of wig styles might show this as an area in which fashion is present. Certainly there seem to be changes in the length of wigs, the colors, the arrangement of the coiffure, and the ornamentation added. Therefore, a systematic study of the depiction of wigs in Egyptian art might produce some interesting results.

Rome

Roman dress was not complex in style and construction, for example, basic garments like the T-shaped tunics. Many others were draped and, except for the toga, which was roughly circular, were square or rectangular, the shape of the fabric as it came from the loom. The technologies basic to the Roman dress depicted would have been needles with which to sew, devices with which to cut cloth, ability to procure fibers through cultivation and/or trade, spinning, weaving, and finishing processes to improve the appearance and the feel of the wool fabric, such as bleaching and compacting the fabric through fulling. It does not appear that Roman garments required or benefitted from radical technological innovations.

Dress Description

The man depicted in the statue in Figure 3.4, from the first century CE soon after the establishment of the Roman Empire, is identified as a magistrate, a public official. He is wearing two visible outer garments. The unseen undergarment worn closest to the skin would have consisted of a loincloth, probably made of linen. The partially visible garment worn closest to the skin is a tunic, has short sleeves, and ends at about knee length. It is T-shaped, rather similar in form to an elongated loose modern T-shirt with cap sleeves, and was made of either linen or wool. It could be dyed for some types of wear; however, a proper Roman tunic worn with a toga was white and made of wool. Over the tunic this Roman citizen wears a draped wool garment called the *toga*. The toga was the badge of Roman citizenship for men. The identification of this individual as a magistrate probably results from the apparent difference in color of the band at the edge of the neckline area of the toga, a feature which Croom (1970: 42) points out.

Magistrates wore a toga called the *toga praetexta* that had a band of fabric dyed purple at the toga edge. The purple dye required complex processing, and would therefore probably have been an extra piece attached by sewing to the edge of the toga. By the time of the Roman Empire, the toga was roughly circular in shape, with one side having a section that folded over to form the toga into a semi-circle. The toga was draped with the folded edge placed at the center of

Figure 3.4 Example of basic Roman attire (source: Vanni Archive/The Art Archive at Art Resource, New York)

the body and extended almost to the floor, the bulk of the garment was drawn over the left shoulder, then pulled across the back, and under the right arm, then taken across the front of the body and pulled over the right shoulder again. Sometimes the fabric across the back was pulled over the top of the head when participating in ceremonies. Roman satirists often speak of the difficulties of keeping this garment in place. Footwear could have been shoes, as seen here, sandals, or boots. In some periods men were clean-shaven, in others bearded.

Technologies required

The tunic and toga would not have required innovative technologies for their production, but would have relied on well-established weaving processes that may have been adopted from earlier civilizations. The fibers available to the Romans were linen, wool, hemp, cotton, and silk, the latter two being luxuries and more likely used for women's dress than for men's, as silk fabrics were viewed by some influential leaders as effeminate. Cotton was imported from India and silk made its way across the trade routes from China. The technologies used to spin these fibers into yarns were part of the civilizations where they originated. Weaving was sometimes done before fabrics were transported; however, both materials were very costly, so they might also arrive as yarns to be woven into cloth by the well-developed Roman weaving technology. Ready-made clothing was available, and cities such as Rome had specific districts where one could shop for shoes, jewelry, cloaks, and other garments, many of which were imported from across the Empire.

Although the toga worn by ordinary citizens was white, some variations such as that of the magistrate proclaimed the wearer's status by the addition of color. Wool was the predominant fabric in Ancient Rome. It could be dyed, but different colored fleece from different breeds of sheep were more likely to be used in their natural colors. If wool had to be dyed, the Romans preferred to dye the fleece before the yarn was spun and the fabric woven. Linen was harder to dye and was generally used in its natural color or bleached.

Sebesta et al. (1994: 66) views the wide variety of textiles and colors available as "a fashion industry developed around Roman women." She notes a selection of fabrics either closely or loosely woven and the skill of dyers in producing such varied colors as marigold yellow, reddish orange, sea blue, and sky blue. Although the basic form of dress in Ancient Rome may not have been subject to fashion change, apparently the colors were. One group of dyers specialized in importing the aforementioned purple dye, made from sea snails and imported from Tyre. It was needed not only for bands of color on the *toga praetexta* and bands of color on other officials' togas, but also on dress for the nobility. Togas worn by those who held specific offices were made in specified colors and with ornamentation that immediately conveyed the status of the individual. Dyeing, therefore, was an important part of textile technology.

Maintenance of clothing was also essential. The fuller not only processed fabrics during the manufacturing, but also served the same function as a cleaner in the twenty-first century. Roman togas and other woolen garments required frequent cleaning, a task undertaken by the fuller through soaking the cloth in a mixture of warm water and urine, which had been collected in public places for this purpose. Workers stood in the vat and stamped on the cloth to agitate it so as to separate dirt from the cloth. The cloth was rinsed, wrung – two men were required to wring out a toga – and then hung out to dry. The surface was brushed or combed to restore its appearance. To whiten the cloth, it might be subjected to smoke from burning sulfur.

Although the illustration of Roman men's dress does not show his footwear clearly, shoe-making was sufficiently sophisticated that the Romans distinguished between the skills of shoe-makers, boot-makers, and sandal-makers. This would indicate that technologies for tanning and working with leather were well developed. Furthermore, metallurgy was needed to make nails that held the sandals together. Archeologists are able to date sandals they find in excavations by the type of nails that were used (Curry, 2012).

Just as garments such as the toga communicated the wearer's status, footwear also signified status. Various types of footwear were to be worn for specific venues and occasions. The one shown on the magistrate is what the Roman's called a *calceus*. It was worn with the toga. Croom (2002) sees its closest modern equivalent as an ankleboot or shoeboot.

Relatively little cutting and little sewing was needed to correctly shape the fabric for a tunic. Often garments were woven to the correct shape, an advantage because Roman cutting tools have been described as relatively dull. Hand sewing would join pieces as necessary. Needles were made of bone or bronze. The toga, being a draped garment made in one piece, would not have required sewing. The ordinary citizen's toga was an off-white color, the natural color of white sheep fleece.

Those who took great pride in their appearance would be likely to have the barber/hairdresser style their hair, and often used a curling iron to create the desired curls that crossed the forehead. The tools essential for grooming, like some of those for making clothing, depended on metallurgy. Scissors, razors, tweezers, and curling irons were essential implements. The quality of cutting tools, whether for cutting cloth or shaving the face, was limited because although the Romans knew and used iron and could make steel, they were unable to process the metal at temperatures high enough to produce steel that would hold an edge. As a result, when imitating an Emperor provided the opportunity to appear bearded instead of with a shaved face, men gave up the daily struggle with a razor, only to resume it when a new Emperor chose to set another style. Was this fashion? Perhaps.

Fashion

Similar styles are worn throughout Roman history and evidence of "widespread acceptance of styles for a short period of time" is not easily identified. Sebesta *et al.* (1994) sees evidence of fashion in changes in the desire among women to adopt the current colors that seem to change often. Toga styles did change, but the motivation for changes in togas is not clear. It seems that over time there was a movement toward a garment that was less cumbersome and easier to manage. Its official status as a garment that was a symbol, and its use stipulated by the Emperor for certain occasions, probably would have inhibited or at least slowed radical changes.

It may be easier to see changes in hairstyles for men and women and in particular in facial hair styles for men as influenced by fashion. The Roman in Figure 3.4 is clean-shaven. Until the late Roman Republic (509 to 27 BCE), men had tended to wear beards. By the time of the establishment of the Roman Empire (31 CE), the clean-shaven face predominated. The Emperor Hadrian (reigned from 117 to 138 CE) is depicted as bearded, a style he may have adopted to hide a scar. Following his example, men tended to wear beards and from this point onward bearded and beardless faces seem to have been associated with current imperial practice. One of the conditions said to be necessary for fashion to thrive is the ability to communicate information about new styles. Emperors were depicted on the coinage of their reign, and those coins were circulated throughout the vast Empire. They generally depicted the head of the emperor, and therefore it was easy even for those living in the far corners of the Empire to see what hairstyle was current in Rome and to follow fashions that originated with the current emperor. So one might see Roman coins as a sort of "fashion plate," as they circulated around the Empire where the fashion-conscious could keep up with current fashion.

4

TECHNOLOGY AND DRESS FACILITATE FASHION CHANGE

(Early medieval period to the 17th century in Europe)

Historians have assigned The Roman Empire a span of the years from 31 BCE to 476 CE. At its maximum the European territory of the Empire had stretched to Britain in the north, the Danube River in the east, and to the Middle East and North Africa. This vast domain was governed from the city of Rome until about 300 CE, after which the Roman emperor Constantine moved the capital to the East in order that it would be more accessible to Rome's eastern territories. This new capital was named Constantinople after its founder. Today it is Istanbul in the country of Turkey. This change effectively divided the Empire into an eastern area called the Byzantine Empire, and into a western section that succumbed to an attack from the north. In 476 CE, the last Roman Emperor in the west was deposed. Gradually the western and northern parts of the Empire developed into a number of independently governed regions. The name assigned to the period that followed the fall of Rome is the Middle Ages, a period that lasted for almost a thousand years. The time from the fall of the city of Rome until the ninth century had been called the Dark Ages, a name reflecting a lack of records needed to document this period. Research has shed more light on the so-called Dark Ages, and as a result historians at present are more likely to call this period the Early Middle Ages. While the Western Empire fragmented, the Byzantine Empire continued to rule over large territories in the Middle East and North Africa. Over the same time the Arab civilizations grew stronger and contested with the Byzantines for control over territory. The rapid spread of Islam served as a unifying force for the Arab states.

The Byzantine Empire

Byzantium maintained ties with the ruling powers in Europe. As a center of culture and the arts, it exerted considerable influence over the Western world. The rulers of European regions imitated the styles in the arts and dress of the more sophisticated Byzantine court. A major element of Byzantine dress was the wearing of silk garments trimmed with jewels. Much of the silk that had become a major status symbol for the Greeks and Romans had originated in China and traveled the Silk Road to Mediterranean ports in the Levant. It came in the form of finished textiles or as yarns or silk fiber.

For centuries China had managed to guard the method of cultivating silkworms and processing the silk they extruded. Little by little some of the countries near to China managed to learn how to produce silk. Chinese immigrants to Korea are said to have taught the Koreans how to produce silk around 200 BCE and soon after 300 BCE Japan was also producing silk. India had long been using wild silk to make silk fabrics and by 300 BCE they were also cultivating silk. Alexander the Great (356–323 BCE) encountered silk when fighting in Persia and his troops carried these fabrics back to Greece and Egypt. Hundreds of years later, demand for imported silk remained strong in the Mediterranean region and in areas influenced by the Byzantine Empire. By this time the Persians had gained control of the trade.

The Byzantines had been using imported silk yarns to weave handsome fabrics, but very much wanted to control production of the fiber, given its high cost. Industrial espionage is not a uniquely modern phenomenon. Feltwell (1990) tells how monks from Persia are credited with smuggling silkworm eggs and mulberry seeds inside hollow staves for the Byzantines. From the fourth to the twelfth centuries on, Byzantine and, to a larger extent, Islamic silks dominated the European silk market, although this began to change as a result of silk weaving being brought to Spain after the Arab conquest in the eighth century, and to the city of Palermo in Sicily in 1147. Gradually silk production spread from Sicily to other Italian cities (Muthesius, 2003: 325).

With the spread of Islam, the Arab presence in the areas controlled by the Byzantines grew stronger. They gained control over the holy places claimed by both Christians and followers of Islam, after which the Europeans launched the first of a series of crusades in 1095 CE. They claimed these wars were to free the Christian holy places in Palestine from Arab domination. These military campaigns had some successes and some failures, but ended in the fifteenth century without achieving their goal. The Byzantine Empire was overthrown when the Ottoman Empire conquered Constantinople in 1453. The Crusades ended with the defeat of the ninth crusade in 1472. Meanwhile, throughout this period, the European territories had gradually formed into nations or smaller political units.

Technological advances

The foregoing provides a cursory overview of the sequence of the political and territorial events that serve as a background to the period from the end of the Roman Empire to what historians call the High Middle Ages (c. 1000 to 1300). As the northern Germanic tribes had gained more influence, clothing styles had altered. Tribesmen wore stockings, trousers, and boots. Clothing for both men and women was made from cut sections of fabrics sewn together rather than being draped from lengths of fabric. Regions were all similar in one respect. The fibers that they could use were linen and wool, produced in Europe, and the imported luxury fabrics, cotton and silk. European silk and cotton production began gradually, and by the twelfth century these fabrics were also being produced in Europe (Gies, 1994). Smaller quantities of natural materials such as bast fibers removed from nettle stems and fibers from the coats of animals domesticated in certain regions were used locally. Each of these fibers required slightly different technologies to turn them into yarns that could be woven into cloth.

Fibers differ in their length and cohesiveness. But all staple fibers go through the same steps in spinning, similar to those described in Chapters 2 and 3.

By the twelfth century, Italian craftsmen were skilled in making both cotton and silk fabrics. The tools that they used were most likely variations of tools used in India, in China, and/or in the Middle East, that had traveled westward as fabric forming technology had advanced. For example, cotton is difficult to separate from the seeds in the cotton boll. A device consisting of two grooved rollers that turned against each other, called a *churka*, was used in India for this task. The Italians then adopted it for their processing of cotton. Gies (1994) notes that this precursor of the eighteenth-century cotton gin had come to them by way of the Arab traders. Probably along with the knowledge of how to make silk fabrics, the Italian silk producers acquired a device that twisted silk fibers together to make a yarn strong enough for weaving. Many see this device as the ancestor of the spinning wheel, which came into use in Europe in the thirteenth century. However, others credit the invention of the spinning wheel to India (Schoeser, 2003).

The spinning wheel was about three times faster than the drop spindle, but it was less smooth than hand-spun yarn and was not strong enough to use in the warp direction, because warp yarn had considerable stress placed upon it during weaving. However, it was suitable for weft direction yarn. This means of more rapid thread production solved the problems of lack of the supply of yarn needed for newer more efficient looms. For this reason, in spite of its drawbacks, the spinning wheel triumphed over hand spinning.

During the Dark Ages, the manufacture of cloth had continued to be done in the Roman way, with enslaved women working in factory-like settings on large estates. Free women worked in the home. Women were assigned the spinning and weaving while men did the finishing processes of dyeing and fulling. Linen was produced and used locally and wool was produced not only for domestic use but also for trading.

The warp-weighted loom and the two-beam loom were still in use. As the variety of fibers being used expanded, adaptations were made. A two-beam loom provided tension by fastening the lengthwise yarns to a beam at both ends of the loom, while the weights on the warp-weighted loom provided the tension. The operation of these two looms was quite similar. The addition of heddles, devices that allowed the raising and lowering of a set of warp yarns, had increased the speed of weaving. The period between 900 and 1200, what Gies (1994) calls the Commercial Revolution, led to further improvements in weaving technology and changes in how cloth was produced.

Fashion in the Middle Ages

In the search for fashionable behavior, many scholars assign the beginnings of fashion in dress to western regions during the Middle Ages. Not all students of dress history agree and some set the beginnings of fashion well after the Middle Ages, while others argue that the fashion process is present in all societies, past and present. Belfanti (2008), in a study of Indian, Chinese, and Japanese clothing systems, concluded that fashion was not a European invention, although it did develop fully as a social institution there, while in the countries he studied it evolved partially.

In order for fashion change to take place, it must be possible for a number of individuals to afford to participate in the acquisition of fashionable dress and there must be means to communicate information about new fashion ideas. Regulations or traditions that inhibit change cannot be so pervasive and rigid as to totally stifle changes. Although it would be possible for a small, elite proportion of the population to exhibit fashionable behavior, a social structure in which individuals can move from one socio-economic class to another tends to facilitate the development of fashion. However, inadequate income will limit some of the population's ability to participate in fashion behavior. Both written and pictorial evidence shows that fashion participation increased as the economies in European states encouraged a newly prosperous middle class to develop. Heller (2007) readily convinces the reader that the literature of the twelfth and thirteenth centuries leads to the certainty that fashion was alive and well in France of that time. She cites Bumke's (1991) caution to those examining dress of the Gothic Period in religious sculpture. He argues that it may tend to reflect conservative values and does not depict fashionable dress. Nevertheless, when compared with sculpted images from earlier periods, there is some cathedral sculpture that does support the presence of fashion changes in areas such as cut and fit of clothing through the torso and at the neckline, length, and fit of sleeve. New garments appear. One is the twelfth-century *bliaut*, an elaborately decorated gown with fitted bodice, pleating, and elements requiring more complex construction. In contrast to the bliaut, early thirteenth-century garments show fairly radical changes to more loosely fitted styles. Changes are clearly present, and are also well-described in the literature of the period (Tortora and Eubank, 2010).

The previously described technological advances in spinning and weaving were related to garment fashions. The new looms produced narrower widths of cloth, and one result was a change in the style of cloaks that had previously been made from one unconstructed rectangular piece of fabric. With narrower widths, cloaks had to be made from pieces shaped into a semi-circular cape. Changes, testifying to the presence of fashion, took place in garment length, fit, and methods of closing; and in neckline shape, the cut of sleeves, and the placement of the waistline, which varied depending on where the belt was placed. Weavers provided more elaborate fabrics to tailors that were made of patterned brocade

Figures 4.1 and 4.2 Women dressed in the fashions through different time periods in the Middle Ages. As seen from the differences in their dress, fashion changes can be documented in examples of women's dress (courtesy of Fairchild Books)

Figure 4.3 The dress of the men in this Italian tailor's shop, the items being constructed, and bundles of fabric all testify to the presence of fashion in dress throughout Europe and the economic importance of fashion in towns large and small (source: Scala/The Art Archive at Art Resource, New York)

and woven stripes. When made into clothing that was tailored rather than draped, tailors had to match these patterns (Pritchard 2003: 369–77). A fifteenth-century fresco from the castle of Issogne in a small town in the Aosta Valley of Northern Italy provides some indication of the complexity of a tailor's shop.

There is no evidence that the fabrics in the painting were woven in the shop. Customers would face the two tailors across a counter on which they are working. The man on the left is seated on the counter to sew together a garment. The man standing behind the counter is cutting fabric according to a pattern laid flat on the counter. Over a horizontal pole at the back of the shop, garments in various stages of completion hang. The shop is obviously on a city street and open to the public passing by, where they can see and possibly be enticed to place an order for a fashionable outfit.

Literature and documents from the medieval period attest to the desire of those affluent enough to afford it to follow current fashions. The acceptance and adoption of advances in textile technology doubtless helped to support these desires. From the complaints of the clergy about fashion excesses to the pride in their fashionable dress expressed by literary heroes and heroines of medieval romances, the connection between dress, technology, and fashion is clear for the upper classes. What is known about dress for those who were part of the subsistence economy is limited. Textile historians are better able to document higher end items available through national and international trade than the dress of the poor.

Textile developments during the Renaissance

By the end of the medieval period, cloth making was well established in Europe, with various regions being known for the excellence of the cloth they made. Advances in textile technology continued and those who could afford it followed current fashion trends. Historians see the beginnings of a new period in Italy in the fifteenth century when philosophers, writers, and artists began to draw inspiration from the creative aspects of classical antiquity. *Renaissance*, the name given to the fifteenth and sixteenth centuries in Western Europe, derives from the French word for rebirth. Italy, consisting of a number of small city-states, was well placed geographically to be the first to be exposed to the ideas about silk design and manufacture. Merchants in towns such as Lucca grew rich on the textile trade that developed. Wealthy rulers commissioned art from artists considered to this day to be among the greatest who ever lived. Some, such as Raphael, provided art that served as the basis of tapestries that hang in museums today. In their day, woven tapestries were a fashionable decorative adjunct to upper-class homes; an illustration of the pervasive nature of fashions that were not limited to dress.

Munro (2003) provides a thorough overview of textile technology from c. 800 to 1500. Earlier note has been made of the well-developed process in Roman times of the fulling of wool and its mechanization. The heavily fulled, felted, and oiled wools were much in demand, which helped to stimulate Northern European and British woolen industries. But as fashion preferences continually changed, these high-quality wools gave way to fashions for lighter wool fabrics. Such fashionable fabrics were made on an upright vertical loom that was better suited for lighter fabrics than the older broad loom, a clear case of fashion demand stimulating technology.

Another change in fabric manufacture, which came about as a result of the higher demand for lighter weight fabrics, was the construction of fabrics made not from wool alone but by blending wool and silk, or wool and cotton. Linen was essential for undergarments. Those mechanized techniques that were applied to wool or, later, to cotton fabrics were not suitable to linen production. A suitable mechanized wet spinning process for linen was not developed until the 1820s (Clarkson, 2003: 478).

In an essay on the Western European wool industries, Van Der Wee and Munro (2003) say that the impact of new weaving technology c. 1500 was "relatively as important for medieval Europe as those of the 'industrial revolution' were for eighteenth- and nineteenth-century England." Men became the weavers and women did the spinning, as the warp weighted loom and a horizontal loom that incorporated some automated elements replaced the two-beam vertical loom. The weaver sat in front of the loom to weave. Treadles activated by feet were connected to heddles so they could be raised and lowered without using the hands. This freed the hand to manipulate a shuttle with pointed ends that held the yarn. The weaver raised the appropriate heddles by pressing the foot treadle while throwing the shuttle through the shed and catching it with his other hand. Then he raised a different set of heddles and returned the shuttle to the other side, inserting the next row of weft. The weaver beat the inserted yarn to make the weave smooth and tight. A new beater shaped more like a comb was built into the loom and could be pulled by the weaver against the forming fabric. The horizontal, treadle looms, documented first in China and later in Syria and in Egypt in the sixth century, were three times as productive as the older upright looms (Schoeser, 2003: 78). These loom improvements made possible the weaving of more complex decorative fabrics.

Additional devices to improve the efficiency of fabric production included metal carders to replace wood, or bone combs to straighten fibers and devices to speed up preparation of the warp yarns. By 1530 there was a new spinning wheel, the saxony wheel, that could spin either wool or flax and which also produced higher-quality yarn. A water-powered fulling mill appeared. Fulling was the only fully mechanized textile process to be developed before the Industrial Revolution.

New types of textile constructions

New textile constructions were added to the available fabrics for fashionable men and women. Hose were an important part of men's dress, and in the Middle Ages they were made by cutting fabric on the bias, the diagonal direction, which stretched more than the lengthwise or crosswise directions of the fabric. Even with the increased stretch, the result was a garment that wrinkled and bagged on the leg. Knitted fabrics have greater stretch and as a result proved to be more satisfactory for constructing hose than woven cloth.

Knitting is so well known and so widely practiced today that it often comes as a surprise to learn that Europeans seem to have learned how to knit in the medieval period and probably learned the skill from the Arabs after their conquest of Spain c. 711–712. At first, most likely a domestic craft, industrial production appears to have begun only in the 1500s. By the late 1500s, the production of knitted stockings, still a hand process, spread quickly and was important employment not only for women but also for men who could knit while doing other tasks such as sheep herding or carrying packs from one place to another. Englishman William Lee invented the first mechanized device for knitting stockings in 1589. His knitting frame was rejected when he sought permission from Queen Elizabeth I to develop and market his invention. Elizabeth saw the device as having the potential to replace hand knitters, and therefore an economic threat to her subjects. Unsuccessful in England, Lee eventually went to France where he was able to take advantage of the greater interest in his knitting frame. Its use gradually spread throughout Europe and it returned to England in the early 1600s (Thirsk, 2003).

Lee's knitting frame made a whole row of stitches at a time instead of forming one stitch at a time along one needle as hand knitting required. The frame had a separate needle for each loop. Placing the yarn over the needles was still a hand operation. Full mechanization of knitting was not to come until the Industrial Revolution. Nevertheless, as Bailey (1998) notes when reporting on knitting productivity on these frames, the knitting frame did speed up knitting. A skilled hand knitter averaged a hundred stitches a minute compared to the production rate of 600 on the frame.

Another new type of fabric appeared around 1500: lace. Two types of lace developed in Europe: needlepoint lace and bobbin lace. The former grew out of embroidery techniques. Precursors were attractive fabrics or trimmings made by drawing threads from fabric in decorative patterns and embroidering to create an elaborate open-work pattern. This work was known as cutwork and featured complex patterns of embroidery stitches such as buttonhole stitches that were raised, free from the background. The second form of lace is bobbin lace, or bone lace, named after the small, bone bobbins that were manipulated to knot or twist threads together into delicate, elaborate patterns. The work was done over a pillow, and as a result these laces were also called pillow lace (Schoeser, 2003).

Needlepoint lace was more expensive and fashionable at first, but bobbin lace soon came to rival needlepoint lace. The techniques produced fabrics similar enough that both were known as "lace." Different communities developed different lace patterns. These laces were named after the towns where they were said to have originated (i.e. Alencon lace or Chantilly lace) or after some characteristic of the lace, such as blonde lace or rose point lace. Some countries actively marketed the products of their towns. While the early popularity of lace grew out of the novelty of these new fabrics, over time fashion played an important part in the popularity of specific laces and of decorative touches on fashionable dress. Lace, however, did not benefit from technology until the mechanization of making nets on which lace patterns could be created by hand in the late eighteenth century and the fully-mechanized production of lace in the nineteenth century (Levey, 2003).

Other aspects of dress

Armor

Cloth and leather were not the only materials with which men surrounded their bodies. Armor played an important part in warfare in Western Europe. It may seem strange to begin this discussion with dress for horses, but scholars who focus on protective armor for warriors see the use of the stirrup, the device in which a foot was placed while on horseback, as directly related to developments in the metal dress used in medieval warfare. The stirrup originated in the East, specifically in the second century BCE in India, where it was present in rudimentary form as a loop that was minimally useful to barefoot horseback riders in keeping their balance. It then appeared in developed form in China, traveled with Avar invaders to Hungary, and from there came into use throughout Europe. The connection to metal armor is in the advantage it gave to mounted warriors who used stirrups to secure their balance and could deliver stronger blows to enemies by using the increased thrust provided by a galloping horse. Full coverage by solid metal plates of armor protected the man on horseback. Armor was expensive, so only royalty and the military leadership wore this metal garment. The mounted soldiers of lesser status wore mail, a protective covering made from small circles of metal joined together. These coats of mail weighed as much as ninety pounds (forty kilograms). The only metal garb worn by the lowest status troops was a metal helmet (Gies, 1994).

Blacksmiths had learned through experience how to heat the metal to a very high temperature and hold it there for a time in order to make it tough and strong. The changes that took place were not understood, but modern metallurgists recognize that it was the absorption of small quantities of carbon from the charcoal over which the metal was heated that was turning the iron into a type of steel.

The suits of mail could either be made of joined iron rings or of iron rings sewn onto leather (Gies 1994: 64). Upper-class men who engaged in tournaments – kinds of games in which they demonstrated their skill – might have highly decorated plate armor. This metal garb became obsolete when bullets began to replace swords (Williams, 2000). The armor suit reflected the current fashions in dress for men, in part because the clothing worn beneath served as padding. But their styles also reflected the medieval desire to be considered fashionable. Sometimes fashionable dress evolved from the armor worn. One example is the *pourpoint*, a padded jacket worn by soldiers either under or over armor. Civilian men added sleeves and started wearing this garment about 1340.

The role of communication technology in spreading fashion information

One of the factors necessary for fashion to exist is a means of communication. The place of print media in twenty-first century fashion is obvious to anyone wanting to find out what kinds of changes are taking place in current fashions. Fashion magazines available at supermarket checkout counters can provide not only the latest news about the current fashion trends but also plentiful illustrations showing the styles. The Middle Ages had no similar printed fashion information. What, then, were the beginnings of fashion journalism?

The Chinese had been making paper since the first century CE. Printing came later. The earliest Chinese block printed book is dated at CE 868 and moveable type is thought to have been used beginning around CE 1041 to 1048 (Scarre, 1993: 1050). Block printing had been used to print fabrics in Europe as early as the thirteenth century. Block printed books became available in the early 1400s. Several factors stimulated the development of printing in the West. The supply of paper had increased significantly and with more paper, prices declined. At the same time the bubonic plague had killed many of the scribes who could produce hand-written manuscripts. With more paper and fewer and more expensive scribes, there was a need for a way to automate writing. Block printing was an improvement, but the printing blocks wore out rather quickly. Also, many of the block printed books had blocks prepared for a specific book. What was needed was moveable type that was durable and that could be moved about so the same type could be used to print a number of different books. Johann Gutenberg of Mainz in Germany is credited for solving this problem by inventing the printing press in the mid-1400s, although other individuals in other locations have also been suggested as producing such a breakthrough at about the same time (Burke, 1978).

Olian (1977) identified twelve printed costume books published in the late sixteenth century. Of these she noted that they did not claim to show coming fashion trends, but rather depicted current styles in major cities; some showed clothes from earlier periods, and still others the dress of faraway places. Some were clearly imaginary and the styles definitely not authentic. Nevinson (1967) described the precursors of fashion plates. These were printed illustrations intended to show the latest styles, presumably so that those buying the plates could dress accordingly. He noted two early books by men whose careers took them to various European courts: one, an entertainer, a jouster, and the other a diplomat. The jouster depicted kings and princes of the courts he visited and the diplomat showed the clothes he wore, apparently intended to educate the reader as to how to dress for the occasions described.

In Nevinson's view (1967: 9), Wenceslas Hollar, a Polish artist, who in 1640 published a series of plates showing the dress of individuals in England, was either "the father of the fashion plate" or "its most important ancestor." At about the same time, a large number of engravings showing current styles were made in Paris. The transition to journalism was complete when a French publication, *Le Mercure Gallant*, was the earliest magazine to pay attention to fashion. On 15 May 1678, this magazine published an article on fashion that was illustrated with fashion plates. This innovation has led some scholars to identify *Le Mercure Gallant* as the first fashion magazine.

Subsequent improvements in printing techniques contributed to the development of a wide variety of magazines directed to the interests of women that published depictions of fashion plates. Until the development of color printing in the nineteenth century, if color was wanted, these plates were hand-colored, usually with watercolor paint. They served as an increasingly important way to present new styles and were the early ancestors of modern fashion magazines such as *Vogue*, *Elle*, and the like. The contributions to fashion of printed and other communications technologies in the nineteenth to the twenty-first centuries are discussed in Chapter 13.

Jewelry

Even if individuals are rich enough to purchase the best jewelry available, materials and technology limit the jewelry they can buy. Images of Byzantine royalty and courtiers show great quantities of gems and pearls used both as jewelry and as ornaments on their clothing. The technology used did not differ much from that used by the Romans for working gold and mounting gems; however, the way in which these stones were placed borrowed from the way gems were used to the east of Constantinople. Precious stones were also augmented by *cloisonné* made by pouring colored enamels into variously shaped metal frameworks.

While Byzantine jewelers utilized a wide variety of materials, tribes living in Northern Europe did not have the craft skills and resources of the Byzantine world. The Romans had called these people "barbarians." The word now has a pejorative meaning but it originated as a Greek description of the sound of the languages spoken by non-Greeks that to Greek ears sounded something like "ba, ba ba." These northerners dressed quite differently from the peoples around the Mediterranean Sea, whose garments were draped and/or wrapped. Northern European men's garments were tailored, not draped, with trousers and more closely fitted shirt-like tops. Capes and cloaks were used as outdoor garments for both men and women. These required some kind of fastener. For the more affluent the fasteners may have been jeweled fibulas, round brooches, and other pins or clasps. Made by inlaying solid slabs of gemstones, the gems used were often garnets and almandine.

The pins and brooches placed on clothes became less important by the fourteenth century, when buttons gradually replaced or added to earlier closures such as pins and lacing. Jewelry brought back from the Middle East by the Crusaders brought Byzantine influences to Northern Europe. When following fashion became important to increasingly urban and more affluent Europeans, the use of glass in jewelry increased. Researchers do not find many examples of jewelry made with valuable gems, because the settings for these stones would be melted down and the gems reset into the more fashionable jewelry, thereby extending the life of the decorative stones through later generations of owners. The most common items of jewelry appear to have been rings, brooches, belt buckles, and clasps for closing mantles. New technology was reflected in innovative techniques for making jewelry. These included *champlevé* and *basse-taille*, types of translucent enamel. For the former, a trough was shaped in a metal base and this was filled in with liquefied enamel. For the latter, the base metal was engraved and the engraving was visible through the translucent enamel, giving the appearance that the engraving was molded in the enamel.

Renaissance jewelry owed its splendor to the discovery of the Western Hemisphere. Gold and silver and new types of gems arrived in the ships that brought the wealth of the Americas to Europe after 1492. Once again improvements in the design of sails and ships contributed to developments in dress. With more plentiful supplies of these components, affluent consumers could participate in the fashions for elaborate jewelry (Philips, 1996).

In the centuries that followed the Renaissance, changes in styles of dress had much to do with the popularity of certain types of jewelry. Heavily decorated and jeweled dress of the sixteenth century gave way to simpler gowns with lower necklines, giving necklaces a more prominent place. Some new technologies such as the painting of colored enamels on gold gave the artisans a palette on which to depict in enamel scenes ranging from flowers to religious pictures. With strong consumer interest in jewelry, new technologies exploited a desire for imitation pearls. A process to make these pearls was used by a Parisian jeweler, Jacquin, in 1680. A hollow sphere of clear thin glass was filled with silver-colored fish scales and white wax. Cultured pearls had been manufactured in China since the thirteenth century by introducing irritants into river pearl mussel shells. The mollusk secreted pearl nacre around the irritant to reduce the discomfort and a pearl was formed (Yarwood, 1988: 317). Gemstones of many varieties were imported from the East, and new methods of cutting these stones were developed.

The breadth of the time included in this chapter has served to place a heavy concentration on the textile technologies that in a shorter time period would not have seemed to follow each other so quickly. A great many of the improvements grew out of the exposure of Europeans to technologies that traveled west from China and India, to the Middle East and the Arab states and then to Europe. Global spread of such ideas continued as various European regions passed technologies from one to another. New devices often produced labor force changes. Women's tasks changed as some equipment required greater strength, making women the spinners instead of the weavers. As a result, unmarried women became known as "spinsters."

Conflict spawned dress made from metal as the Crusaders and participants in local wars or in jousting tournaments attempted to protect themselves. Even here fashion was evident in the shape of suits of armor with the lines of contemporary fashions. The greater emphasis on fashion among those affluent enough to participate both affected and were affected by the trends in textile fabrics, an interaction that has continued ever since. New types of textiles continued to contribute to fashions. Knitted stockings were a practical garment that achieved a better fit. Knits had not yet achieved a place in the fashionable world, while lace became an important element of fashionable dress.

European colonizers of what eventually came to be called the Americas contributed to increased interest in jewelry as the materials from which it was made became more available. Art depicting the upper classes shows many jewels applied to ornamentation of garments and accessories.

Looking at relationships through illustrations

Although few actual garments remain from the periods discussed in this chapter, art works abound and one can draw conclusions about dress, the technologies needed to create the elements of dress, and the presence or absence of fashion. In this chapter a garment from the medieval period and one from the Elizabethan era will serve as the basis of an analysis of technology, dress, and fashion.

The depiction in Figure 4.4 is of William of Hatfield who died in infancy. He was the son of King Edward III of England. William appears on his father's tomb as a weeper (a mourner). He is depicted not as a child but as a young man. His dress is typical of the dress of upper-class young men at the time of his father's death, the 1350s. Newton (1980) identifies the garments worn at this time as being a shirt placed under a tunic and over these an outer tunic. This style marked a major fashion change from a longer, more loosely fitted garment. The new garment was short, around knee length, a length previously associated with lower-class men. It fitted the body closely. The textile technologies described earlier in this chapter would have been in use to create the fabric in the depicted dress, which was probably wool.

Buttons and belts

In order to achieve this new tighter fit, the wearer could have laced the garment closed, which was the common closure in earlier centuries, but as can be seen in the illustration, a prominent row of buttons runs vertically up the front of his tunic. An elaborate belt is placed over the garment at hip level. Although button-like devices had been used prior to this time, it is likely those used in earlier periods were ornamental. Buttons appear in substantial numbers from this time forward, and surviving textile artifacts indicate that buttonholes were sewn into fourteenth-century garments. While buttons could be made from stuffed round cloth shapes that passed through buttonholes, a considerable amount of technology went into the creation of solid buttons. Egan and Pritchard (2002) divide British medieval buttons into three types: cast buttons of lead/tin that had bronze or embedded wire shanks; composite buttons made from stamped metal sheeting to form two spherical copper-alloy pieces that were then soldered together; or the aforementioned cloth buttons, made into a ball and sewn together.

Belts, called girdles in the Middle Ages, were a decorative item of dress by which the wearer could display status, rather than, as belts are used today, a practical device that holds up part of a garment. The hip-level band that circled

Figure 4.4 Medieval dress, c. 1350. Edward III Weeper, William of Hatfield, Westminster Abbey

the body was made either from leather or woven fabric. The leather for this use, as for any other, had to be tanned and treated to remove any organic matter clinging to the skins. Archeologists have identified the fibers used in cloth belt artifacts from London as being linen, worsted wool, silk, or a blend of silk and wool. Artifacts from archeological excavations vary from simple girdles with metal buckles to those of the type shown in this illustration with a number of mounts attached. These are the rectangular items seen side-by-side on the hip-circling girdle. Usually, but not always, made from the same metal, mounts were held in place with metal rivets. Shapes could be rectangular, circular, or variants of circles such as quatrefoil, cinquefoil, etc. or star, seashell, or similar shapes. Some had designs stamped on them.

Buckle shapes varied widely and displayed fashion trends that changed. Archeologists are not always able to determine whether particular buckles were used on belts, on other items of dress, or even on horses. Buckle frames were made of iron, while the pins that close the buckle might be iron or copper alloy or, less often, other alloys. Only rarely were mounts made of precious metals or with jeweled ornaments found. This is not surprising as it was common to recycle valuable materials when an item of dress had outlived its usefulness or gone out of fashion. Ceramic and stone molds for making buckles provide evidence of mass production of standard buckle types (Egan and Prichard, 1991: 123).

Shoes

The style of shoe worn by William of Hatfield is unclear. Even so, some attention should be paid to the subject of footwear and the technical aspects of shoe-making. Those who made shoes would most likely have been members of a guild. Shoemakers made shoes to order but also are shown in art with shoes ready to sell in their shops (Mussarelli, 2011). Some cobblers would make shoes in the homes of wealthy customers. On his excellent web site, Carlson (2001) lists and depicts the tools utilized in making shoes during the Middle Ages. A variety of types of awls and knives were essential, as were needles and a wooden piece called a seam block that was a device enabling the sewing of some types of seams. Foot-shaped forms or lasts are depicted in paintings of cobblers' workrooms. A special mallet was required for turning the shoe inside out, as well as a stick that helped in the turning of the shoe. The types of shoes made included boots, long-toed shoes, footed hose, and a number of basic shoe forms that varied in their closures or shapes. William of Hatfield seems to have been wearing one of the basic shoe types. He does not wear a *poulaine*, a style of shoe that first appeared in the twelfth century and was not used for a time and then returned as a fashion in the mid-fourteenth century. This style of shoe with an exaggerated extended toe must have presented particular challenges to the shoemaker. Shoemakers' assistants complained in court about the extra work required to make the long-toed shoes, because of the difficulty of making the shoes that had large amounts of stuffing that had to be inserted into the toe. The judge, however, ruled that the workers had to make the shoes in whatever form the customer required. Other supports used for the elongated toes were sticks of wood, bone, and whalebone (van Buren, 2011: 314).

William of Hatfield's hose are shown as closely fitting the leg. This is probably artistic license, as hose were generally cut on the bias or diagonal direction of fabric. Bias has greater stretch, but still would most likely have been somewhat baggy. A better fit would be achieved with knitted hose, but machine-knitted hose were not available until after the reign of Queen Elizabeth.

Queen Elizabeth I would have been a woman whose dress set the styles for those at her court, Figure 4.5 shows a portrait of her from c. 1592 displaying the sumptuousness of royal dress toward the latter part of her reign. She died in 1603.

Undergarments

The items of dress she would have worn, both those visible and those underneath, were these. The undergarments worn closest to her body would have been made of linen fabric, loosely fitting and, given her status, probably ornamented with embroidery and possibly lace. Women did not wear drawers at this time. Additional underwear supported and established the shape of the outermost garment. These consisted of one garment called "a pair of bodies" – what today would be called a corset. The corset was rigidly stiffened to produce a flat appearance at the front of the bodice. A narrow waist was not the objective. Queen Elizabeth's wardrobe records report that she had a number of these garments made using leather, stiffened buckram, or whalebone (Arnold, 1985). Wood might also be used. The corset of this period was probably made in two parts that were laced together. A stiff device, called a busk, was inserted in pockets at the front of the corset. The portrait shows clearly the flat appearance that was created. A sort of barrel-shaped hoop called a farthingale supported the skirts of the gown and was made from wood, cane, whalebone, or wire, probably mounted into a petticoat. Sometimes a padded roll was placed around the waist as well. The large sleeves also required support, and that was provided by wire, reeds, or whalebone (Cunnington et al., 1972).

Davenport (1948) provides a detailed description of the materials in the dress in this portrait (Figure 4.5). Her enumeration of the jewels on the surface of the white satin fabric illustrates Phillips' description of the jewelry of the Renaissance

Figure 4.5 Portrait of Elizabeth I, c. 1592, showing royal dress that set the style for those at court (source: National Trust Photo Library/The Art Archive at Art Resource, New York)

as being of extraordinary splendor (Phillips, 1996). On Elizabeth's gown were coral, pearls, rubies, and sapphires, mostly mounted in gold studs. Pearls appear in lengthy ropes around her neck and pinned into what appears to be her hair, but this is undoubtedly a wig.

Accessories

A number of accessories appear in the portrait. These other aspects of the Queen's dress also influenced fashion. By 1592 Elizabeth wore a curled wig the natural color of her hair, which had been auburn. Fashionable ladies of the court therefore dyed their hair auburn or wore similar wigs. In order to hide signs of ageing, she wore heavy white make-up. Before the twentieth century, make-up was generally either made at home or purchased from an apothecary. Little was known about the advantages and disadvantages of chemical materials, and as a result the substances used were often toxic. The preferred cosmetic used to whiten the face, an effect observable in this and other royal portraits, was ceruse, which was made of white lead. Another, known as Soliman's water, intended to eliminate blemishes on the skin, was made of sublimate of mercury, and destroyed the outermost layer of skin, after which it corroded the next layer of flesh. Color added to the lips might be achieved with mercuric sulfide.

Lace ruffs of various shapes were fashionable. The Queen wears a standing, heavily starched lace ruff. A very sheer wired veil edged in jewels stands behind her head. In her left hand she holds a pair of gloves that are brown with slashed gold cuffs, and in her right hand is a folding fan (Davenport, 1948: 446). The fan held by Elizabeth was a new device. Earlier fans had been rigid but hers is a folding fan, a device from Japan brought back to England by the trading companies. The folding fan made its way from the Mediterranean Sea to the French court from which it reached England during Elizabeth's reign where it became a popular fashion, especially when perfume was added to the fan. Gloves were also perfumed, scent being added to a number of items of dress, probably because baths were infrequent. Pomanders, containers filled with fragrant herbs and/or flowers, were carried or hung from belts.

5

SOME ASIAN DEVELOPMENTS IN TECHNOLOGY, DRESS AND FASHION

(End of the Neolithic period until the 17th century)

The civilizations of Asia were becoming increasingly urbanized at much the same time as those of the Middle East and the Mediterranean regions. Given the enormous distances that separated these early civilizations, at a time when knowledge of geography was incomplete and modes of transportation limited, it is not surprising that what direct contact there was between these areas was limited. Even after contact increased, attitudes toward other parts of the world tended to be culturally biased, with people in Western countries seeing those living in other parts of the world as "backward" and "primitive." It was not until Joseph Needham's massive work (1954 and after) on the history of science and civilization in China that English-speaking people began to learn of the various technologies developed and used in that part of the world that had made their way to other parts of the world. Earlier accounts of visits to China, such as that by Marco Polo, were mistrusted and thought to be fanciful. For many centuries, China and India had a virtual monopoly on the cultivation and production of two important textile fibers: silk and cotton. Not only did they supply these textile fibers and fabrics to the rest of Eurasia, but over time and with trade, the technologies they developed also made important contributions to textile manufacture in other parts of the world.

China

Trade with nearby regions began early in Chinese prehistory. Ornamental objects of dress such as pendants made from jade from as early as 5000 BCE have been found in Chinese areas distant from where this stone originates. In order to engage in trade with the Western world, the Chinese had to send their products by land along a route that served as the means of communication between the Mediterranean and China. The route had several variations and as goods made their way along one of the routes, products changed hands many times. Some products made the complete journey, but far more were added and subtracted at various trading centers along the way. Nor was all of the material being traded going in one direction. Cotton, which originated in the Indian sub-continent, made its way east to China as well as west. Over its long history, the people at one end of the road would never have met those at the other end. Nineteenth-century German geographer Ferdinand von Richthofen named these routes "the Silk Road" after silk fabrics, one of the most important items of trade. Much of this silk was traveling west. A second very important product carried along the silk roads that related to dress was the aforementioned jade. This prized green stone was carried east to China from where it originated in the region of Khotan on the southern route of the Silk Road. The techniques for shaping this tough, difficult to work stone included polishing with abrasive sand in combination with wooden tools or hemp cords to drill holes. The Chinese used jade for utilitarian and decorative objects and personal ornaments. For the Chinese, jade was a symbol of high status (Wood, 2002: 26–7).

Cultivation of silk originated with the Chinese. After thousands of years that knowledge was spirited out of China to other parts of the world. It appears that some auxiliary equipment used for silk production may have served as a prototype for subsequent technological developments in textile production in European countries, and that the route traveled often came by way of the Arab civilizations of the Middle East and North Africa. Examples include the horizontal treadle loom and the draw loom that served as a basis for the eighteenth-century Jacquard loom.

On the other hand, the origins of the spinning wheel are less clear, though it is accepted that it was probably Asian in origin (Munro, 2003: 201). A device used to twist silk fibers together into a yarn that is strong enough to be used in weaving is said to date to the eleventh century in China. The earliest European reference to spinning wheels is c. 1280. Temple (1986: 120) reports Needham's suggestion that Italians brought the idea back after a trip to China and that soon after that visit, manufacturers in the Italian city of Lucca were using such machinery. Others claim that the spinning wheel derives from an Indian device.

Influences on the Chinese also traveled there by way of the Silk Road, as missionaries from many religions used the trade route as a means of bringing

Figure 5.1 Chinese draw loom. The weaver on the left works at floor-level. A draw girl sits above the weaving level manipulating the yarns that the weaver's pattern indicates must be in a raised or lowered position in order to form the design (source: RMN-Grand Palais/ The Art Archive at Art Resource, New York)

their philosophies eastward to new regions. Dress scholars note the foreign influences in dress from Central Asia in the Tang dynasty. And it is argued that fashion was very much present at this time.

Basic fiber technologies

The technologies required to transform textile fibers into textile fabrics can be divided into those used for preparation of the fiber, spinning the fibers into yarns, uniting the yarns into a fabric structure, and providing special characteristics to the fabric though processes called finishes. Color and other ornamentation can be added to the completed fabric by dyeing, printing, embroidering, or by using decorative weaves. The formation of yarns using the spindle described in Chapter 2 was used for bast fibers such as linen, hemp, nettle, cotton, and wool. Silk was sufficiently different that it required specialized techniques and equipment.

The Chinese learned to raise silkworms (*Bombyx mori*), feeding hungry caterpillar larvae leaves picked from a species of mulberry trees that was grown for this purpose. After the caterpillars reached maturity, they spun cocoons. Some of the cocoons were selected as breeding stock for the next generation. Those moths were allowed to hatch, emerge and lay eggs for the next generation. The rest of the cocoons were subjected to steaming, baking, or soaking in salt water to kill the chrysalis inside the cocoon. In this way none of the silk fibers that made up the cocoon were broken by the exit of the moth. Some floss, consisting of short broken fibers on the outermost layer, was removed. This material might be used as insulation in padded winter garments (Collier et al., 2010).

The gummy material that held together the fibers in the cocoon is called sericin and was removed by soaking and agitating the water. This sericin removal is known as degumming. After this, the fiber was unwound from the cocoon. Up to this point, the equipment needed was minimal, but as the journey from fiber to fabric continued, more specialized tools were needed. Silk fibers are not strong enough to be used alone for weaving, so two or more filaments were combined in a process called reeling.

Neolithic archeological sites have yielded a number of tools used in textile production. These include needles that would have been used to separate fibers, devices for reeling, and spindles to insert twist in yarns. These spinning devices were dated at 5000 BCE. They could have been utilized with other fibers such as hemp (Vainker, 2004). The earliest actual silk samples in poor condition have been dated to 3630 BCE. More evidence is present by 2570 BCE. Some of these artifacts attest to the development of looms. Examples include weights used for twining yarns that had to be stronger for use in the lengthwise (warp) direction of woven cloth; shuttles used to carry cross-wise (weft) yarns in weaving; and blades (battens) used to beat weft yarns into place after insertion and actual looms. From the Shang Dynasty (1500–1050 BCE, considered to be the first historical period in China), come additional written records that attest to a highly sophisticated weaving technology. This leads Vainker (2004: 16–17) to conclude that "Weaving implements and practices are one of China's contributions to world technology." Desire for silk outside of China was a major impetus to the development of world trade.

As silk technology continued to advance, the Chinese created a wide variety of beautiful fabrics with complex ornamentation. One device that made complex pattern weaving possible was the draw loom (Figure 5.1), When this loom was first used in China is not clear, but Vainker states that a draw loom is depicted in a seventeenth-century drawing in a Chinese Technology manual. Although claims have been made for much earlier origin, by the Tang Dynasty (618–907 CE) such looms were definitely in use. Operation of a draw loom required two people. One sat at the loom, inserting the weft yarn, the other on a framework over the loom where the drawboy or girl could raise sets of yarns so that only the yarns needed for the pattern were incorporated (Bradley Smith and Wen, 1973). Ornamentation was created not only by complex weaving achieved by constant improvements in looms, but also by the superb embroidery skills of textile workers, by painting the cloth, and by attachment of sequins or other ornamental objects.

Traditional textiles were not the only Chinese inventions put to use for dress. Paper was another early invention of the Chinese, c. 300 BCE. From the second century and after, paper clothing was apparently used as protection against the cold. To some extent the description of pounding and using the fibrous bark layer of the paper mulberry tree sounds like the use of bark cloth in the Pacific islands such as Hawaii. An archeological excavation in China uncovered a paper hat, belt, and shoe dated at 418 CE. Other paper was made from hemp fibers. Accounts exist of using paper for armor, with its advantages being noted as its lighter weight, making troops more maneuverable. The paper is described as being made of "silk and cloth," lined with cotton one inch thick, fully pleated and knee length. The account dates from 1629 (Temple, 1986: 82–3).

Another invention, the umbrella, is noted by Temple, reporting on Needham's work, as an innovation of the Wei Dynasty (CE 386–534/535). Needham assigns the collapsible umbrella to the first century CE. Umbrellas that protected against both rain and sun were made of oiled paper said to be made from mulberry bark. Colors appear to have been assigned by status, the Emperor carrying one of red and yellow, while those for ordinary folk were blue. By the fourteenth century, silk umbrellas were in use, the evidence being an Imperial decree restricting the use of silk umbrellas to the royal family. When umbrellas made their way to the West or when Westerners also discovered the usefulness of these devices is not clear.

Fashion in China

Steele and Major (1999: 16) make a valuable contribution to the question of whether one can find evidence of fashion in Chinese dress. Westerners have tended to see Chinese dress of the past as unchanging. These authors differentiate between traditional China and contemporary China of today, saying that traditional China dress was "not simply a matter of fashion or taste or social status, although it was all of those too; it was perhaps most importantly a signifier of cultural identity." Hints of concern about the incursions of fashion are noted in Ming Dynasty (1368–1644) records, with complaints about changing clothing styles. But it is the dress of the Tang dynasty that generates the most comment about fashion.

The Tang dynasty united China after a period of some four centuries of political division. Its control of China lasted from 618 until 907 CE, though it was not without political strife at times during this period. The usual practice was for men to occupy the highest offices and hold the throne; however, for a time in the late seventh century until 713 CE, women ascended the throne and gained the power that went with that high office, until revolt against their rule removed them from power. The period from 712 to 755 CE is often called the Golden Age of China, a period both Zhou (1984) and Benn (2002) agree was "the most prosperous age in the Tang for the largest number of the people." This prosperity was in large measure due to the reign of the Emperor August, which lasted forty-four years.

The Tang was notable for extensive contacts with territories to the west. Writers speak of foreign influences from as far away as Turkey, with Schafer (1963) quoting a poet of the period who complains about women in cities who copied eastern (Turkish and East Iranian) make-up and wore foreign furs and fleeces.

Tang society has been described by historians as both highly stratified and hierarchical, with sumptuary laws regulating "quantity, quality, size and adornment" of dress. But apparently sumptuary legislation was much ignored in some periods of the Tang, as women abandoned riding dress that completely covered the body and the head and adopted Turkish caps and a masculine form of riding clothes and boots. At the same time men sported hats of leopard skin. They copied Iranian style tight sleeves and fitted bodices. Skirts were pleated and stoles draped around the neck. Hair styles and make-up were described as being of "un-Chinese character." Apparently these practices varied, with some communities holding firm to traditional styles, while others adopted foreign styles (Schafer, 1963).

Another aspect of fashionable dress was the custom of using scents and perfumes. An interesting technology supported this practice. Hollow metal globes with ornamental piercing held burning incense. These censing baskets were hung from gimbals (devices that kept the globes upright) as the containers were passed under clothes and also bedding and other household textiles.

The variety of textiles available for use was extensive. Silk was of course the fiber most often utilized, but ramie (a bast fiber related to nettles), kudzu (a vine), hemp, banana, and bamboo all provided fibers. Wool was used for felt. The foreign contacts provided other fabrics. Japan and Korea sent China raw silks made into shantung fabric, and Persia in the eighth century produced decorative silks with foreign patterns. Cotton had come originally from India, but by the Tang period was being cultivated and produced in China. Written records from the Imperial Office of Weaving and Dyeing listed these types of fabrics: pongees, damasks, nets, gauzes, linens, and woolens and in addition five kinds of cords and ribbons and four kinds of spun threads. Benn reports that warp twills were the most characteristic weave, that satin weave was a Tang invention, and that true brocades could be woven (Benn, 2002).

Textiles were decorated not only by weaving patterns in fabrics like brocades but also could be printed using wood blocks. The surface of the wood was cut into designs, the fabric laid between the blocks, and color poured into the hollow spaces between the blocks where it came in contact with the fabric. Colors used by dyers working for the court included "five official colors other than white: blue, red, yellow, black and purple." Colors were obtained from plants that included a local Chinese indigo for blue, madder for red, gardenia for yellow, acorns for black, and gromwell, a plant in the borage family that produces a purple dye. The foreign textiles that arrived in China often influenced the design of Chinese textiles (Benn, 2002). Cahill (1999) describes contributions to Chinese technology for weaving as coming from imported textiles. Metallurgy that came from Persia contributed to ornamentation added to decorative hairpins that supported elaborate hairstyles.

The Indian sub-continent

People on the sub-continent of India were also exchanging a life based on hunting and gathering for one based on agriculture c. 4000 BCE. The civilization that developed is known either as the Harappan Culture (from the important city of Harappa) or the Indus Valley culture, after the Indus River that flows through the region. This civilization had its full flowering from c. 2500 to 1500 BCE (Schulberg, 1968: 31). In the video *The Story of India*, interviewer Michael Wood reported that estimates indicate that the population during the height of this culture may have reached as much as five million people and was home to 2,000 towns and villages (Wood, video).

The ports situated along the coast were active and well equipped. The largest was Mohenjo Daro. From this port and others, a number of items important for dress were shipped: cotton, especially dyed cottons, and for jewelry gold, copper, lapis lazuli, and ivory. Much of this trade was with Mesopotamia. Gernsheimer's report (1984) of finding shells from the Indus Valley in archeological sites in Mesopotamia is just one example of research that confirms these early trade connections. For unknown reasons, the Indus Valley civilizations disappeared after about 1500 BCE. One hypothesis is that changes in the monsoon rains may have had a negative impact on the ability of agriculture to support the population. An alternative suggestion is that people whose economy and lifestyle were not adapted to urban civilizations invaded and conquered the cities. A combination of such factors may have been responsible. The evidence of decline differs in Harappa and Mohenjo Daro (Schulberg, 1968: 33).

Even without the support of an active trading culture, cotton continued to be an important element of Indian agriculture and dress. In later periods, trade resumed as India once again developed a high level of civilization under cultures dominated by invaders called the Aryans. Subsequent periods such as the sixth century BCE brought intense philosophical exploration and a concurrent development of religious thought.

Other powers that sometimes dominated territory on the Indian sub-continent also played a role in Indian history. The region occupied by the country now known as Iran has had a number of names. Not all of these civilizations occupied all of present-day Iran and some were much larger. The earliest history of the region was tied to the history of its close neighbor, Mesopotamia. In the period from 3000 BCE, some would have known it as Elam. It reached the summit of its power around the second millennium BCE, declined, and grew powerful again later when it was more likely to be known as Persia. It was the leading power in the Middle East, and the names of its kings are familiar. Cyrus the Great, Darius and Xerxes engaged in hostilities with Greece from c. 550 BCE until Alexander the Great defeated Darius in 331 BCE (Loveday *et al.*, 2005). In the third century CE, the Mauryan Empire, described by Schulberg (1968: 73) as the first great empire of historic times in India, replaced Persian and Greek forces that had conquered and settled the Indus Valley and the Punjab. The Persians had controlled the region for two hundred years, until their defeat by Alexander the Great who moved in to establish Greek settlements in the area. Indian forces were able to re-establish control over these regions under a leader called Chandragupta. From this point on, the history of the sub-continent of India includes periods of invasion from the north, development of additional empires, and then in the 1500s CE came under the control of the Mughals. Led by people who claimed descent from Genghis Kahn, the Mughals gained control over most of the sub-continent of India from the sixteenth to the early eighteenth centuries. It was during this period that contact with European traders grew substantially.

Just as silk played a pivotal role in Chinese trade, cotton was the textile at the heart of the Indian cloth trade. Lying as India does along land and sea trade routes, textiles were readily exchanged with other regions. Trade goods from other regions passing through these ports contributed design influences to both textiles and garments. Among the areas to which Indian cottons were first sent were China and Indonesia; later to Persia and Egypt, and still later to Greece and Rome.

Cotton fibers are relatively short and light in weight. As a result, cotton required a different type of spindle than linen; one that was small and light and was supported so as to avoid putting too much pressure on the yarn as it was formed (Barber, 1995). The special requirements for successful spinning of cotton fibers into delicate, soft fabrics, this fineness being one reason these fabrics were so highly prized, led to additional improvements in spinning. Some scholars credit the development of the spinning wheel to India, others to China, and others to Iran. Pacey (1990) after examining this question concluded that the evidence is not clear enough to establish the precise origin of this important tool for textile production. He suggests that the exposure through trade to Chinese silk and Indian cotton may have stimulated local responses, unique to handling of different fibers.

Indian technology was responsible for excellence in dyeing and weaving that created beautifully patterned cloth. Samples of cotton fabrics dating to the Harappan period that are colored red with the plant dyestuff madder support the conclusion that even in this early period Indian dyeing technology had reached a very high level. Dyeing cotton with madder requires a mordant. Mordants are compounds, often metallic salts, which combine with the dyestuff to make the color stronger and more durable. A Greek physician of the fifth century BCE has been quoted as saying that bright colored Indian textiles were popular with the Persians. Woven patterns, checks, and stripes appear in Indian paintings (Dhamija, 1989). Evidence of trade in textiles with India has also been reported in Egypt, ancient Rome, and eighth-century Anglo-Saxon England. After the Fall of Rome, trade between Europe and India fell off and revived again once Arab trade with Europe increased in the Middle Ages. The names of the traded fabrics often reveal either their point of origin or the ports though which they passed. Examples include: fustian, an important fabric in medieval Europe that was named from Fostat, an Egyptian port city; calico, named after the Indian city of Calicut (modern Calcutta); or chintz, the name deriving from the Hindi word *chint,* descriptive of its multi-patterned appearance, meaning "variegated" (Geijer, 1989).

Fairservis (1971), in his exploration of dress of the East, sees the division into three zones of the Indian sub-continent, based on their ethnic and historical roles, as useful for the study of dress. Subbaro, an Indian scholar originated the concept, calling them the Zone of Attraction, the Zone of Relative Attraction, and the Zone of Isolation. The Zone of Attraction includes the Indus and Ganges river valley systems of northern India in both India and Pakistan. This area was the region where foreign invaders were most likely to enter the Indian subcontinent, and as a result dress styles were the most varied and likely to change. The Zone of Relative Attraction includes much of the peninsula that makes up India. Here changes and outside influences were fewer, and the Zone of Isolation, as its name implies, was made up of indigenous tribes and pastoral nomads who were subject the least to outside influence and as a result retaining the strongest attachment to traditional dress.

Trade developments and their impact

By the close of the Middle Ages advances in ship design and building – especially the compass, the full-rigged ship, and the quadrant, not to mention the desire to enrich themselves, led adventurous mariners to voyage farther and farther from their own shores. Spices were the products that first enticed explorers to risk these hazardous journeys. In a period when preservation of food was difficult, spices provided a means of preserving foods or making food palatable that was past its prime. Most of the spices used in Europe came from Africa and the Far East, and their scarcity made them extraordinarily valuable. Sea voyages seemed a better alternative than the long and arduous journeys by land that brought these and other Asian products to Europe. At the same time Christopher Columbus sailing for Spain believed that by sailing west he could arrive in the Indies. When he reached what was recognized later as a new continent, he was certain he had reached his goal, the proof being native people wearing cotton garments. In 1492, Europeans knew the source of cotton to be India, having no idea that South America had its own species of cotton.

The first European country to undertake these oceanic explorations had been Portugal. Through their voyages around the Cape of Good Hope, and into the Indian Ocean, the Portuguese succeeded in dominating the spice trade. Other countries followed, getting support from their governments for explorations intended to let them enter the spice trade as well. The Dutch then joined the competition, and quickly established relationships that would stymie the first of the English efforts by the East India Company, chartered by Queen Elizabeth I in 1600. The already-established trading organizations had learned that not only was there money to be made in the spice trade, but that other goods such as silk and cotton could be profitable too. Shipping them to Europe was not the objective initially. For the most part, these textiles were carried from one country in the region to another. For example, there was a ready market for printed fabrics from South India in Java and Sumatra. European trading companies happily and profitably obliged (Wild, 1999).

British successes in establishing trade in Indian cottons among local Indian Ocean communities led them to establish what they called "factories" in the areas of India that produced these textiles. These were trading posts where goods were stored, processed, and readied for export. A factor, the title of a representative of the company, was the manager of the factory. Eventually they realized that the goods they were selling to the Indian Ocean region could also have a market in Europe, and soon piece goods (this business was known as the piece trade) were becoming fashionable, not only for dress but also for household interiors.

McKendrick *et al*. (1982) introduce the concept of a consumer revolution, and tie it to the printed chintz and muslin cotton textiles carried to Britain from India in the seventeenth century and the imitations subsequently produced in the factories of Britain. Describing the enthusiasm for these fabrics as a craze, McKendrick goes on to ascribe this as marking the origins of fashion in dress. Other authors disagree about the beginnings of fashion. McCracken (1988) sees clear evidence of fashion in the Elizabethan period, and in Chapter 4, I have discussed not only evidence of fashion in the Middle Ages but also the current tendency to note the Western bias present in claiming fashion as a solely Western phenomenon.

Cotton had been present only to a limited extent in Euro America before the European trading companies brought these attractive fabrics back from the

Figure 5.2 Indian cotton chintz fabric made into a dress for a resident of Albany, New York. Colorful cotton fabrics painted and mordant dyed in colorful and costly fabrics became increasingly fashionable in the 1780s and 1790s (source: The Colonial Williamsburg Foundation, gift of Mrs Cora Ginsburg)

East. Costly as they were, only the Indian skill in handling cotton and the ready supply of cheap labor made it possible for the wealthy to afford the fabrics (Figure 5.2). Cotton's short fibers were difficult to spin into strong yarns that could be used in the warp direction of fabrics and it required thirteen days of labor to produce each pound of cotton thread. By comparison, silk required only six (Bernstein, 2008: 253).

Attempts to establish trading relations with Japan by the Portuguese and the English were thwarted by the Dutch. The English desire to have silks woven in Britain focused their silk trade on importation of raw silk fiber for British mills. Other products, most notably tea, porcelain, and gold bullion dominated the China trade. India was the most fertile ground for the English traders, and textiles one of the major imports. Both imported cottons and silks were enthusiastically received, so much so that British textile workers protested and manufacturers lobbied, leading to the enactment of legislation passed in 1700 that prohibited the use or wearing of imported silks and cottons from Persia, China, or East India. Other European countries followed, but the chief effect of these laws was to stimulate the growth of smuggling. To take advantage of the demand for Asian silks, manufacturers in China and India began to produce silks in patterns preferred for European fashions. Indian cotton design also responded to European preferences (Wild, 1999: 48).

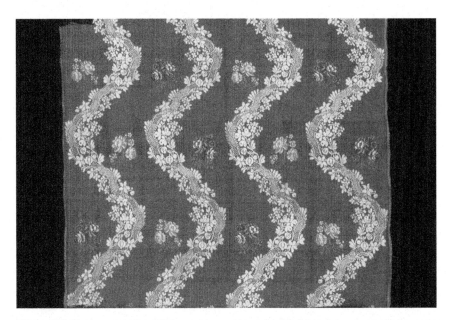

Figure 5.3 Trade goods from China were used to make this intricately woven silk brocade pattern, c. 1775. Imported goods were often made in patterns like this one, which were known to be favored by European customers (source: The Colonial Williamsburg Foundation, museum purchase)

Over time, particularly in the period between 1740 and 1860, the trade systems and practices in the rest of the world became increasingly westernized. One of the major factors in this change was the Industrial Revolution that was beginning in Europe. The superior technologies that flowed from industrialization made it possible for Britain to dominate India, not only economically but also militarily, so that by the 1770s, the British controlled "British India" (Curtin, 1984).

The products of the textile industries of China and Japan had been in demand in Europe since Greek and Roman times. After colonies were established in the Americas, the settlers also bought the imports. While an exploration of the history of the dress of China and India as it relates to technology is beyond the scope of this book, the technologies that developed in these civilizations cannot be overlooked, as they played an important part in the development of technologies that made their way around the world. Even more important, as will be seen in subsequent chapters, the popularity of their products s timulated the development of the technologies that jump-started the Industrial Revolution.

At the same time, a brief look at the presence of fashion in the Tang period does reveal that fashion in dress is not an exclusively Euro-American phenomenon. And that contact between different cultures and the spread of technologies can play an important part in motivating some individuals to experiment with new fashion ideas.

Looking at relationships through illustrations

These examples of dress in India and China come from textile-rich civilizations that had long engaged in trade; both export trade of their products and import trade from others.

Figure 5.4 shows a painting of a lady from the Tang dynasty, providing an example of one style of dress for an upper-class woman of the court. She is wearing a multi-layered garment that would have been made from several different types of fabric. Her accessories and grooming reflect court practices.

According to Benn (2002), women of this period removed their eyebrows by plucking and used pigments for painting eyebrows of fashionable shapes. This lady appears to have painted her blue eyebrows in the popular shape of moth wings. Indigo coloring matter was one of the preferred pigments. As noted in Chapter 9, the processing to produce indigo blue from plant material was quite complex. Her hairstyle also conforms to the practice of piling the hair high on the head. The high hairstyle provided a place to add ornaments. This lady has

Figure 5.4 Painting of a lady from the Tang Dynasty showing dress style of middle-class women of the court, c. 730–800 CE (source: bpk, Berlin/The Art Archive at Art Resource, New York)

arranged flowers on top of her head, and has inserted into the arrangement a variety of filigree hairpins, something Cahill (1999: 104) notes had benefitted from Persian metalwork technologies that came into China through trade.

A wide variety of silk fabrics were available to court ladies. Although the structure of all the woman's garments is not clear, one can see at least three different types of silk fabric. The small triangular lower section appears to have either a woven or embroidered pattern. Sources note that foreign influences do appear in patterned fabrics. Another layer is a solid red colored fabric, one of the colors deemed suitable for court wear. Although the precise type of fabric cannot be ascertained from the illustration, the fabric appears heavier than the other fabrics and could have been satin, a heavier-weight fabric being made at this time. Covering the other layers, she has an extensive, very sheer shawl-like garment that appears to be extremely fine and delicate. At her shoulder a white section appears to join several edges of the sheer fabric. These appear to be similar to a knotted or crochet-like structure and as China was producing cotton by this time, it could be cotton. The variations in the fabrics testify to the high levels of skill in textile manufacture possessed by Chinese weavers.

Mogul emperor's dress

The textile technologies used to create Mogul dress had been developed over the millennia preceding the period of Mogul rule on the Indian sub-continent. The skills in weaving cotton fabrics and in dyeing them to an exceptionally wide range of colors, some quite subtle, have been noted above. Block printing techniques, painting, and embroidery skills were well-developed. Silks, both domestically produced and imported, were available. These could all be used in the dress of the imperial court. Dotted and checked fabrics were often made using tie-dying techniques.

Harwood identifies male garments at the time of Akbar (1542–1605) as consisting of five basic components: a turban (called a *pagri*), a coat (*jama*), shawl (*patka*), a sash (*katzeb*), and trousers or a loincloth (*dhoti*). In the illustration shown in Figure 5.5, moving from head to toe, the aforementioned elements can be seen, except for the shawl. The figure at far left is wearing a shawl.

The technologies necessary to create these garments would have been those described for spinning and weaving, especially those that created patterned fabrics. One decorative element, the light dots on the jacket of Akbar, could have been created by a type of resist dyeing process in which the areas that create the design are covered by some substance that prevents the fabric from absorbing the dye in the design area. Not a new technology, this method is and has been used in many parts of the world.

Both Muslim and Hindu people lived in this region. Hindu's religious beliefs rejected the wearing of shoes and of leather, whereas the Muslim Mogul rulers did not. The figures in the illustration are, therefore, wearing shoes. These generally had an upturned toe and did not have a raised back at the heel.

Figure 5.5 Painting of a Mogul emperor showing the wide range of coloring of textiles (source: Newark Museum/The Art Archive at Art Resource, New York)

Harwood notes differences in styles of elements of dress that vary with imperial reigns and with religious affiliation. These would appear to vary sufficiently from one part of the Mogul period to another to be considered fashions, at least within court circles.

PART TWO

THE INDUSTRIAL REVOLUTION AND FIRST STEPS TOWARD THE FASHION INDUSTRY

6
DRESS AND FASHION MOVE THE INDUSTRIAL REVOLUTION FORWARD
(18th century)

By the beginning of the 1700s, ships were sailing east to what the Europeans called the Indies and west to the Americas where the British had established colonies in eastern North America, the French in the Caribbean and North America, and the Spanish and Portuguese in South America. After 1700, new commodities made up the bulk of cargos brought from the East to both Europe and America: coffee, sugar, tea, and cotton (Bernstein. 2008: 243). Not unknown in the West, cotton had been a luxury fabric in Ancient Rome and had gained a foothold in Europe, arriving by way of Spain after its conquest by the Arabs in the eighth century and in Italy from Sicily. Arab traders traveled far and wide, and the major items of trade and manufacture in the Mediterranean in the years between 600 and 1000 were raw textiles and textile products (Vogelsang-Eastwood, 2003: 158). When manufactured in Europe, cotton was usually mixed with other fibers, so once the all-cotton and superior quality Indian cottons appeared they set a higher, more desirable, standard. Lemire (2003: 494) notes that by 1684 more than a million pieces of cotton were being shipped to England, making up 84 per cent of the English trade with India. In discussing the beginnings of the cotton trade, Bernstein (2008: 252–64) observed: "At that early stage no one could imagine that the trade in these textiles would eventually ignite the Industrial Revolution . . ."

Protecting the textile industries

Silk was another textile that had a ready market in the West. No other textile fiber could compete with silk. As the only filament fiber, it did not need to be tightly twisted before it could be woven. As a result, the fabric reflected light, producing a high luster that enhanced the elaborate designs into which it was woven. This, together with a luxurious feel, made it a symbol of affluence. The wide variety of types of cloth made with silk fibers alone or in combination with linen, worsted, or wool and the variations in designs applied, demonstrate the importance of fashion by the Early Modern Period (c. 1500 to 1780). As styles in art and architecture changed, so too did the ornamentation of fabrics. Both unwoven silk fiber and finished silk textiles were imported. Silk industries had developed in the Mediterranean region as well as in those countries to the east. Other European countries, including Britain, had also begun to produce silk (Rothstein, 2003b: 528–30).

Britain had long been known for its wool production. In fact, the first trade voyages from England had set out to trade British wool for spices. Unfortunately, the climate of the Far East was not one that required the warmth of wool garments and successful trading of these goods was rare. At the same time, the trading companies were eager to sell the trade goods they had acquired in the Far East. The East India Company played an important role in manipulating the demand for imported Indian cotton fabrics. As early observers of fashion's trickle-down effect, in which fashions originate at the uppermost levels of society and are then imitated by those on lower social levels, the company made sure that British royalty were well-supplied not only with financial shares in the company but also with the products they brought back to the home country. Others in the nobility were similarly gifted. As a result, silk and cotton had reached an enviable position at the top of the status ladder by the early 1700s (Bernstein, 2008). The imports of textiles from the East to Europe soon created threats to the European textile industries. Manufacturers' and workers' demands for protection ultimately led to a 1721 ban by the British government of East Indian fabrics, a ban intended to protect their home industries (Lemire 2003: 502). Other Europeans enacted similar regulations.

While European Britain banned imported goods, the American colonies were not subject to these restrictions. Costly fabrics of cotton and silk were carried directly to the colonies where they were very popular among the more affluent. At the same time the colonists were not able to import French silks, these being prohibited because of legislation that banned trade with the French, the Navigation Acts. French silks finally made it into the hands of the Americans after the American Revolution did away with British laws. The appetite for silk in the colonies before the Revolution could not be fully satisfied by imported Indian or Chinese silks, however, and the largest part of these shipments came from the silk mills of England. Although some English silks were made in colors and patterns similar to those of Chinese manufacture, they can be distinguished because the Chinese wove wider silks than the British (Baumgarten, 2002).

Technological requirements for cotton manufacture

Before looking at the specific technological advances in the making of textiles that resulted from the Industrial Revolution, it is essential to understand the steps required to manufacture cotton fabrics. It was cotton manufacture and the need to speed up the steps in the process that stimulated the burst of inventive energy that was the Industrial Revolution. As we have seen, the cotton fabrics and yarns that went into the fashionable dress of the seventeenth and early eighteenth centuries came largely from India. Some cotton was planted in the Caribbean Islands and in the American South. But no matter where the cotton originated, these are the steps it had to go through.

The fiber is found in a cotton boll, the mature seedpod of the cotton plant. Fibers must be separated from the seed, a slow process that was done by hand until tools were invented to do the separation mechanically. Once the fibers are separated, they must also be cleaned of any accumulated dust and dirt. Before the fibers can be made into a yarn, they must be brought into at least some degree of alignment. This process is called carding and a device with a brush-like surface structure is used to straighten the fibers. The resulting strand of fiber is known as the sliver. However, if a finer, smoother yarn is wanted, the carded fiber may also be combed, or subjected to further straightening and removal of excess short fibers before being formed into the sliver. The sliver is drawn out somewhat and formed into the roving, which is given a slight amount of twist to improve cohesion, then coiled and ready for spinning. These preliminary steps can be and were done by hand until the development of machines to do the work of twisting textile fibers into the yarns that were needed to feed the looms that transformed them into woven cloth.

Hand spinning had been superseded in many parts of the world by the spinning wheel well before the eighteenth century, but the problems of supply and demand provided strong incentives to speed up all the steps in making all kinds of textiles. The importance of fashion in stimulating demand for cotton fabrics in Western Europe and North America made this particularly urgent. Any bottleneck in moving the cotton from one step to the next as it made its way to the waiting consumer was an impediment to making a profit. The supply of raw cotton had increased substantially once cotton cultivation expanded in the American south. While these plantations had the effect of lowering costs and increasing the supply of this textile, they were also the reason for beginning the horrendous African slave trade through which men, women, and children were forcibly shipped across the Atlantic to work in the cotton fields.

The aforementioned steps are reflected in the inventions and patents that began to appear rapidly in the eighteenth century. In 1737, Englishmen John Wyatt and Lewis Paul invented "drawing rollers to draft fibers so spinning of yarn would be possible by machine" (editers *Encyclopedia of American Fabrics*,

WOOLLEN MANUFACTURE.

SPINNING JENNY.

Figure 6.1 James Hargreaves' invention of the spinning jenny in 1767 moved spinning from a single spinning wheel making one yarn at a time to a device that allowed multiple yarns to be spun at once (source: HIP/The Art Archive at Art Resource, New York)

p 166). In the same year, the first cotton mill opened in Birmingham, England; however, it burned down only twelve years later. Elements that would be important in mechanical carding were invented in 1748 and a patent for a carding machine was taken out in the same year. A major step forward was the invention in 1767 by James Hargreaves of the spinning jenny, a device that allowed one worker to spin multiple spools of yarn at one time.

This device was one of many that succeeded, because the high demand for cotton yarn had fueled the need for rapid production. Two years later, Richard Arkwright invented the spinning frame (horses supplied the power for operating this machine), and in 1779 Samuel Crompton combined principles from the spinning jenny and the spinning frame in the hybrid mule spinning machine.

In the interim period, improvements had been made to carding, to drawing, and to producing the roving as well as to spinning. The first "great cotton mill" was built in 1771 in Derbyshire, England. It used the aforementioned spinning frames. And it hired children (1972 editors, *AF Encyclopedia of Textiles*).

Figure 6.2 Cotton mill in England (early nineteenth century) is indicative of the importance of cotton manufacture to the Industrial Revolution (source: Shutterstock/ Neveshkin Nikolay)

All of these improvements were faster than the old hand processes, but were hindered by the lack of cotton fiber. The slow hand process of separating the cotton fiber from the seeds caused that blockage in the route to a cotton fabric. The problem was solved in 1792 when American Eli Whitney invented a machine, the cotton gin, which automated the separation of cotton seeds from cotton fibers.

Now cotton could flow uninterrupted from field to factory, and thence to merchant and consumer.

Textile technology comes to America

British legislation had restricted American colonists from manufacturing textiles, so that British merchants could profit by selling their products to the Americans. The absence of restrictions on purchase of Chinese silks and Indian cottons and the prohibition of purchase of French silks by American colonists can be seen as an indication of the power and influence of the trading companies that had permission to sell their imports abroad. These restrictions did not entirely succeed in stifling textile production in the Americas, but did keep the mechanized equipment of the budding Industrial Revolution away from the colonies.

Figure 6.3 Eli Whitney's cotton gin made it possible to detach cotton fiber from the seed so that it could be spun into yarns. The cotton, above left, enters, passes through jagged teeth that separate the fiber from the seeds, and the clean fiber exits the machine at the front, while seeds fall out below the machine (source: Culver Pictures/The Art Archive at Art Resource, New York)

All this changed when the United States declared their independence from Britain and prevailed in the ensuing war. McCauley's fictional account (1983) chronicles the history of a mill in New England. This book provides an interesting overview of technological changes in manufacturing. He begins with a water powered mill, noting that in America textile fibers were not spun using water power until 1790; however, water did power fulling mills that used hammers for beating wool fabrics. In his fictional town, a water-powered cotton mill is built in 1810 as a result of the need to make southern cotton into fabrics in northern towns. Water power moved systems of gears, shafts, and pulleys in the machinery that produced the fabrics (McCauley, 1983).

By this time cotton manufacturing had begun in Rhode Island (1788). Then in 1789 Samuel Slater secretly left England for the United States. Settling in Rhode Island, Slater proceeded to build a textile mill. Taking plans from England was illegal, and Slater brought all of his plans inside his head. The technological processes were all recreated from his memory (*AF Encyclopedia of Textiles* 1972: 170).

Other fashions benefit from technology

It may seem that the only eighteenth-century fashions that benefited from technological advances were those in the textiles used for dress. One of the elements of dress that fashionable women consistently sought was jewelry. Gems were incorporated into the most valuable of these. The popularity of many gems has been related to their "sparkle," a quality resulting from the amount of light they reflect. The amount of light reflected from the surface of a gem is related to the way in which the gem is cut. Cuts before the eighteenth century were fairly simple, and did not reflect light as well as several new cuts that were developed and used in the 1700s. The introduction of the "rose cut" in the eighteenth century produced more glitter and shimmer and the more complex cut called the "brilliant cut" resulted in even more sparkle. As a result, art critic Mastai (1981) has called the eighteenth century "the age of the diamond." She also notes the first appearance of "paste jewelry," made of glass that was cut in the same manner as gemstones. As a result, this jewelry could be purchased at much lower cost but used in greater quantity to give the impression of more valuable ornaments. This was also the period during which Josiah Wedgewood pottery was popular. Wedgewood created ornaments that simulated the appearance of cameos that, set in gold or faceted steel and mass-produced, could be sold at moderate cost (Mastai, 1981).

With this chapter we begin to see the important role played by textiles in stimulating the technological advances known as the Industrial Revolution. Affluent European consumers could acquire the popular imported silks and cottons. But their prices placed them beyond the reach of the working classes. But when the competition from imported goods led European governments to ban their importation and sale, the only products available were inferior copies of the fabrics. The commercial world was ripe for the technological innovations that would release the pent-up consumer demand.

Historians and economists have debated and disagreed about the importance and uniqueness of the period known as the Industrial Revolution of the nineteenth century. A considerable number of scholars challenged the idea that this was a "unique turning point in economic and social development". Berg and Hudson (1992: 24) counter this viewpoint and argue effectively that the research supporting this view is biased by research methods that are too limited. At least for textile technology, dress, and fashion, the Industrial Revolution was unique in its immediate and long-term impacts. While it is true that Chapter 4 discusses many important advances in textile technology, it would be difficult to find an historical period in which invention and technologies had such an overwhelming impact on dress as the nineteenth century.

Looking at relationships through illustrations

Figure 6.4 shows an upper-class French woman and her son wearing garments of white cotton muslin that would have been imported from India. The garments

Figure 6.4 Madame Serizat and her son, 1796 (source: Erich Lessing/The Art Archive at Art Resource, New York)

would probably have been constructed in France. The European cottons could not compare in quality with the very costly imported goods, especially soft, white muslin fabrics. As a result, they were the height of fashion, and at the same time conveyed this wearer's status as the wife of one of the high-ranking politicians who emerged from the Revolution and later became important in the Napoleonic period.

The ability to spin these fine cotton yarns depended on a labor supply, like that available in India, willing and able to do the slow and difficult job of freeing the cotton fiber from its seeds, after which it was spun into delicate, fine yarn and woven into cloth superior to anything made in the West. Demand for the fabric was high; so were the prices.

The dress Madame Serizat wears is simple in contrast to the elaborate styles of the pre-revolutionary years. Styles became even simpler in the next decade. Ribero (2002: 789) points out that contrary to the common assumption that styles changed radically at the time of the Revolution in 1789, there was no abrupt break in clothing styles. The change, instead, came in a faster pace of fashion change. This post-war dress would have been cut and sewn together by hand by a skilled seamstress. Male tailors made men's clothes. The flowers in her hand lead to the conclusion that she is dressed for summer. Women wore head coverings out of doors, and this appears to be a straw hat in the bonnet style that is ornamented with silk ribbons and bows, and ties around her chin. The brim of the hat is not overly wide. The technology for making straw hats is not complex. Straws of different kinds come in various widths. Sometimes groups of straws are handled together. They must be soaked to make them flexible. A braid is formed, and then wound into the desired shape and the strands stitched together with needle and thread.

The process for creating a top hat such as those worn by men of the period was complex and dangerous. The materials required were the hair of an animal such as beaver trapped in North America and shipped to Europe to make into hats. This was such a lucrative practice that the official seal of the state of New York to this day includes a depiction of a beaver. The beaver fur was combined with wool so it could be made into felt. Felting is a process of shrinking the hair and wool together so that the scales on the surface of the wool fibers will hold the beaver hair firmly in place. A mixture of mercury and nitric acid was applied to the hair to facilitate the felting. The fumes released by the chemicals eventually caused a condition called "hatters' shakes" and a suspiciously high level of mental illness was thought to be another result of working as a hatter. This is reflected in the character of the mad hatter in *Alice in Wonderland*. The manufacture continues through steps to make sure that the fabric of the hat is uniform in thickness and that the crown will be the proper shape when pieces are joined. Crown shapes were subject to fashion, with some periods when crowns were higher or lower or wider at the top or bottom according to the latest fashion.

Figure 6.5 Man on the right is holding a top hat, early 1800s (source: author's image)

Some additional shrinking must be done before blocking the hat into the desired shape and forming the brim. Ginsberg (1990: 70) describes this complex process in detail, quoting an eighteenth-century woman who observed and counted ten separate steps required to make a man's top hat.

7

THE CENTRAL ROLE OF DRESS AND FASHION AND THE INDUSTRIAL REVOLUTION
(c. 1800 to 1860)

Much of the Industrial Revolution may have been focused on textile technology, but its applications were quickly applied to other types of manufacturing, so that factories powering machines by water or steam soon crowded the landscape. Even so, textile technologies maintained a central place in the increasingly mechanized world. And a formidable interaction between fashionable dress and technology drove each. We have already seen how the popularity of Indian chintz and muslin cottons and Chinese silks were powerful fashion influences that served as economic incentives to mechanization. As the Industrial Revolution progressed, it is sometimes difficult to determine whether the fashion stimulated the mechanization or the ability to produce the fashions by mechanization created the fashion.

The cotton gin and the Muslin Empire dress

One of the clearest examples of how technology, dress, and fashion interconnect is in the fashions that emerged in the closing years of the eighteenth century. The European market for Indian cotton was strong and even with greater cotton production in the American South, cotton supplies remained scarce, the fabric very costly, and at first limited to royalty and the wealthy.

It is relatively rare that fashion changes suddenly. More often styles evolve gradually. Even by the close of the French Revolution, the tightly fitted bodices and full-skirted women's dress styles of the 1770s and 1780s through a gradual,

L'ANGLAISE.

Figure 7.1 Male and female dancers wearing the mass fashion of the early 1800s. The costly white cotton dresses became far more affordable once the cotton gin contributed to increased supplies of cotton fabric. Its lines simplified when fashions were inspired by ancient Greek and Roman women's dress became fashionable; women in a wider skirt with an empire waist and men in the trousers that replaced the knee breeches of the previous century (L'Anglaise, etching and watercolor on paper mounted on card, ca. 1815, courtesy of the Victoria and Albert Museum/Lebas)

though more rapid than usual, evolution had been replaced by dresses that had the appearance of those depicted on Greek statues. Puffed sleeves, high waists, and softly gathered skirts were made from white cotton muslin.

The style had probably been stimulated by an awakened interest in classical antiquity, and reinforced by the political ideals of the Greek and Roman republics that accompanied the French Revolution. This fashion was widely adopted at the court of the Emperor Napoleon Bonaparte of France, and the high-waisted skirt style that is revived periodically has been known ever since as the empire waist. It was also fortuitous that this change came about at a time when the floodgates opened and released an abundance of cotton fabrics that could not only be manufactured rapidly, thanks to Eli Whitney's cotton gin, but that also became affordable not only to the rich and royal, but also to the ordinary citizen. Mass fashion had become possible. For the first decade of the nineteenth century, the empire waist predominated and American southerners proclaimed cotton to be king! This ready supply of cotton provided the raw material for the continual change in fashions.

Figure 7.2 The very fashionable Empress Eugenie of France weaves a flower on the new Jacquard-type loom that mechanized the weaving of patterned fabrics. This invention derived from the earlier Chinese draw loom principles illustrated in Figure 5.1 (source: Shutterstock/Marzolino)

The draw loom and its impact

Weaving complex designs into fabrics by hand is time-consuming. The Chinese silks that were carried west by traders were prized for the beautiful patterns painted, printed, or woven into the fabric. To make these magnificent silks with woven patterns, they used a modified loom called the draw loom, described in Chapter 5. Scholars are uncertain about whether the draw loom was an invention of the Chinese that gradually traveled west or whether it was independently invented in Middle Eastern areas, where local fabric artifacts woven on the draw loom have been found in Iran and Syria. It was in use during the Byzantine Empire to make woven patterns after the Byzantines began producing silk fiber from which they wove fabrics. European silk weavers in the Middle Ages also utilized this technology (Rothstein, 2003b: 528).

Even relatively simple figured textiles woven on a horizontal or vertical loom required a great deal of time to set up the loom. As a result, the complexity of the fabrics woven on these looms had limits imposed by the number of treadles and the number of patterning rods that could be added to a loom. By contrast, the draw loom required an overhead structure into which a number of leashes (cords) that encircled the warp yarns could be fastened. By lifting a leash, the yarn held by that leash was lifted. Creating a woven pattern required the warp and weft yarns to intersect in a certain sequence. Lifting the leashes in the prescribed order allowed the weft yarns to intersect the warp yarns as required to make the pattern. Grouping the leashes allowed repetition of the lines within a pattern. The draw loom also required an extra worker, who sat on the upper framework and lifted the leashes that lifted the yarn. A mistake would create a flaw in the fabric (Schoeser, 2003: 82).

As automation was taking place in textile production, it was only natural that some way of speeding up the production of patterned fabrics would be desirable. A number of inventors had made attempts to devise an automated process, so that there was a body of work on which to build. Joseph-Marie Jacquard of France made his first effort toward the end of the eighteenth century, but the invention did not become fully realized and operational until about 1818. Even then, additional time passed before the concept was finalized. Gone was the assistant sitting on an overhead framework; gone were the cords and the leashes. Instead each warp yarn passed through the eye of a metal needle. A card with punched holes was prepared for each warp yarn. When the weaver depressed a treadle, the metal needles were raised to where the punch cards were held on the upper part of the loom. If the needle encountered the solid card, nothing happened, but if the needle passed through a hole in the card, the warp was raised. The preparation of the cards was as time-consuming as setting up the draw loom had been, and two workers were required to prepare the cards. Given these costs, the loom was only economically advantageous when long yardages of elaborately patterned fabrics were made (Rothstein, 2003a: 793).

The jacquard loom, as it came to be known (Figure 7.2), was a major factor in stimulating the fashion for Kashmir shawls. The Kashmir shawl, named after its place of origin in the Indian sub-continent, was a garment for men in India. When it was imported to Europe, it became an outdoor garment for women. It was made from the wool of the Kashmir goat, a soft, warm fiber. Its pattern was distinctive. Called by the people of the region, a *boteh,* suppositions about what it represents vary from a leaf to a mango fruit. Once established in the West as a design motif, it was generally known as "a pine," because the shape is not unlike that of a pine cone. Ultimately it came to be called a paisley pattern.

The first India-made Kashmir shawls were imported to England, and later to other European countries around the mid-1700s. They were fearfully expensive, but very appealing. Having learned that earlier Asian imports could be successfully

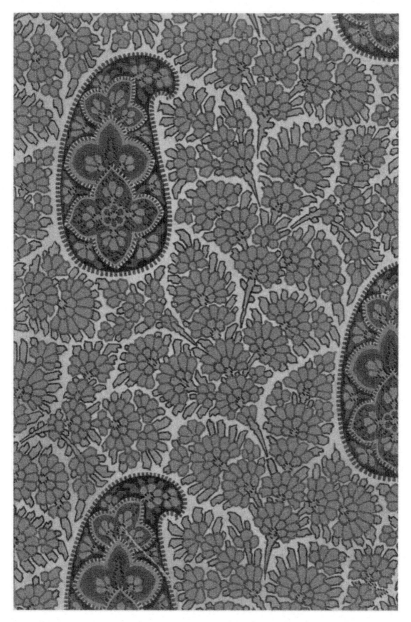

Figure 7.3 British design for a fabric that could now be woven on Jacquard looms to be made into the immensely fashionable paisley shawl (courtesy of the Victoria and Albert Museum/Presented by George C. Haité, Esq., RBA)

copied and marketed, manufacturers in Edinburgh and Norwich produced copies. By the first decade of the 1800s, the town of Paisley had started manufacturing them too. And somehow it was the name "paisley" that came to describe the typical paisley pattern. How did it happen that these shawls, made all over Europe, came to be known as paisley shawls? The jacket of Reilly's (1987) book summarizes this well: "Superior piracy and plagiarism combined with determination and inventiveness to see the town of Paisley triumph and make its own a pattern that endures to this day" (Figure 7.3).

The town of Paisley had invested in some of the new jacquard looms by the mid-1820s. Paisley is credited by Reilly (1987) as probably the first among British weaving centers to carry out jacquard work on a large scale. The availability of this new technology is doubtless responsible for its popularity as a mass fashion. When the cost of a shawl was from 210 to 315 British pounds, they remained an affluent woman's choice, but when the first imitations dropped to 20 pounds, there were more customers. Paisley shawls were an important garment for outdoors in the period from 1830 to 1870. And the automated manufacturing processes continued to cut prices, so that by the mid-1860s costs could be as low as twenty-seven shillings and one penny. Printed imitations went for as little as three shillings and sixpence. Fashion played an important part not only in making paisley shawls mass fashion but also in their disappearance.

Maskiell (2002) traces the history of consumption of Kashmir shawls and sees the decline of the style as related to import and manufacture practices. However, it seems likely that when the bustle styles of the 1870s became the dominant silhouette, wearing a large shawl was logistically difficult. Over the full skirts of the previous forty years, the shawl was a natural outer garment, but with the back fullness of a skirt supported by a bustle jutting out at the back of a skirt, a short waist-length cape or jacket was more comfortable. Although the paisley shawl is no longer fashionable, the paisley pattern has remained an important part of fashion in the years since its first appearance in Western dress.

Hand crafts are fully mechanized

Knitting

Chapter 4 described the first steps in the mechanization of knitting that came with the development of the knitting frame, used mostly for making hosiery – it was known as "the stocking frame." Even after the availability of this device and until the end of the eighteenth century, the actual manufacture of knitted goods remained largely in the hands of individual workers who owned the frames. Chapman (2003: 824) associates two factors with the transformation by 1845 of this formerly domestic British industry into a more concentrated system

Figure 7.4 The paisley shawl was an ideal outdoor garment to wear over the wide hoops of the 1860s (La Mode Illustree, courtesy of Dover Publications, inc)

located outside the home. The first was the acquisition and transfer of ownership of the equipment from the workers to the capitalist class. The second was regional concentration of the industry. Furthermore, creating a knitted structure such as hosiery was a great deal more complex than either spinning or weaving yarns or fabrics. When a flat woven textile was cut, its interlocked yarn structure maintained its integrity, whereas the loops in a flat weft-knitted structure would unravel, unless pieces were quickly joined together with firm secure sewn seams.

Progress in overcoming these obstacles was made gradually. Patents in 1861 and 1864 imitated the motions of hand knitting sufficiently to produce needed shapes for knitted goods, especially hosiery. A key factor, called fashioning, was the ability for the machine to drop and add stitches in order to shape the item being produced. Among the notable contributions to industrializing knitting was the latch needle (1849), which is credited with making possible circular knitting, a type of production that became very popular in the United States. Prior to the late nineteenth century, most knitted goods were weft knits in which yarns interlaced horizontally, although a hand-operated warp knitting machine had been invented in 1768 and the warp knitting machine was mechanized in 1791. Knitting machines are classified as either flat or circular. The former can make either warp or weft knits, whereas the circular machines are used mostly for weft knits. Warp knitting, in which the interlacing is vertical, is generally done on flat machines. Knitting technology progressed in the nineteenth century, but the more dramatic developments took place in the twentieth century (Chapman, 2003: 1028).

Lace

By the time of the Industrial Revolution, lace making had become a profitable industry for many European regions. The traditional designs frequently carried the names of their place of origin, so the geographic spread of cities and countries involved can be visualized by looking at the list of names of laces in any textile dictionary that are associated with areas of Europe as far apart as Ireland, Paris, Venice, and Crete. With mechanization of textile manufacture moving ahead rapidly in the late eighteenth century, inventors recognized that machines used in an area such as lace making could be profitable.

Lace had become less fashionable by the late 1700s and was more often used as edging and trimmings than incorporated into dress as a major part of both men's and women's apparel. This contrasted with the many ways lace had been used in earlier centuries as essential elements of dress (Figure 4.5). The most popular laces at the end of the nineteenth century tended to be small patterns placed on a net ground (Kratz, 1989). As a result, the first machine patented c. 1764 that can be viewed as a forerunner of a lace-making machine produced a machine-made net on which small patterns could be hand-embroidered. This saved the tedious labor of constructing the ground, the name for the base fabric of the lace. The device on which the net was made was a stocking frame. The earliest of these nets were made from one continuous yarn, but if that yarn were broken, the structure of the net was compromised. Earnshaw (1994: 17) describes the subsequent progression of improvements as coming with a square net (1777–1830), a point net with a hexagonal mesh (1780–1820), and a diamond-shaped net (c. 1830 and after).

Fashion played an important part in the technological journey of lace manufacture. As long as the embroidered nets made up the largest part of lace production, net manufacture and hand embroidery co-existed. The transition from Empire fashions to fashions of the Romantic Period, with its revival of interest in styles of earlier centuries, called for much larger expanses of laces with elaborate patterns, which proved to be an incentive for greater mechanization of the process. The wider market that came with more women from all socioeconomic levels following fashion trends created a market for both costly hand-made and less expensive machine-made laces, thereby motivating inventors to work toward full mechanization. A bobbinet machine patented in 1808 by John Heathcote was the precursor of the machine that proved to be the breakthrough to full mechanization. The Leavers brothers lace machine was described dramatically in the American Fabrics *Encyclopedia of Textiles* (1972: 378), saying it could be "compared in strength with an elephant, and, in delicacy of performance, and creative ingenuity, to the spider. It is undoubtedly the most complicated and difficult piece of textile machinery the ingenious mind of man has been able to contrive." By the 1840s, lace making profited from the availability of the jacquard loom that could be used to control the complex patterns that typified the more elaborate laces. However, it is not the jacquard that makes the lace. That is done by the Leavers machine. Successful in accomplishing the mechanization of lace manufacture, the basic principles and design of the Leavers machine have continued to be used. Subsequently, additional fabrics with lacelike appearances emerged in the twentieth century as a result of additional technological advancements.

As each new item of textile equipment facilitated production of fabrics, fashionable dress benefitted; beginning with empire-style dresses, made by women sewing at home or by skilled seamstresses, and progressing to the paisley shawls produced commercially. Soon machine-made lace could be purchased. Although knitting had to wait until equipment was refined, basic garments such as stockings knitted on machines were available. Later chapters tell of the wide uses of manufactured knits.

Looking at relationships through illustrations

The woman in the center of the fashion plate in Figure 7.5 is dressed in the styles of 1851. The extensive lace panels that cover her skirt testify to the ready availability of machine-made lace. Many of the fashion plates from this period depict extensive use of lace fabrics, which had become an important part of fashion again.

Parasols

Another element of her dress that generally appears in outdoor scenes is the parasol that she carries (Figure 7.6). A pale complexion was considered fashionably desirable, and parasols helped to preserve that look. One of the innovations in parasol construction was the development of the carriage parasol. The carriage parasol was constructed so that the stick that held it aloft had a hinge placed about half-way up its length. With the hinge, the lady could fold the stick in half. This combined with the frame that closed made the parasol small enough to be held in the hand while riding in a carriage (Figure 7.7).

Bustles

The round hoop-supported skirt gradually shifted its fullness to the back of the skirt and by 1870 required a change in the undergarment that supported the back fullness. Various solutions included a petticoat with horsehair ruffles placed at the back (Figure 7.8) and several wire constructions, important when bustles grew more rigid in shape. One was a braided wire bustle (Figure 7.9) and another was a coiled wire spring (Figure 7.10) that benefitted from improvements in metallurgy.

Figure 7.5 Woman dressed in the style of 1851 showing extensive use of manufactured lace (source: author's image)

Figure 7.6 Diagram of
parasol carried when
outdoors (courtesy of
Fairchild Books)

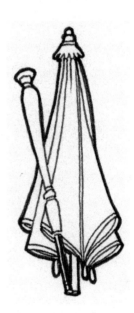

Figure 7.7 Diagram of a
carriage parasol that
could be folded in half
when entering a carriage
(courtesy of Fairchild
Books)

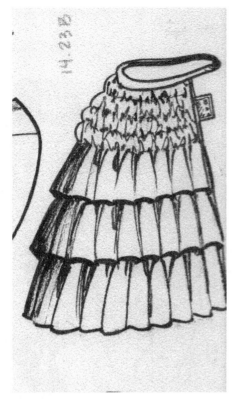

Figure 7.8 Sketch of a petticoat with horsehair ruffles placed at the back to support a bustle skirt (courtesy of Fairchild Books)

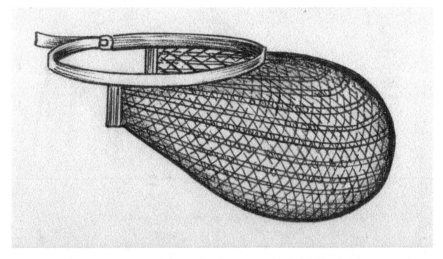

Figure 7.9 Sketch of a braided wire bustle (courtesy of Fairchild Books)

Figure 7.10 Sketch of a coiled wire spring bustle (courtesy of Fairchild Books)

8

DRESS, FASHION, AND SOCIAL CHANGES FOLLOWING THE INDUSTRIAL REVOLUTION
(19th century)

The Industrial Revolution began in Britain; its duration less than 200 years. Marked by an astounding burst of inventive energy in many different areas, it began in the eighteenth century and closed toward the end of the nineteenth. Previous chapters chronicled the ways the textile industry stimulated the industrialization that characterized the period. This chapter explores the differences this revolution made in the lives of the population of Britain where the Industrial Revolution had its start. Through them we may be able to answer these two questions. What changes in Western society can be identified as having been somehow related to the Industrial Revolution? And what did this have to do with dress and fashion?

Life in Britain before and after the Industrial Revolution

The bulk of the population of Britain (there were around six million in the late 1700s) was rural. Most people worked on the land. Only about one-fifth of them lived in towns. Most of the work they did was an outgrowth of agriculture (Hicks, 2010: 4). What industries there were, were small-scale. Even textile-related work was done using agricultural products: linen from the flax plant and wool from sheep. Linen was not generally produced in England, Scotland, or Wales. It was brought from Ireland, where there were more favorable growing and processing conditions (Ashton, 1968: 22–3).

In all parts of the world, textile production had been one of the earliest industries associated with those living on the land. In Britain, the government provided a variety of regulations of wool production in order to safeguard this product. These ranged from prohibiting the emigration of wool workers to forbidding the importing of competing fabrics, and even insisting that the dead be buried in wool garments. All members of the household had tasks relating to wool production. Women sorted, cleaned, and spun the fiber. Assignment of this latter task to women, including those unmarried, is reflected in English in the word "spinster," as well as in "distaff," the staff on which bundles of fiber were held prior to spinning, a word that has become a synonym for female. Men did the weaving. By the eighteenth century, the finishing steps in making the fabric were more likely to be done in local mills where wool was fulled (compacted), fibers were brushed up on the surface in a process called napping, and the cloth was dyed. The power source for these latter activities was provided by horses or by water.

Imported textile fibers that were not yet made into fabrics such as silk, linen, mohair, and cotton did not follow the pattern of the family-produced woolens. With these fibers, an employer who funded the operation gathered a group of perhaps half a dozen looms in central buildings, described as garrets or sheds (Ashton, 1968: 24). In a few more specialized areas, a merchant distributed (described as "putting out") fibers and/or yarns from which a local weaver (male) wove the cloth. Often additional finishing was done in establishments owned by merchants. From these descriptions, it is easy to see how a kind of factory system in infancy was developing.

Production of completed items of dress is described as "relatively small and unimportant," as garments were most often made by the family or by a seamstress or a tailor hired for this purpose. Specialized items such as hats usually had an identifiable regional center where they were made. For example, hats made from beaver fur imported from the American colonies generally came from London, while stockings were knitted by hand in Scotland and Wales or on a mechanized knitting frame in London.

One of the first of the mechanical inventions that set the textile industry on its way to the Industrial Revolution had been the flying shuttle, invented in 1733 by John Kay of Lancashire. This device allowed one man instead of two to insert the shuttle across the full width of the cloth. Hammers activated by pulling a cord provided sufficient momentum to pass the shuttle through the full width of the shed. Workers fearful of losing their jobs to this mechanical device opposed its use, and it was not fully accepted for about thirty years, gaining its place in the textile industry only after 1760.

The mechanization of the production of formerly hand-made products described in Chapter 7 was not accepted without opposition. The movement toward mechanizing machines such as the stocking frame and the opening of factories of various kinds, along with a depressed economy in England, led disadvantaged workers to engage in machine breaking – a weapon used by workers to gain some leverage when negotiating with owners. Probably the most famous of the campaigns waged against the new technologies is that of the Luddites, a name derived from Ludd, the pseudonym adopted by the leaders of a revolt against the use of wide knitting machines that made three or four stockings at once. This excess quantity of stockings lowered the prices and exacerbated the economic decline of these textile-working families. Groups of workers revolted against their situation, broke into premises housing the hated machines, and broke them up. This rebellion continued sporadically from about 1811 to 1817 and was centered largely in Nottinghamshire, Yorkshire, and Lancashire. The British government eventually stamped it out with arrests, executions, and penal deportation. The memory of the movement lingers on in Luddite, a term that has come to mean a person who objects to modern technology.

While mill and factory production increased, it did not completely eradicate the home production of textiles and apparel. Thompson (1988) reports some 50,000 hand loom cotton weavers in the 1850s and notes that the combing of fibers remained a hand process. But by the latter decades of the nineteenth century, the move to factory production of textiles was largely complete. However, textiles as they came from the loom were not ready to wear as clothing or use in the home. Shoes and stockings were produced by local craft persons and often sold to a local clientele. When sewing machines became available in the nineteenth century, work on making clothes could be either put out to workers at home or produced in a factory setting. The first ready-to-wear was predominantly menswear, but by the 1880s and 1890s, blouses and dresses for women were also being made (Thompson, 1988: 36–7).

In the late 1800s, Britain looked entirely different than it had a hundred years before. The population had grown to twenty million, and more than half of those lived in cities. In the earlier period, power had been supplied by horses, wind, and water. Working from a background of earlier patents that were not fully successful in trying to harness steam as power to run an engine, James Watt patented his steam engine in 1769. Watt's use of coal to produce the steam was a boon to the coal industry. As the population grew, manufacturing tended to be located in towns and cities where there were more workers. In the factories, work was divided into specific tasks and each worker was assigned an operation, the origin of the assembly line in which work flowed from one logical task to the next. This factory-based manufacturing and the wealth of new machines to speed up the production line was beneficial to the entrepreneur, but workers had no control over working conditions and schedules. Fifteen- and sixteen-hour days were the norm. Safety and health issues were plentiful. Women and young children did much of the work and there was no regulation of child labor. Most of the factories were located in overcrowded cities and towns where poor housing, crime, and disease were rampant. The novels of Charles Dickens were often set in these neighborhoods and provide a daunting picture of life for the working classes. Over time, improvements did come as social reformers fought for better working conditions, shorter hours, and imposition of laws regulating child labor.

Britain was not alone in its progress through the Industrial Revolution. Other western countries experienced similar evolutions in their industries. Many Europeans saw emigration to the United States in the nineteenth century as an opportunity to improve their lives. And the United States as it too moved through the Industrial Revolution found these workers, some with excellent skills in sewing and tailoring, a great resource as that country began to develop its ready-to-wear industry.

Dress responds to social changes

The Industrial Revolution was not the only revolution of the eighteenth century. The French Revolution (1789–1799) and the American Revolution (1775–1783) were not without impacts on dress. Dress for upper-class and royal French men and women in the decades before the French Revolution was ornate and decorative.

Made of luxurious fabrics imported from the Orient or created by European textile firms such as those in Lyons in France, and Spitalfields in London, England, dress of the affluent clearly displayed their wealth and status. By the time these revolutions had ended, the dress of men was on its way to a radical change. Eighteenth-century men of the upper classes had worn knee breeches, lace-decorated shirts, and over the shirt a vest. The finishing touch was a jacket. For formal occasions, fabrics were opulent. For less formal wear, matching fabric of good quality was often used for the breeches, vest, and jacket. Only peasants and working-class men wore trousers. By contrast, nineteenth-century men dressed for business and office work would have worn suits consisting of trousers, a radical change from the knee breeches of the previous century, a vest, and a suit jacket, the fabrics in all three made of matching fabric. Gone was the lace-trimmed shirt. Instead, the shirt was generally white, which gave rise to the distinction between those who worked in offices or other business settings and those engaged in physical labor. A white shirt worn in an office would not become unduly soiled. These "white collar workers" contrasted with "blue collar" workers, manual laborers who were more likely to wear blue or colored work shirts. White collar and blue collar became a sort of shorthand for middle class and working class respectively.

Fashion was not absent from this new style of dress for men. Gradual changes in the fit and cut of all of these garments and preferences for particular accessories can be documented, but differences were more subtle than in earlier centuries.

Figure 8.1 This suit consisting of knee breeches, a vest, and outer jacket is typical of upper-class men's dress of the 1700s. The vest and jacket varied in their length and cut, but the basic elements remained the same. Compare it with Figure 8.3, dress for men as it developed in the next century (courtesy of the Victoria and Albert Museum)

Affluent men could afford more expensive fabrics, and could have their suits hand-tailored, while those with lower incomes bought their suits "off the rack," slang for "ready-made." Dark colors predominated. Some fashion historians see the changes as a demonstration of the new, egalitarian values that can be credited to the democratic attitudes and values that emerged after the American and French revolutions. The color shift is ascribed by others to a practical response, a way of hiding soiling from the soot and dirt spewed out from factory chimneys. Probably both motivations played a part.

Women's styles were more colorful and decorative. Fashion changes came about frequently and were more obvious than those in men's dress, especially when the predominant silhouette changed. Differences also could be seen in accessories such as the size, shapes, and materials from which headwear, hand-carried accessories, gloves, shoes, and jewelry were made. In general, it took about twenty years for a new silhouette to replace an older one. The empire silhouette had evolved into a more hourglass shape by the early 1820s and by the middle of the 1830s women's skirts were full, bodices fitted, and sleeves enormous. By the 1860s, skirts had grown still wider, but by 1870 the fullness moved to the back of the skirt, supported by a bustle. The bustle changed its configuration several times, but persisted until in the 1890s it disappeared, being replaced by an hourglass silhouette not without some resemblance to the shapes of the early 1830s.

Middle class

Blumin (1994) notes that the term "middle class" described by poet Walt Whitman in 1858 as "the men of moderate means," rarely appeared two generations earlier, although print uses of the words lower and upper classes seem to have been around longer. Trying to divide Americans into classes is a task sociologists have undertaken in developing research tools. The results may be useful for academics, but for my purposes in this discussion it suffices to say that it is clear that the Industrial Revolution resulted in increasing the population that we might call middle class, a group that could afford to acquire fashionable goods of many kinds including dress. But when I say fashionable, that no longer has to be a synonym for costly.

As the number of individuals described by historians and sociologists as middle class increased, a stereotypical view of what that middle-class family should look like developed. Thompson's (1988) criteria for placing families in the middle class were "separation of work from home" and "separation of women from work." The nineteenth century was not without its feminists seeking rights for women; however, the fact that the vote for women was not enacted into law until two decades into the twentieth century in the United States and three decades in Britain, indicates that social life in the Victorian Period (1837–1901) was not structured to encourage women to enter all spheres of life. Most men and women would have accepted without argument the platitude that "a woman's place is in the home."

But who was included in this "middle class?" And how did a middle class come into being? Bushman (1992) sees it first developing after the Renaissance in the European courts, in what would have to be called, in terms of income and social status, upper middle classes. With English colonization of North America, the concept spread westward. At first confined to great merchants and planters, clergy, professionals, and officers of government, Bushman claims the obligation to be genteel was part of the value system inherent in being part of the middle class. By the beginning of nineteenth century, the middle class had grown, and consisted of smaller merchants and professionals, well-off ordinary farmers, successful artisans, schoolteachers, minor government officials, clerks, shopkeepers, industrial entrepreneurs, and managers.

European history differs from American in that the colonies did not evolve from a feudal state, nor did North America ever have a class comparable to European peasants, who were agricultural workers working lands owned by others. In order to move or change occupations, they had to buy the land to which they were bound. Instead, North American settlers, other than the enslaved population, were predominantly independent landowners and entrepreneurs and as a result social conditions developed differently. The British class system was such that middle-class people could not be "in society." Individuals could only belong to society by right of birth and family connections. Even so, since the nineteenth century, British individuals who could be identified as middle class have increased in numbers and influence (Hibbert, 1975: 29).

The categories of workers that Mills (1956) classifies as "old middle class" were farmers, businessmen, and free professionals, while after 1870 he lists occupations in these expanded classifications: managers, salaried professionals, salespeople, office workers.

In viewing the effects on society that follow not only from the increase in the middle-class population but also the Industrial Revolution, Mills stresses the importance of consumption of consumer goods beginning in the nineteenth century and continuing to this day. In his view, mass production resulting from industrialization produces so many goods that this glut of goods requires "great stores" in which to house and sell them. Those "great stores" would be the department stores, a merchandising mechanism that appears first in the mid-eighteen hundreds. In addition, the goods to be sold must be transported to the markets. Once again the Industrial Revolution was responsible for the mechanized transport that carried the products of mass production. This ample stock of consumer goods was enough to supply not only department stores, but also specialty shops that dealt with one or several items such as footwear or jewelry. Mills does not confine his analysis to dress, but does pay considerable attention to fashion, noting particularly the elements of planned obsolescence that are part of the fashion cycle. His view of fashion has something in common with the analysis of another scholar, this one writing in 1899. Thorstein Veblen, an economist and sociologist, developed a theory that has interested scholars of dress and fashion ever since. Veblen (1899) identifies three means of displaying economic status: conspicuous leisure, conspicuous consumption, and conspicuous waste. He saw dress as a prime example of these practices and used fashionable dress to illustrate his ideas.

In his principle of conspicuous leisure, he argued that wearing dress that does not permit the wearer to do serious physical work shows that one is sufficiently affluent that one need not labor to support an affluent lifestyle. In the history of fashionable dress, one example that is sometimes noted is the *chopines* of Renaissance Italy. However, such examples of class distinctions may not always be so clear. Chopines were platform-soled shoes so high that women wearing them had to be supported by attendants walking beside them. They were very obviously not intended for women who had to engage in manual labor. However, as they were worn by both Venetian prostitutes and patrician women, they are not a clear-cut example of class distinctions (Harold Koda (*www.metmuseum*)). Other examples of conspicuous consumption abound in dress history. Any portrait of Tudor monarchs of the sixteenth century can serve as an excellent example of the principle of conspicuous consumption. And conspicuous waste can be associated with the practice of discarding garments or other items of dress, not because they are no longer serviceable, but simply because they are no longer fashionable.

The styles of Veblen's youth – he was born in 1857 – could have led him to see the bustle styles of the 1870s and 1880s as exemplifying conspicuous leisure, in that even the simpler, though still cumbersome, women's daytime dresses would not have been comfortable for housewifely tidying or cleaning. Moreover, these fashionable clothes were elaborately ornamented with ruffles and V-shaped ornamental edgings called vandyking. Many had elaborate embroidery or beading applied. They were very good examples of conspicuous consumption, requiring as they did large yardages of heavily ornamented fabrics. The skirts were multi-layered and draped. Far more fabric is consumed in these garments than would be needed to make a serviceable garment and with the rapidity of fashion change in the bustle period, they would have been discarded long before they were worn out (conspicuous waste).

While one can understand how the upper classes could afford to obtain the sumptuous garments that would proclaim their family's wealth, it was not just the upper classes that followed fashion. Fortunately, technology came to the aid of the less affluent. The sewing machine was well established as a household tool, as well as a tool for dressmakers by the 1870s. With the aid of this equipment it was possible to construct the decorative edgings and ruffles that were a prominent part of women's dress. Sewing machine manufacturers sold not only the sewing machines but also attachments for the machines that could make ruffles and pleats, and could gather fabrics into ruched sections, thereby eliminating the time-consuming handwork that would otherwise have been required. Long seams on trained skirts and overskirts no longer mandated tedious hand stitching. And if the styles changed markedly, remodeling could be done more quickly and efficiently, whether this was done by the lady of the house or by a seamstress. Furthermore, by the last three decades of the century, mail order catalogs offered a wide range of machine-made decorative braids and laces that the casual observer could not tell from the handmade varieties. Jacquard looms produced handsome silk brocade fabrics. Jewelry made from imitation gems was readily available.

But both Mills and Veblen fail to recognize that the fashion industry, growing as it was in the late nineteenth century, was not the cause of an insatiable demand for novelty and change. What they overlooked is that participation in fashion has been a part of human behavior in many cultures and periods of time. In fact, it may be a basic form of human behavior in that it allows both self-expression and conformity. The fashion industry utilizing the products made possible through the Industrial Revolution has effectively exploited these behaviors, building a complex industry structured to allow its customers to satisfy their desires for self-expression within the parameters of current fashionable dress. In other words, through fashion we not only show that we belong, but can also express a personal style within the context of the explicit or implicit limits of custom. Some cultures may set restrictions on allowable personal style and require close conformity to these mores. Others may have few restrictions and reward innovation.

But while the Industrial Revolution did not create fashion, its technologies clearly provided the raw materials of fashion – the textiles, the equipment for making items of dress – ranging from garments to a host of accessories, which expanded the means to transport these products to the marketplace, and provided incomes that enabled many more individuals to participate in the fashion process. By the close of the nineteenth century, the stage was set for increasingly complex relationships between technology, dress and fashion.

This chapter provides some description of social changes that people who lived at the time of the Industrial Revolution, especially those who were in some way associated with the production of textiles and dress, may have experienced. Style changes in men's dress that the development of the theory of conspicuous consumption, which Thorstein Veblen drew from observations of women's dress of this period, is explored and illustrated. While women were more likely to use fashion and ornamentation to display their affluence, men's dress showed its cost in more subtle ways. Bespoke (made-to order) men's tailored garments were a symbol of wealth.

Looking at relationships through illustrations

Conspicuous consumption

The dress c. 1881 worn by this English woman in Figure 8.2 serves as a visual example of Thorstein Veblen's theory of conspicuous consumption. The dress

Figure 8.2 Young woman wearing bustle dress (courtesy of the Victoria and Albert Museum/ Given by Mrs G.T. Morton)

Figure 8.3 Young man of late 1800s wearing a suit (source: author's image)

was designed by the most prestigious design firm of the period, the House of Worth. Wearing clothing designed by Worth would have been a proclamation of wealth. To select the gown the customer would have had to travel to Paris, order the gown, and be available for fittings once the dress was finished. The silk satin fabric and pearl embroidery trimming were costly; the amount of handwork required to make the draping and the trimmings all tell the viewer this is an expensive and very fashionable item. At the same time the gown also displays

Veblen's conspicuous leisure, another mark of affluence. The structure of the dress, especially the elaborate train, tells us that this woman does not need to engage in physical labor of any kind. And finally, it is the height of fashion for its time; however, it will not be more than a few years before this type of bustle will be replaced by a very different style. And it seems most likely that this well-to-do woman will abandon the dress for a new fashion when that change comes, an example of Veblen's principle of showing status through conspicuous waste.

The contrast between men's dress of the eighteenth and nineteenth centuries is clear in the two examples shown in Figures 8.1 and 8.3. The ornate vest, part of a three-piece suit, dating from about a century earlier, would have been cut and sewn by hand and made by a tailor for a particular person. The ornamentation was added by someone of consummate skill at embroidery. The contrasting photograph here is that of a young man about 100 years later, the second half of the 1800s. He too wears a three-piece suit; however, by this time sewing machines would have been used to construct all the pieces of the garment. From his appearance one would conclude that he is probably not especially affluent. He most likely would have acquired his suit as a ready-made garment, probably manufactured in a factory. If he were of a status similar to the man of the 1700s, his suit would have the same elements (trousers, white shirt, vest, and jacket). His sack suit jacket, a garment new in the 1840s would, however, be of more costly fabric and would have hand tailored details that the discriminating upper-class man would have noted. His white shirt, bow necktie, and stiffly starched collar would mark him as holder of a "white collar" job and a member of the middle class.

9

TOOLS THAT ENABLE FASHION CHANGE AND INNOVATIONS IN DRESS
(19th century)

The textile machinery developed in the eighteenth and early nineteenth centuries made fashionable fabrics from which to cut and sew garments available in greater quantities at lower prices, making it possible for women of more modest means to wear the latest styles. Accessories of dress and components of undergarments also benefitted from new technologies. Nineteenth-century consumers saw even more radical changes as technology not only made it possible to use natural materials but also led to the invention of processes that altered natural materials in ways that allowed them to be put to new uses. But the most radical changes of all were those that resulted in entirely new materials.

Contributions from metallurgy and chemistry

Mechanization contributed to the increased availability and affordability of dress accessories made from or with metal. The plating of gold on silver was a process known and used as early as the Middle Ages, but the plating of gold on other base metals had to await the development of the Galvanic cell, an early application of electrical technology. Invented by Alexander Volta in 1796, this device gained its energy from chemical reactions taking place in the cell. Scientists recognizing the potential of this tool experimented with gold plating from 1837 onward and some filed patents. By 1840, the process had been commercialized.

The lower cost of these materials made them affordable to the now larger numbers of middle-class men and women. Industrial processes made it possible to stamp metals into a variety of shapes, and techniques for enhancing the appearance of glass gave it the appearance of gems. By the 1870s, advertising flyers were offering gold-plated buttons and silver-plated jewelry items such as finger rings for fifty cents or lockets, medallions, neck chains, and chatelaines for a dollar.

Before the successful plating of base metals with gold, gold jewelry and ornamental items such as buckles, buttons, pocket watches, and the like were a luxury product, unaffordable except for the affluent. The industrial processes of the mid-nineteenth century made possible the creation of jewelry with the appearance of gold through gilding, gold plating, and rolled gold, a thin layer of gold laminated to a less expensive metal (Figure 9.1). The lower cost of these materials made them affordable to the now larger numbers of middle-class men and women. Industrial processes made it possible to stamp metals into a variety of shapes.

Not only jewelry but also undergarments benefited from advances in metallurgy. Fashionable dress styles of the 1840s had very full, gathered skirts. These were held out by stiffly starched petticoats called "crinolines" (the name deriving from the practice of sometimes making them with horsehair (*crin* in French) that was incorporated into the fabric, to give the cloth more body and stiffness. Women found these petticoats heavy and cumbersome. Earlier periods in dress history also had full skirts that needed to be supported by undergarments. For these a variety of materials such as wood strips, cane, and whalebone had been used to hold out the undergarment in the desired shape, but none were entirely satisfactory as a support for the dome-shaped skirts of the 1850s.

Just who originated the idea of making hoopskirts from tempered spring steel is not clear, but narrow strips of steel cut from thin sheets of the metal were used as the supporting material for what became known as the cage crinoline or hoopskirt. In this structure, a series of steel hoops were covered with fabric tape and attached by eyelet fasteners (patented in 1858) to vertical tapes to create a network that widened gradually from the waist to the bottom. Light in weight (eight ounces to less than two pounds), the cage crinoline was certainly a factor in extending the fashion for full skirts for another decade. The manufacture of hoopskirts was a precursor of what was to come in the fashion industry of the 1900s, with one factory in New York hiring sixteen hundred young women to create these affordable skirts (Green, 1997: 45). The Cheap Store of Boston advertised hoopskirts in 1868 as on sale for four cents per "spring" (steel hoop), reduced from five cents a spring for anywhere from six to sixteen springs mounted on seven tapes (Figure 9.2). Perhaps the price reduction was a harbinger of the changing styles as hoopskirts gave way to bustles, another device requiring a supporting structure, around 1870.

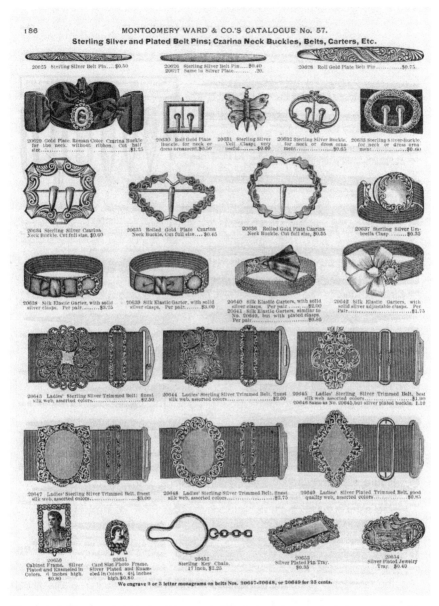

Figure 9.1 Silver- and gold-plated items of all kinds (on this page: belt pins, neck buckles, and garters) occupied a prominent place in the Montgomery Ward mail order catalog of the summer of 1895 (courtesy of Dover Publications, inc.)

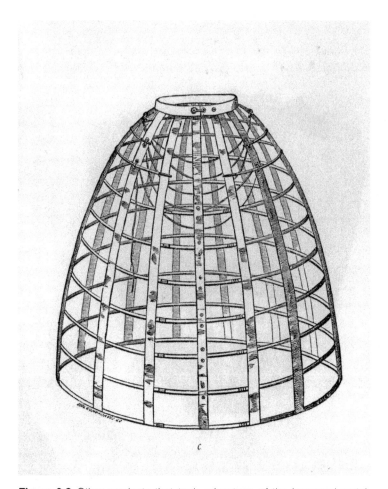

Figure 9.2 Other products that took advantage of the improved metal-working tools included hoops on which the devices that connected the steel parts of the hoop are visible (Godey's Lady's Book, courtesy of Dover Publications, inc.)

Another aspect of dress that benefited from improvements in metallurgy can be seen in garments from the mid-1800s. The outermost garments must have a means of opening and closing so that the wearer can don the garment. Buttons and lacings had served that purpose, but by the mid-1800s hooks and eyes were much in use. These were not new devices, having been used for centuries, generally made of sturdy bronze wires shaped so that a hook on one side of an opening clasped an eye, a metal loop, on the other side of the opening. In 1840, designs for "new, original, and ornamental designs for articles of manufacture" were made patentable by the US patent office, but only if these designs were "new and useful improvements." In the 1840s, four patents for hooks and eyes were filed, in the 1850s only two, and in the 1860s there were fifteen. Subsequent decades saw fewer, but in the 1890s there were forty-six patents filed. Improvements focused on durability, performance, ease of use, and some made use of iron instead of brass. The substantial increase in the 1890s may have been related to the introduction of a design with a safety catch that was intended to reduce embarrassing accidental unhooking. Also, over time, smaller diameter iron wires replaced heavier bronze. Hooks and eyes are still used in ready-to-wear dress and continue to be sold in notions departments in department stores today. They are similar is design to those with safety catches that appeared in the late 1800s, though they are now supplanted in many uses by zippers and Velcro (Chapter 16).

Before the nineteenth century, dyestuffs for coloring textiles, just as the textiles themselves, had been made from natural materials. Techniques for dyeing had been developed over the millennia and many of the most valuable of these dyes had to be applied using technologies that had been developed over thousands of years. The most prized colors often came from far away and some, like the royal purple discussed in Chapter 3, commanded prices that only the rich could pay. Many colors could be problematic in their color retention and inconsistent in the color produced. Along with advances in industrial textile production in the nineteenth century came an interest in and experimentation with organic chemistry. As a result of attempts in 1856 to synthesize quinine, a medication, British chemist William Henry Perkin accidentally produced a synthetic dyestuff, aniline purple, more commonly called mauveine or Perkin's mauve. Perkin set up a factory and began producing mauveine in 1857. After Empress Eugenie of France wore mauve and British Queen Victoria wore a mauveine-colored dress to a royal exhibition in 1862, the color became very fashionable. Although it is not certain that Victoria's dress was dyed with the synthetic dyestuff, the publicity surrounding her color choice helped to launch the modern synthetic dye industry. More and more chemically based dyes were made.

After his retirement in 1874, Perkin made another important contribution to technologies affecting dress, but in quite a different area, that of perfume. He was the first to synthesize coumarin, which formed the chemical basis for the synthetic perfume industry.

Red had always been a problematic color. Perkin's success with mauveine led others to experiment. The Spanish conquistadors in 1519 had found the Aztecs of the Americas had a red dye that produced a superb, strong red. It was obtained from cochineal insects and had become such a prized substance that these insects were raised in Mexico, and put through a careful process that included drying these very small insects. It took at least 70,000 dried insects to make one pound of dyestuff. Until the development of synthetic dyes, cochineal maintained a prominent place as an important element of trade for Spain, but once the synthetic dyes were available they were preferred (Greenfield, 2005: 39).

The basis of the color obtained by processing the shellfish from which royal purple was obtained, and similar colors from indigo, and from woad (a plant native to Europe) rests in the similar chemical structure of the dyestuff in these sources. All have been used to produce colors in the blue range. The process required to produce indigo blue color was very complex. The leaves of a number of different plants cultivated in different parts of the world have been the source of indigo dye. Balfour-Paul (2011: 100–107) classifies extraction into three different methods that have been used. These are:

1. putting fresh leaves into a dye pot;

2. fermentation of the leaf mass of the plants without extracting the dye; or

3. full extraction of the dyestuff from the leaf mass.

Each method incorporated additional steps and each was suitable depending on the level of sophistication of the practitioners. Method 1 was most suitable for small-scale production and Method 3 was the most effective overall.

The complexity of chemical composition of the indigo dyestuff was such that a suitable synthetic dye called Indigo Pure did not appear until 1897. For a time, natural indigo and synthetic indigo were both utilized, but gradually synthetic indigo, for the most part, replaced the natural. By the twentieth century, natural dyes had become a craft activity and few natural dyes could be found in the mass market.

From natural to regenerated materials

Two of the most important non-textile natural materials used in dress in the nineteenth century were rubber and gutta percha. Rubber is a latex that is obtained from under the bark of *Hevea brasiliensis*, commonly called the Pará rubber tree, sharinga tree, or the rubber tree. First encountered by Europeans in Brazil when they colonized South America, these trees were subsequently planted in other parts of the world. Processing of rubber in a factory began in Britain in 1820. In 1823, a Scotsman Charles Macintosh developed a process for waterproofing fabric by making a veritable sandwich of two layers of fabric with a layer of rubber between. Gaining popularity for raincoats, these waterproof coats were and are still called "macs" in British English. Waterproof shoes and boots were also produced (Figure 9.3). Rubber was softened by heat and therefore any severe heat wave was the cause of customer returns of the defective products.

Figure 9.3 The boot known to Victorians as a congress boot had a V-shaped elasticized insert that increased the comfort and fit of shoes. It was introduced only after the vulcanization process improved the performance of rubber (courtesy of Fairchild Books)

American Charles Goodyear solved the problem in 1839 by adding sulfur to the process of producing rubber. A British manufacturer coined the name vulcanization for the process that eliminated the heat sensitivity problem.

Due to its elasticity, pieces of rubber became components of many garments and accessories. British Patent Office Records note its incorporation into low-cut boots known as elastic-sided boots in the form of gussets of India-rubber material in 1837 (Cunnington and Cunnington, 1970: 147).

By 1895, the *Montgomery Ward Catalog* was selling items including suspenders, rubber diaper drawers for toddlers, rubber boots in many lengths, rubber coats, and the sewing department offered elastic cords and garter elastic. Some shoes had rubber soles and there were black tennis oxfords with rubber soles, precursors of today's sneakers.

Gutta percha was another natural material, the sap of the paraquium tree native to Madagascar. Indigenous people used gutta percha for its quality of softening in hot water, after which it could be pressed by hand into various shapes. Upon cooling it became very hard. First used in 1860 as a durable covering for underwater telegraph wires, this material gained favor in a wide variety of objects, including items and accessories of dress: waterproof soles on shoes, and boots for outdoors. But as it too softened when too close to heat, wearing such footwear near a fire was problematic. It was used for jewelry, canes, and even inflatable bustles.

The next step on the way to plastic was the transformation by chemical processing of natural materials that were not usable as found in nature, a technique called regeneration. Cellulose, the natural substance in plant-derived materials such as cotton and paper, was treated with acids (nitric and sulfuric) and camphor. The result was called celluloid and the process for making it was patented in 1860. But commercial success came only after 1869 at which time natural ivory was becoming scarce. Celluloid could be made both transparent and colored and could be made to appear like ivory and also tortoise shell. Both of these natural materials had been used in dress in a variety of ways, ranging from buttons to jewelry, decorative hair ornaments, fans, and even dental plates. Celluloid was put to these uses. Removable collars and shirt fronts that had come into use in the late 1820s could be washed and starched separately from shirts that were not soiled. Celluloid alternatives that imitated linen collars, cuffs, and shirt fronts were marketed as practical replacements that did not even have to be washed and starched but instead could just be wiped off to be cleaned. Other early attempts to create plastic materials included a German invention, galalith, made from milk protein and used for small buttons. This proved to be unsatisfactory as consumers complained that they smelled like sour milk. Early attempts to create a new fiber from cellulosic materials that could not be spun into yarns began the 1800s, but these did not become commercially viable until the 1900s and will be discussed in Chapter 10. The first true plastics synthesized from chemicals and not related to natural materials also appeared in the twentieth century.

The sewing machine

Machines that could sew two layers of fabric together had been patented as early as the 1840s. But cost, at least one hundred dollars, discouraged their wide adoption. Even a lower priced machine, invented by a Virginia farmhand, James Gibbs, and sold for about eighty dollars did not result in widespread use. The American Civil War and Isaac Singer, inventor and mechanic, were the primary factors in the successful marketing of the sewing machine. The beginning of hostilities in the American Civil War (1861–1865) created an immediate need for uniforms for the troops. The North required at least a million and a half uniforms each year. Sewing machines (Figure 9.4) made their manufacture possible. This demonstration of the benefits of this technology was one more step toward the development of mass production of garments. Another was also a by-product of

Figure 9.4 Once the sewing machine had been widely accepted by manufacturers of uniforms during the Civil War, it went on to success with manufacturers and home sewers and served as the basis for mechanized embroidery machines. The logical outcome was the development of mass production and the fashion industry (source: Shutterstock/ Kruglov_Orda)

the Civil War. In order to produce uniforms in standard sizes for the military, men were measured and these measurements used to produce standard sizes. This data became useful to ready-to-wear manufacturers for men's clothing.

In 1851, Isaac Singer had patented improvements in a sewing machine, for which Elias Howe had obtained a patent in 1846. Howe sued for copyright infringement. Both men went on to manufacture sewing machines, but Singer's great gift was in marketing and publicizing his machines, using such methods as setting up showrooms where attractive young ladies demonstrated and taught the use of these machines. He sold sewing machines on the installment plan and in order to give them the aura of respectability sold them to church and church-connected organizations, expecting that many women would see and use them there, and then want one for their home. He allowed a generous trade-in reduction of fifty dollars for an old machine when a customer bought a new one.

The sewing machine had a significant impact on fashions. Ready-made garments such as the hoopskirt and capes and cloaks for outdoors could be made rapidly, mass-produced, and therefore were much less expensive than if they had to be hand-sewn. This contributed to their acceptance as current fashions. But even for the seamstress or home sewer, the sewing machine made it possible to keep up with current fashions. A style feature called a bustle characterized the styles of the period between 1870 and 1890. Skirts supported by stiffened petticoats and hoops had altered somewhat in their shape in the years from 1850 to 1870. Initially round, gradually the fullness became more oblong, with more fullness in back than in the front, and by the last years of the 1860s, skirts had higher waistlines, were more fitted at the waist, and fullness had been concentrated toward the back. At the same time, thanks to attachments for sewing machines, it was easy to sew on braid, and to tuck and pleat fabrics, which led to more ornamentation.

Historic dress collections often include dresses that had originated in the 1860s and were in the process of being restyled to meet the newer bustle fashions, which incorporated large quantities of fabric into the enormous and complex draperies of the first phase of the bustle period in the 1870s. With the sewing machine, reconstructing earlier styles required much less labor than if the long, straight seams needed for making the draperies on these skirts had to be done by hand. The scalloped, vandyked (V-shaped trim), and ruffled trims were far easier to make by machine, whether it was a home sewer or seamstress who was doing the work.

A more subtle point about the impact of technology such as the sewing machine is made by Anne Hollander in her book *Sex and Suits*. She cites men's suits and synthetic fabrics as examples of how such new technologies are at first used to imitate the way dress was made before the arrival of the new technology. In the case of men's suits, she notes that even though they are made using new materials and stitching techniques, the objective is to give them the appearance of hand tailoring. And in the case of the new fibers of the twentieth century, they are often blended with natural fibers or given special finishes to create the appearance of natural fibers. Hollander says, ". . . only slowly does new technology affect style as a whole" (Hollander, 1994: 72).

Other stimuli to ready-to-wear

Home sewers also benefitted from another innovation, the manufacture and distribution of paper patterns in the mid-1800s. The earliest paper patterns were made in one size and it was the task of the sewer to adapt the pattern to fit the wearer. In 1863, Tailor Ebeneezer Butterick introduced what appears to have been the first sized paper patterns.

Rapidly successful, Butterick expanded from men's shirt patterns and children's clothing to women's clothing as his business expanded. Dress scholar Carol Anne Dickson (2010), writing in the *Berg Encyclopedia of World Dress and Fashion*, reported that in 1871 six million patterns were sold by Butterick and Company. She describes a growing number of American companies that began producing sized paper patterns. The availability of lower cost paper made from wood pulp contributed to this industry.

One of the steps in the manufacture of ready-made clothing that was very time-consuming was the cutting of the garment pieces to be sewn together. The first invention intended to address this problem was a device with a long knife that moved up and down through slots in a table. This hand-operated device could cut 18 layers of cloth at one time. A steam machine that turned out to be awkward and cumbersome to move was introduced in 1872. Once electricity was available to power machines (c. 1890), improvements were made that had the advantage of smaller size and ease of operation. Twenty-four layers were cut by the first of these, and those that developed later increased that number to one hundred.

By the middle of the nineteenth century, the stage was set for changes in the way dress was obtained in America. Until this time, dress for women was, for the most part, made by professional seamstresses or women sewing at home. Tailors created men's wear and some clothing could be purchased ready-made. Rob Schorman, a scholar who studies retailing history, points out that widespread commerce in clothing was facilitated by expanded production of affordable textiles in England, and especially in the American Northeast, thanks to the technological advances in textile manufacture, and the growth of transportation networks across America, an outgrowth of the transportation revolution in which canal building, riverboats, and railroad-building linked the expanding country. Entrepreneurs took advantage of the system by having tailors cut garments and other less-skilled workers assemble them. Schorman (2010: 87) says, "By 1860 clothing was the biggest manufacturing industry in New York City, which was the city with the greatest amount of manufacturing in the United States." He goes on to point out that these beginnings were largely confined to men's dress. For women the growth was slower, highlighted by outdoor capes and cloaks after the mid-century; tailor-mades, which were tailored suits for women; and shirtwaists (blouses) in the last two decades of the century. Dresses had to wait until the early decades of the twentieth century (Schorman, 2010: 87–96).

Sociological factors that enabled mass production

The ready-to-wear industry in America, which experienced rapid growth around the turn of the century, required labor as well as the aforementioned technologies in order to succeed. The great wave of European immigration between 1865 and 1918 brought 27.5 million people to the United States. Many among these immigrants brought with them tailoring and sewing skills. Often living in metropolitan centers near their ports of entry, they found employment there. This was also the period when more women, many of them immigrants, were entering the workforce in large numbers. No matter the area of their employment, working full-time outside the home meant they had little time for sewing clothes for their families, so the demand for ready-made clothing grew and has never slackened.

The nineteenth century utilized the products of industrial technology in aspects of fashion ranging from coloring fabrics to manufacturing accessories. It also produced tools (sewing machines like those in Figure 9.4 and sized paper patterns such as in Figure 9.5) that contributed to the development of the ready-to-wear industry, first in the United States, and later throughout the world. It was a century that witnessed the first regenerated products made from natural materials transformed to create dress and synthetic materials created from chemicals that found a place as replacements for natural materials such as ivory and tortoise shell that had long been used for fashionable accessories.

Looking at relationships through illustrations

The dress in Figure 9.6 dates from 1885. Its skirt is held out by a bustle (Figures 7.8, 7.9, and 7.10). The sewing machine was now in wide use, so the garment would have been sewn together using such a machine. This and other newly developing technologies could have contributed to the ornamental nature of this garment. From the fashion plate it is not possible to be absolutely certain about the details of the ornamentation on the original garment. This discussion will focus on what these might have been! Three different types of fabric appear. The bodice and skirt are of a pale colored fabric. The techniques available to create the ornamentation on this fabric were printing, or hand- or machine-made embroidery. Switzerland took the lead in commercializing embroidery. The first commercial embroidery operation, done by hand, is said to have been in New York in 1848. The Swiss owner was Jacob Schiess. By the 1870s, Schiffli embroidery machines, using techniques related to those used in the operation of sewing machines, were sold abroad and have been used ever since, though

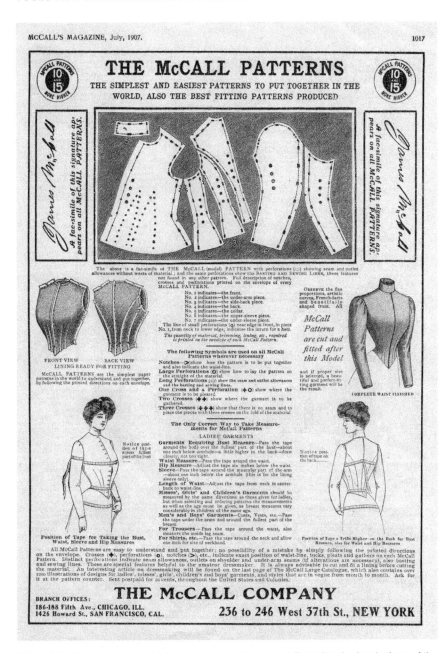

Figure 9.5 The development of sized paper patterns contributed to the beginnings of the fashion industry. The older, labor-intensive method of printing a pattern of one size required the seamstress or tailor to increase pattern elements to fit the person who would wear the garment. When the customer could buy a garment of a standard size, manufacturing on a large scale became possible (source: author's magazine collection)

Figure 9.6 Fashion plate, 1885 (source: author's image)

their exportation was curtailed during World War II. At present, computers play an important role in this technology.

A second fabric is used for the draperies that ornament the bodice, the upper part of the skirt, and swags that fall over the back and front of the skirt. Running vertically on the front of the bodice the fabric is pleated. This brown fabric is probably some type of silk. The fashion plate is French, and the silk was probably manufactured in France, possibly in the textile center in Lyons.

Yet another fabric appears along the left side of the pleated fabric on the bodice. This appears to be some type of lace. As noted in Chapter 7, lace production had been automated in the early 1800s.

Lingerie dress

Toward the end of the nineteenth century, a type of dress known as a lingerie dress had become fashionable (see figure 9.7). Worn for warm weather, usually made of lightweight white or off-white cotton or linen, a wide variety of matching ornamentation ranging from embroidery to applied lace, braids, and ruffled trims decorated the dress. The name lingerie dress was given to this garment because it resembled the frilly, lacy lingerie worn by women. The fashion continued on into the first decade of the twentieth century and fashions inspired by this dress have appeared occasionally since then. It was very much the product of mechanization, with the fabric being woven in factories and dress elements sewn together using a sewing machine. The various trims once requiring hours of hand labor to construct were now available for purchase from the notions departments of department stores and the growing number of mail order catalogs.

Figure 9.7 The lingerie dress (source: author's image)

PART THREE

THE FASHION INDUSTRY IS BORN

10
TOOLS AND PROCESSES EXPAND OPTIONS FOR DRESS AND FASHION
(20th and 21st Centuries)

Until the twentieth century, consumers had a very limited number of textiles from which they could choose. All were fibers found in nature. All were widely used and most were available either through local production or trade. Textile technologies that provided new raw materials in the form of regenerated fibers, made by processing natural materials, and synthesized fibers, made from or with the use of chemicals, were developed in the twentieth century. These began with processes for regenerating useful textile fibers from materials unsuitable for spinning into yarns. The earliest commercially successful examples were rayon and acetate.

Manufactured fibers

The first of the new fibers were made from natural materials that could not be used as textile fibers. But chemically they were similar to natural textile fibers. All natural textile fibers and manufactured textile fibers are long-chain molecules called polymers. The first manufactured fibers were made from cotton fibers too short to be spun into yarns or from wood chips. The process to transform these materials into useable fibers requires several steps. The cellulose material is dissolved in chemicals using specified technical processes and some further treatment, after which the solution, called viscose, is filtered to remove any impurities. It is then pushed through small holes in a device called a spinneret into a bath of diluted sulfuric acid that causes the fibers to regenerate into cellulose, and to coagulate in the form of long, continuous fibers. Because this fiber is cellulose, it has many similar characteristics to cotton, but also some differences.

When first marketed in the early 1900s, this fiber was called artificial silk. Its long continuous length put it in the classification of a filament fiber and also gave it some characteristics similar to silk, but consumers were confused by the name, and in 1924 its name was changed to rayon. Several variants of the production process existed, and while the resulting fibers were all cellulose, confusion about terminology remained. While the public continued to call all of the resulting fabrics rayon, the generic fiber name registered with the US Federal Trade Commission is viscose rayon and in some parts of the world the fiber is now called viscose.

Figure 10.1 Acetate, one of the regenerated fibers, was popular in the 1930s and after for dressy garments where its high luster made it desirable, (source: Shutterstock/Karkas).

A chemical relative of rayon was the next regenerated fiber. Beginning with the same materials as for rayon, the chemical process for this fiber differed in ways that created a chemical variation of cellulose called cellulose acetate. This fiber was also called rayon at first and was also a filament fiber. However, cellulose acetate had characteristics that were markedly different from viscose rayon, and in 1953 the US Federal Trade Commission required that the fabrics be given different names, and viscose rayon retained the name rayon and cellulose acetate became acetate. The other early rayon product is now called cuprammonium rayon. This fiber has not been manufactured in the United States since 1975, due to the difficulties in handling the chemical pollution of water produced in its processing. Rayon also presented pollution problems and it too is no longer manufactured in the United States at this time. Both of these fibers are still manufactured elsewhere and imported products made from them are available in the United States.

The characteristics of the fabrics made from each type of fiber can be one of the factors that add to or detract from its popularity. There are times when the fabric may contribute to the development of a new fashion or the predominant fashions may have a negative impact on the use of a specific fiber. Rayon's closest competitor in the 1920s would have been silk. The predominant styles of the 1920s had soft lines, draped well, and many were colorful. Rayon satisfied all of these needs. Its price, compared to silk, probably had a positive effect on its acceptance. In the 1940s, during the wartime period, silks were not available because they were produced in parts of the world where the war was raging. As a result, rayon stockings replaced the more luxurious, more sheer, and better-fitting women's silk stockings. Viscose rayon stockings tended to stretch and bag, but as the only option available they were widely worn. After the end of the war the first of the synthetic fabrics, nylon, entered the market and their superior performance quickly drove the sheer rayon stockings from the market.

The regenerated fibers, made from natural materials, had been joined in the late 1930s by nylon, the first of the synthetic fibers made from chemicals. Though nylon was not actually the first fiber to be synthesized, that breakthrough was for a fiber that was not commercialized at the time, but which eventually became the most widely used synthetic fiber: polyester. Encountering difficulties with his work on polyester, Wallace Carothers, a chemist with the DuPont Company, turned to a chemical group called polyamides and synthesized a fiber that the E I du Pont de Nemours and Company named nylon. Introduced in 1938, the fiber's initial commercial success was interrupted by the beginning of World War II. It was put to use for wartime needs such as parachutes and consumers did not begin to use nylon products until after the war, when its aforementioned rapid acceptance for women's sheer stockings made "nylons" a synonym for women's hosiery.

The post-war period saw the introduction of many additional synthetic fibers and a few regenerated fibers. Table 10.1 lists the most widely used manufactured fibers created in the period between 1945 and the present and the major uses to which they have been put for dress and identifies some fashions they have influenced. High tech fabrics and their impact on fashion are discussed in Chapters 15 and 16.

American post-war consumers accepted these new fibers in part because housewives in the rapidly spreading suburbs were receptive to the producers' advertisements of the easy care qualities of synthetic fibers such as nylon, polyester, and acrylics. Slogans such as easy care, drip-dry, and wash and wear appealed to the suburban families, owners of a new generation of washers and dryers. Fabric producers developed special finishes for textiles that made them permanent pressed, wrinkle resistant, and stain resistant. Blending natural and manufactured fibers such as polyester and cotton provided some advantages. The natural fiber made the fabrics more comfortable, because they were more absorbent, and the synthetic fibers conferred wrinkle resistance.

Designers in haute couture were less enthusiastic about the new fibers. Based on the contents of editorial descriptions of new styles in fashion magazines of the post-war period, the featured high style fashions tended to be made of natural fibers, although stocking and undergarment advertising prominently featured mention of their nylon fiber content and men's dress shirts emphasized the Dacron polyester fiber that made them easy to care for. Post-war improvements in laundry equipment facilitated sales of the synthetic fibers, a technological contribution to the adoption of these new fibers. Manufactured fibers obtained couture status only when the fiber producers worked with designers, providing economic support for special promotions.

The introduction of manufactured fibers (called man-made fibers until the rise of feminism) was not without its consumer problems. A major concern was the change from a time when it was easy to tell a cotton fabric from silk or wool; perhaps not so easy to tell cotton from linen or silk from rayon or acetate. With the manufactured fibers and blends of manufactured fibers with natural or other manufactured fibers, consumers were not only unable to tell the fabrics apart, but without knowing the fiber content, decisions about how to care for fabrics were more difficult. Legislation addressed the problem. In the United States, the TFPIA (Textile Fiber Product Identification Act) was passed in 1960. It required labeling of wearing apparel as to its fiber content. In actuality this legislation was an unsuccessful attempt to discourage buying imported goods as the place of origin also had to be listed. The care problem, however, was not solved until further legislation (1972) required that permanent labels be affixed to garments that told the customer how to care for the purchase.

With all of these new fabrics now available, what was the impact on fashion? A few examples from US experience may serve to show how the fibers and their

Table 10.1 *Major manufactured textile fibers used for fashionable dress in the twentieth and twenty-first centuries**

Generic fiber name	Date introduced and early trademark name	Notable properties	Major uses for dress	Impact on fashions	Comments
Viscose rayon	c. 1900 artificial silk. After 1924: rayon	Stretches and shrinks, drapes well. Better to dry clean than to launder	Fashionable wearing apparel	Less expensive than silk, so used in competitive products	
Cellulose acetate	Acetate silk until 1924, rayon until 1953 when called acetate	Lustrous, attractive appearance, melts at high temperatures	Apparel, especially decorative fabrics used in formal wear	Attractive appearance and luster makes it appealing for formal and bridal gowns	
Nylon	Introduced in 1938 using name Nylon® Becomes generic name in US	Excellent strength, stretches easily and recovers from stretching, a durable fiber, easy to care for	Women's hosiery, wide variety of other products range from sheer fabrics to durable luggage	Very much in demand when again available after World War II	
Modacrylic	1949 Dynel®. Initially included in same generic category as acrylics, then given separate generic name in 1960	Relatively weak, maintains shape well, easily texturized to provide special qualities, good flame resistance	Used in pile and fleece apparel, and in fabrics that simulate furs	Stimulates interest in pile fabrics; can look like fur but made in wide variety of colors	Early slogan used in advertising: 'It's not fake anything, it's real Dynel®'
Acrylic	1952 Orlon®	Relatively weak, launders well when directions are followed, can resemble wool in appearance and feel	Used in areas where wool has been used such as hosiery, knitted sweaters	Lower cost and similar qualities when made into knitted fabrics lead to uses similar to those of wool	

(continued)

Table 10.1 Continued

Generic fiber name	Date introduced and early trademark name	Notable properties	Major uses for dress	Impact on fashions	Comments
Polyester	1953 Dacron® and in Britain Terylene	Relatively strong, launders well. Produced in varying strengths and cross-sections that affect its hand (the way it feels) and appearance	Wide range of wearing apparel, easy care fabrics, blended with other fibers	Made into pants suits	Often blended with natural fibers to make easy care products. Inferior quality gave the fiber negative reputation for a time, but introduction of microfibers made the fiber very popular
Olefins: polypropylene and polyethylene	Specialized non-textile uses from 1949 and in 1960s in textiles where polypropylene has more textile applications	Strength good, elasticity excellent, nonabsorbent. Low melting point	Disposable diapers, active wear, insulation in gloves, footwear, and apparel, clean suits, protective garments for toxic waste clean-up	Becomes important in active wear, because of its ability to transport moisture from perspiration away from the body	
Spandex	1959 Lycra®. Other generic categories for elastic fibers include elastomers and elastane	Weak compared with non-elastomers, but stronger than rubber; high elongation and excellent recovery from stretching, resists deterioration from chemicals and sea water	Used in combination with other fibers in dress such as swimwear and in combination with a wide variety of apparel ranging from undergarments to outerwear	Initially spandex was used in apparel for sports, and in underwear for figure support, but by 1980s and after it was appearing in a wide variety of garments for all occasions, as a way of making garments fit the body more closely	

*Data derived from Collier et al. (2009)

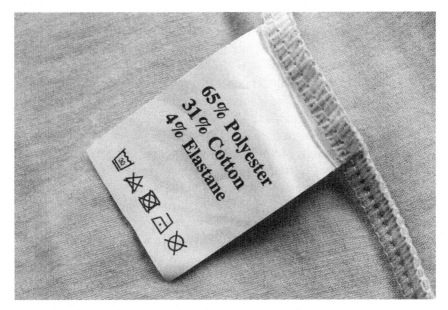

Figure 10.2 In the post World War II period, many manufactured fibers were developed and marketed. The blending of natural fibers with synthetic fibers made identification of the fiber content of fabrics difficult, so legislation was passed in some countries that required identification of fiber contents of garments. Eventually a series of symbols also conveyed information about how to care for the item (source: Shutterstock/Tarzhanova)

special characteristics affect specific fashion developments. In some cases the fibers helped fashion trends to accelerate. In others, the impact could be negative, nylon providing an early example. During World War II, nylon was unavailable and had not yet been fully accepted by consumers before the war, although it had been on its way. The styles of the 1920s and 1930s revealed women's legs and flesh-colored stockings were preferred. Women who could afford them had worn full-length silk stockings by choice before the advent of nylon. The alternative was rayon, which was esthetically less appealing, as it was not very elastic, did not fit the leg closely, nor was it as sheer as silk. During the war, silk was no longer available, and stockings were generally of rayon, cotton, or wool. Nylon stockings became available once the war ended. Newspapers ran stories and photographs of long lines of women waiting to buy the newly labeled "nylons." These stockings could be made in very sheer, light-weight knits that fit the leg closely. They were both less expensive and more durable than silk. Their innate characteristics, of high strength, resiliency, and stretch made them a successful fashion. The design features changed from time to time with some having seams while others were seamless. Some had decorative figures called clocks knitted into the fabric. Nylon pantyhose (stockings and underpants combined into one garment) replaced pairs of stockings, especially once girdles and garter belts were no longer much used. The fashion for very short miniskirts reinforced the practicality of this hosiery. Nylons had become a permanent fixture in the fashion world. Later, when women took to wearing trousers as an alternative to skirts, nylon anklets and mid-calf hosiery were worn.

Polyester, marketed by DuPont under the trademark name of Dacron, was another of the early entries into the manufactured fiber market. Used frequently in blends, polyester was successful in easy care fabrics. Until the 1950s, women had worn trousers only as casual wear, but had not seen them as appropriate for business or evening wear. At the same time as women's liberation movements began to examine issues relating to the status of women, fashion designers introduced pants suits, similar to men's business suits, but intended for women. With the availability of so many new fibers, many ready-to-wear clothing companies began to make pants suits for women from polyester double knit fabrics. Some of these fabrics were of inferior quality and the term polyester pant suit became a derogatory description. While pants continued to be popular with women, polyester pants suits lost favor and by association so did polyester. Fiber manufacturers continually looked for improvements in their fibers, and one of the areas that could be manipulated to produce different qualities was the diameter and the shape of the fiber. Polyester benefited from advances in textile technology in this area. Fibers with exceptionally small diameters are called microfibers. The very fine polyester microfibers had a more pleasant feel, superior draping qualities, and in tests many times consumers were unable to distinguish between microfiber polyester fabrics and silk. The improvements were such that the negative image of polyester was obliterated and polyester regained its place in fashion.

Another example of the interactions between synthetic fibers and fashion is the impact of spandex fibers. As noted in Table 10.1, the fiber called spandex in the United States and elastane in some other countries, is used largely because of its elasticity. Compared to its predecessor, rubber, spandex has advantages in resistance to damage from sun and chlorine, so making it suitable for use for swimwear. It can also be manufactured as finer diameter fibers. Spandex and rubber share the need to be used in combination with other fibers, otherwise these fibers would show bare filaments. The need to combine spandex with other fibers led to its incorporation into body-hugging active sportswear for swimming, skiing, biking, and other sports, where a streamlined body offered athletes an advantage. Once used in competitive sports these garments influenced fashions for many kinds of recreational sports and casual wear. After 2000, designers and manufactures created fashionable dress items for women and for men, in which spandex was combined with other fibers to produce fashions that were more form-fitting and maintained garment shape more effectively. This was another clear example of the characteristics of the fiber driving its use in fashion.

The impact of warp knitting technology on dress and fashion

Weft knitted garments had an advantage, in garments such as hosiery, sweaters, and some types of undergarments, of being completely formed by the knitting process. As noted previously, although both weft and warp knitting machines had been available during the nineteenth century, warp knitting did not reach its full potential until the twentieth century. When compared with weft knits, warp knitted fabrics are both smoother and flatter, less elastic, and more resistant to runs. Different warp knitting machines were invented that made different kinds of knits. These included tricot, simplex, and raschel machines. Tricot machines came into use in the 1940s. They utilize a type of needle called a compound and can be constructed to have a more or less secure connection of the yarns, referred to as one, two, three, or four bar tricot. More dense fabrics (three and four bar) are used for dresses and men's suits, and two bar for undergarments, sleepwear, blouses, and the like. The least stable one bar tricot is not often used in garments, but may be used as linings attached as an inner layer on bonded fabrics. Tricots can also be made into satin-like fabrics where some yarns are allowed to float across the back surface of the fabric, can be brushed to create a napped surface, and can be manipulated to create a lacelike appearance. Simplex knits are similar to tricot, but have a denser texture and are used in products that need a sturdier fabric: gloves, handbags, and fabrics given a simulated suede-like texture. Raschel knits may appear more woven or lacelike in appearance. Used in the 1950s and after, this versatile machine can produce fabrics for a wide range of products ranging from power nets to simulated embroidery, "fake" furs, and hand-crocheted fabrics (Collier *et al.*, 2009: 338–41).

Raw materials and fashion design: the relationship

With the availability of these diverse kinds of knits and further twentieth-century developments in new fabric structures, the range of materials available to textile designers was enormous. Gale and Kaur (2004) explore the relationship between textiles and fashion designers thoroughly, making clear the importance of textile materials in the design process. Although their discussion focuses on present-day designers, fabrics obviously had been equally important to nineteenth and early twentieth-century designers such as Worth and Poiret. Certainly Madeline Vionnet with her use of bias cut fabrics and Gabrielle Chanel who introduced wool jersey to the couture were known for innovations in textile use. With the availability of new materials came new possibilities. The plastics that were new to the 1920s led to innovations in jewelry.

Non-textile materials for dress

Williams (2000) assigns the birth of the plastics industry to 1909 with the US patenting of Bakelite. Plastics can be divided into two categories: thermoplastic and thermosetting. Thermoplastic materials will soften with heat; thermosetting materials will not. Karima Parry, specialist in vintage plastic jewelry, says of these collectables that they were cast, laminated, inlaid, carved, and tinted almost any color of the rainbow.

Bakelike, unlike its predecessors, was thermosetting. It was very fashionable for jewelry in the 1920s and 1930s and these Art Deco jewelry designs have become quite collectable and their styles have been revived in the twenty-first century. Plastic materials continued to be developed and gained use in jewelry and ornamental closures such as belt buckles and buttons, as well as for elements of dress ranging from headwear to footwear. Synthetic fibers and plastic materials are closely connected. Synthetic polymeric material can be given form by extrusion; in some cases as a sheet of material and in others as fibers. In this latter case, the fibers must then go through processes needed to form them into fabrics, whereas sheets of the same material can be cut and used in various forms and for various purposes, including becoming part of functional or fashionable dress.

Footwear, before the synthetic era, was generally made from leather or cloth. Leathers have long been used for items of clothing such as jackets and coats, gloves, hats, and a wide range of garments for men and women. Treatments are given to leather that render them more supple and comfortable. Imitations of leather footwear made in plastic have had limited success. Even Corfam, a Du Pont product given an extensive publicity campaign in 1963 and after as a leather alternative that was breathable, did not achieve market success (Meikle, 1995). However, when not presented as "like leather" but as plastic, such footwear as Crocs™ or "flip flops" have become quite fashionable.

Body modification: an overlooked element of dress

Body modification has been alluded to in a number of earlier chapters when discussion has moved to areas such as hair care, treatment and/or removal, whether this be hair that grows on the scalp, on the face, or the body. Other modifications include addition of color to parts of the body; reshaping the body permanently through surgery, binding, or other techniques, or temporarily through garment structure. Technologies to accomplish these tasks range from simple to complex practices or processes that had become available by the twentieth and twenty-first centuries. Fashion, in the form of cultural standards of beauty, plays an important role. The technologies that create or promote these standards of beauty are explored in Chapter 13. For example, print and electronic media of the twenty-first century present the ideal feminine beauty as tall and slender and young. For those twenty-first century women not naturally tall, full-busted, with slim but well-rounded hips, and young, help can be found, for a price. Technologies can create platform-soled shoes to increase height, cosmetic surgery to augment breasts with silicone implants, remove excess fat with liposuction, and smooth away wrinkles with Botox.

Physicians working in the area that is called by some as cosmetic surgery and by others as plastic, aesthetic, or reconstructive surgery, see the origin of this modern medical specialty in the work done for those who received facial wounds in World War I. In the 1920s, the ability to correct what individuals saw as flaws in their appearance received extensive publicity when surgery altered the nose of Fanny Brice, a famous comedienne and star of Ziegfield Follies. A certification process for physicians working in this area was developed and a techniques for procedures expanded as specialists expanded their skills. Haiken (1999) explores the area of body modifications.

Other forms of body modification that move in and out of fashion include areas such as tattoos and body piercing. As noted in Chapter 2, the mummy of the Ice Man from Northern Italy had tattoos on his body. Some Egyptian women's mummies also carried tattoos. Tatooing has been practiced in many periods and in many cultures. It generally requires a sharp device to puncture the skin according to a pattern that can be complex or simple, and the application of some colored substance into the areas where the skin is broken so that when it heals the design will still be visible.

Body piercing is another form of body modification that is often used as a means of anchoring decorative devices. Ear piercing is a common piercing for women. However, with the introduction of punk fashions in the late 1970s, body piercing of various kinds became widespread and a number of sub-cultural groups established their own fashion trends for piercing. With increased knowledge about potential infections from some of these practices, the techniques and the equipment used by skilled practitioners were designed to avoid negative outcomes for those following these fashions.

Hair care and technology

Special treatments for manipulating hair on the head or on the body have changed as scientific knowledge about chemistry and physics has advanced. At

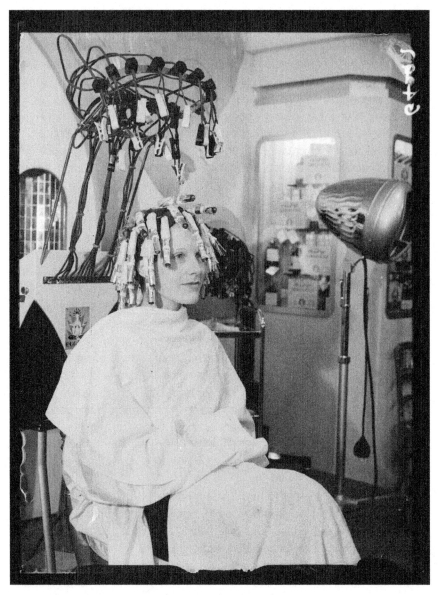

Figure 10.3 Permanent waves of the 1930s required an elaborate machine and an extended stay in a beauty shop (source: Getty)

most times, hair on the head is manipulated in some way. Whether hair on the rest of the body is appropriate is determined by societal custom and fashion. Methods for removing unwanted hair have ranged from tweezing (theoretically a method in prehistoric times may have been using bivalve shells as tweezers), shaving, abrasion with pumice stone, and applying wax and allowing it to harden and then removing it so that the hair comes off with the wax. Advances in chemistry resulted in the development of chemical depilatories that break down the protein in the hair. The most advanced technology relies on electricity and is permanent. In this case a needle applies a galvanic current to reach and destroy the root of the hair.

Social customs generally dictate where hair should be visible. Hair seems to be associated with men and virility, possibly because men usually have more luxuriant facial hair than women. When women in Western Europe were covered almost completely by their dress, there does not seem to have been much concern about hair under the arms or on the legs. But once skirts shortened and sleeveless women's garments came into fashion, it was considered best if this hair was not visible and women's visible body hair was removed by one of the aforementioned methods.

Heredity equips each individual with hair of different colors and textures. The popularity of particular hair colors and hairstyles is generally a result of fashion. As films became an important fashion influence, and particularly after films were made in color, certain hair colors and hairstyles became very popular: blonde hair preferred at one time; red hair at another. Straight hair might be the ideal in one year; in another, curls may be fashionable. Technological processes can straighten hair or curl hair. Before the twentieth century, the technologies for making such changes were temporary. Hair when wet, then shaped with hairpins, rollers, or other manual devices, and allowed to dry will remain in this shape in the form of curls for a short time. If the wet hair is pressed flat, it can remain relatively flat for a time. But eventually it will return to its natural state. Hairdressers were able to find natural or synthetic compounds, or to heat tongs or curlers that would help to hold the styles for longer periods. One of the first successful hairdressers to create waves in women's hair was Marcel Gateau, a Parisian hairdresser who, in 1872, first used curling tongs that he heated over a gas flame, a sort of ancestor of the modern electric curling iron, to set waves into his mother's hair. It was of course temporary, until the next time the hair became wet. This "Marcel wave" became quite popular.

Charles Nestle developed the first permanent wave around 1906. He used an electrically-powered machine attached to hair pads that prevented the heat from burning the customer's head. A chemical was applied that would break down the chemical bonds in hair that give it its natural shape. The hair was rolled on heated cylindrical rollers that were placed according to the style the customer wanted to achieve. This entire process required ten hours. This could only be done in a beauty salon – its popularity helped to increase the number of beauty salons markedly (Figure 10.3). Variations followed these early attempts. By 1932, a chemical process that did not require heat and took much less time was available. The fashionable hairstyles that required curly hair stimulated additional improvements. By 1946, home permanents were available.

In the nineteenth and twentieth centuries, men's hairstyles have generally been less elaborate than women's, but no less subject to fashion preferences. Both men and women were expected to conform to accepted standards in how to deal with body hair. For men, facial hair was the greatest concern. The advances made in metallurgy over time were a great help in this regard. When beards were fashionable, achieving the correct shape and placement of beards and moustaches required some shaving of facial hair. Even after high-quality steel that could hold a good edge was available, many men found it was far easier to have a skilled barber in a barber shop remove the facial hair than to do it themselves. The invention of the safety razor after 1828 was a boon to men. Continual improvements such as two-edged disposable razor blades were welcomed and in the 1960s stainless steel blades kept their edge very well, even though electric razors had gained widespread use in the 1920s and after.

The twentieth and twenty-first centuries are characterized by an explosion of developments in regenerated and synthetic materials used for textiles and for accessories of dress. When there were only the natural fibers, it was easy to know how the textiles made from those fibers would behave and how to care for them. The many new fabrics presented consumers with problems. Some such as nylon fulfilled a need while others had to find an audience. As the technologies matured, it was possible to create a wide variety of fiber variations that were suitable for specialized uses. As obtaining some raw materials required the destruction of wildlife that was endangered, such as elephants and tortoises, manufactured plastics with similar appearance could take their place. Modification of the body has been part of many cultures. With advanced technology, some aspects of body modification became easier and safer.

Looking at relationships through illustrations

Entertainment award ceremonies in the twenty-first century have become a veritable fashion show that arrives in the homes of consumers by way of the technology of color television. Figure 10.4 is an example of one participant, actress Danai Gurira, attending the International Press Academy's 17th Annual Satellite Awards on 16 December 2012. Her dress can serve to highlight some of the aspects of technology that contribute to the fashion statement she is making.

Her slender figure, curved in all the right places, as well as the dramatic dress she wears, can be viewed as the kind of dissemination of photographs that can appear in any of a number of media sources that serve to communicate to viewers the current fashion trends and body image for which they might want to

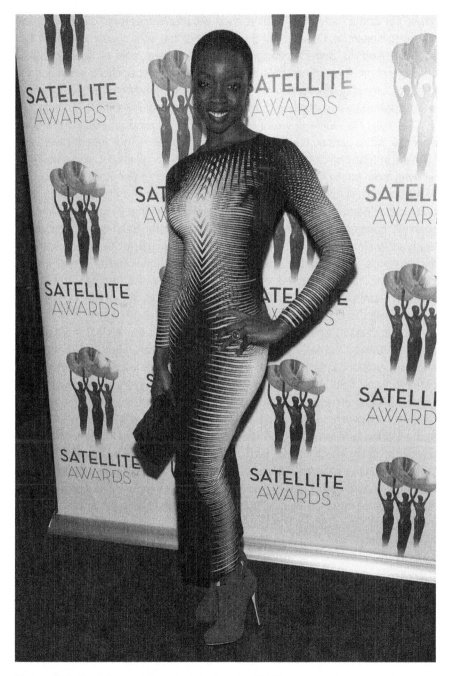

Figure 10.4 Spandex-containing fashion (source: Getty)

strive. For some, achieving such a body will require personal efforts such as dieting and exercise. Others may choose to seek the skills of cosmetic/aesthetic surgery, used to correct changes that accompany age or their inherited characteristics. These range broadly from the relatively specialized techniques of face lifts, breast augmentation or reduction to transgender surgery, all of which are supported by constantly improving medical technologies.

The dress Ms Gurira is wearing is clearly made using an elastomeric fiber. Spandex is the generic fiber name used for this fiber in the United States and elastane in many other countries. It is a fiber that has excellent elongation and recovery from stretching. Similar to rubber in these characteristics, it is superior to rubber in flexibility, strength, abrasion resistance, and is not deteriorated by body oils or perspiration. However, it is rarely used alone. Grayish in color, it is generally covered by other fibers. In the illustration, those fibers are apparently black and white. Initially used in applications such as garments for active sports and undergarments, it became fashionable after the 1980s when it was incorporated into many types of dress for both men and women in order to achieve a better fit. See Table 10.1 for information about the origins and characteristics of spandex.

As described in Chapter 4, cosmetics have also been an essential part of dress throughout human history. This certainly has continued in the twentieth and twenty-first centuries. In the United States, cosmetics were not openly promoted and sold until the 1920s, after which lipstick, rouge, mascara, and glossy nail enamel became common. When blonde movie stars became popular, many women bleached and dyed their hair. Some benchmarks in the development and adoption of cosmetics and devices to aid grooming included: in 1923 a device for curling eyelashes; in 1931 first electric razor sold by Jacob Schick; in 1936 first sunscreen invented; and in 1950 Hazel Bishop Company sold the first non-smear lipstick. New lipstick and nail polish colors were introduced each year as the style of make-up was as subject to fashion change as styles for other aspects of dress.

Ferragamo and shoes

Designer of shoes, Salvatore Ferragamo, created the shoes illustrated in Figure 10.5, in 1948. His earliest training in shoe-making was as a young boy in Italy; he went to the United States at the age of 16 and there became acquainted with the technologies associated with the American mass production and marketing of footwear. Building a successful career designing and selling footwear to screen actors, he returned to Italy in 1927 to hone his skills in making shoes by hand. Ricci (2006) chronicles his subsequent career in detail, and stresses the importance of Ferragamo to technology. Swann (1982) points out

Figure 10.5 Ferragamo shoes (The Metropolitan Museum of Art. Image source: The Art Archive at Art Resource, New York)

the usefulness of the wedge heel during the depression and wartime as a way of covering less expensive materials with leather. While the shoe pictured here is from post-war 1948, it exhibits not only the wedge heel, but also a sculptural effect that originated with Ferragamo. As he developed new and original processes and constructions, he patented them. Four hundred patents registered by Ferragamo have been found in an archive in Rome, which date from the 1930s to the 1950s.

Italy made a concerted effort to make the city of Florence an international fashion center after World War II. Ferragamo was an important part of this effort and his business developed a strong international focus. After his death in 1960, his family took over and continues to operate the firm.

11
TRANSPORTATION AND ITS EFFECTS
(20th and 21st centuries)

Changes in how people get from one place to another generally result from technological advances. Before the invention of the steam engine and the internal combustion engine, both long- and short-term travel were likely to be dependent on human power, animal power, or natural phenomena such as the wind or the currents in rivers. Examples of human power include walking or running, lifting devices such as sedan chairs, pulling wheeled vehicles, or pedal-driven bicycles. Although bicycles have since their beginnings been a means of transportation for a great many people, I am choosing to discuss cycling and its interaction with dress in Chapter 12, where I examine its impact on dress and fashions for sport.

Humans doubtless provided the power to move boats on water until some innovative persons hoisted sails to catch the wind to move a boat more rapidly. Recognition of how a water channel could move goods more rapidly than roads led to the construction of canals, and the use of animals such as horses to pull canal boats.

While giving credit to boats and ships and their role in facilitating trade, not all goods could travel by water-based routes. Roads provided an alternative; however, road development was somewhat sporadic. The silk route, or Silk Road as it has been called, was not a single road but rather many different routes that were utilized for trading goods between the eastern Asian regions and Western Eurasia. Segments of these routes came into and went out of use, depending on a variety of natural and human factors ranging from weather to the willingness of political regimes to permit passage of traffic. In the ancient western world, the Romans constructed an elaborate road system that in some areas is still visible and often serves as the base for modern roads. It linked together the far reaches of the vast Roman Empire, making possible not only the movement of military forces but also of goods and people. Residents of the city of Rome could choose to buy linen from Egypt, silk from China, and cotton from India, some of which had doubtless traveled the Silk Road, the sea, and finally Roman roads from port cities to the city of Rome as part of their journey. In the Americas, the Incas constructed roads to link together their extensive territories. However, these roads were not so much devoted to trade as to activities related to governance and military control of the Incan Empire. It was not until after the invention and use of automobiles and the rise of trucking as a means of moving merchandise that extensive road systems built with modern road-building technologies made their contributions to the spread of fashionable dress throughout the developed world.

Horse power

Animal power, and in particular horse power, was probably the most widely used means of travel for the average person in the western world before the nineteenth century. Like bicycle riding, it could serve as personal transportation or be used for sport. Scholars tell us that horses were probably domesticated in the fourth millennium BCE. However, horses or oxen pulling some type of vehicle do not appear in art until at least 1900 BCE. The earliest associations of horses and humans were in the areas of travel, warfare, and hunting. The technology needed for riding is probably more a part of the dress of the horse than the rider, as saddles, stirrups, bits, and reins improved the riding experience and these were modified over the thousands of years that humans used horses for transit. Bits and bridles were quite likely the earliest devices for controlling horses. Stirrups improved riding – examples of rigid stirrups from China were probably preceded by soft ones of perishable material. As nomadic tribes moved about Eurasia, this technology would have spread. The Chinese seem to have developed a wooden saddle that kept the rider more securely seated between a pommel in front and cantle in back. This device only reached Europe in the Middle Ages (Mckay Smith, 1965).

Greater comfort for the rider and better control over the horses are goals that are reflected in modifications and additions to the dress of the rider. Contact between the bare back of a sweating horse and the bare legs of a rider is uncomfortable. For this reason, clothing made from material that can serve as a moisture barrier is important. In some areas, there may be trailside brush that can injure the rider. Boots that cover the lower leg serve as a protection. It is not surprising, then, that typical dress for those on horseback is likely to include high boots and some water resistant material such as leather or, as these became available, some type of non-absorbent synthetic material. Control over the mount was improved by the addition of metal spurs to rider's footwear. These, and also whips, have been found in Celtic graves dated to c. 400 BCE (Mckay Smith, 1965).

Horses, too, deserve consideration for their part in sports such as racing, polo, and recreational riding, where they have had an impact not only on dress of the riders, but also on fashion. For the most part, the provision of non-human, non-animal sources of power to move individuals and groups of people came after the Industrial Revolution. Railroad trains were the first vehicles that were able to carry large numbers of people. By the 1840s, railroad trains had become a readily available form of transport.

New modes of travel of the nineteenth and twentieth centuries range from railways and Conestoga wagons to autos and airplanes. Often these technologies were in conflict with current dress practices, particularly for women, and especially when transportation forms were first introduced. Examples of initial impacts on dress can be seen, as railroads and Conestoga wagons did not accommodate full skirts very well. The first automobiles were open and clothing had to be protected from dust. When women began driving, long skirts hampered this activity. Special dress was worn in the air by pilots of both genders. As dress for these activities evolved along with the transportation, one can see how modes of transportation have been responsible for some adaptations in fashionable dress.

Fashion and practicality

An example of conflict between fashion and transportation occurred when women adopted hoop skirts and at the same time began to travel by train. Figure 11.1 illustrates the problem. The need to ride in a train or carriage did not kill this fashion, but it is one of the more extreme examples of the sometimes impractical nature of fashionable dress.

By the 1800s, men's dress had simplified sufficiently that it provided relatively few problems in mobility and ease of movement. The same cannot be said for women's dress, as it maintained floor length skirts, usually quite full, and required undergarments that inhibited movement, for example multiple petticoats, hoop skirts, or bustles and tight corsets necessary to support fashionable style lines. In a study of illustrations of women and machines, Wosk (2001) describes many depictions showing women to be inept and averse to technology. However, she says that they also illustrate the effects on dress, providing evidence that women did not avoid, but engaged in, active interactions with technologies.

American women making the trek westward with wagon trains in the nineteenth century were likely to travel in covered wagons that would hold the large quantities of goods settlers required. Much of the period of the westward migration was in the 1850s and 1860s when long, full skirts held out by many layers of petticoats or by hoopskirts were fashionable. Clearly these were

Figure 11.1 Hoop skirts were an inconvenience when traveling by train (source: Gianni Dagli Orti/The Art Archive at Art Resource, New York)

impractical garments, and travelers' accounts speak of their being discarded early on. Some pioneer women found a garment that had originated in the 1840s to be the ideal solution: the bloomer dress. Worn by women's rights activists in the 1840s, it was named after Amelia Bloomer who wore it at speaking engagements. The style derived from dress worn by European women in health sanitariums who needed to be able to exercise more easily. The garment consisted of full bloomers worn under a shorter version of women's dresses of the 1840s. Women's rights activists had hoped that women would adopt this style as a practical alternative to the heavy stiffened petticoats of mainstream fashion, but it became a source of ridicule and fertile source of material for cartoonists. Nevertheless, photographs of pioneer women do show some of them dressed in the bloomer dress, doubtless a far more practical, though distinctly unfashionable, alternative to the wide hoop-supported skirt.

Cartoonists derided hoops worn in other transportation contexts. Their sketches showed women having to remove their hoops in order to get into a carriage. Paintings of the interiors of railroad trains show the advantages of first-class tickets. Passengers in first-class railway cars sit comfortably, while in the lower-class carriages passengers are squeezed together, with women's hoops distorted by the crowding. The width of these skirts was such that it was virtually impossible for passers-by to avoid touching or pressing against the skirt. The result could be accusations from ladies that the gentlemen nearby were being inappropriately familiar.

Automobiles

Automobiles powered by steam or by electricity were introduced in the 1890s. Gasoline powered engine autos followed soon after. Before automobiles lost their status as "a rich man's toy," automobile racing was a popular sport for the wealthy. Uncertainty about what to wear was clear in the dress of the wealthy spectators who came to watch the races in 1905. One woman wore tweed, another a large feathered Gainsborough hat, and another "dripped pearls." Men seemed to prefer riding clothes, but one was in a gray cutaway suit, and W K Vanderbilt Junior combined automobile goggles with a black satin Norfolk jacket, and black leather trousers (Lord, 1965: 108).

The earliest motorcars were without roofs so the driver, whether male or female, required some protective garments to avoid being covered in the dust that these cars stirred up on the unpaved roads. Harmsworth (1904) provided explicit instructions as to the appropriate dress for driving for men and for women. The advice related to protection in the winter from cold and in the summer from dust. For winter, leather was recommended for its quality as a windbreaker. In summer, minute holes punched in leather linings helped allow air circulation and evaporation of perspiration. Fur was seen as good for winter, but authors noted that it could be difficult to shake out dust from fur. Headwear was essential. Women were instructed to wear veils that could both keep dust off their faces and hold their hats in place. Damage to the complexion was seen as unavoidable for ladies. Other perils to be avoided by women drivers were capes (they could blow up into the face and obstruct vision) and any long skirts that could interfere with reaching the clutch. Rain was another hazard – more to comfort than safety – as with the open car the driver would most likely find himself or herself sitting in a puddle. Special outer garments called dusters were designed and worn. When car design changed and cars were roofed and enclosed, these problems were solved.

By the second decade of the twentieth century, skirts for women drivers had shortened somewhat and by the 1920s skirts had shortened significantly. Except for evening wear, when a gentleman escort or paid driver could be expected to take the wheel, full length to the floor skirts have not returned since as the prevailing style for daytime wear. After closed automobiles became the norm, women had largely given up carrying parasols. They exchanged large, lavishly decorated women's hats for smaller fitted cloche hats, and both men and women found wrist watches a far greater convenience than pocket watches.

Indirectly one can probably attribute the rise in the wearing of casual dress after World War II to automobiles. Volti (2004) points out that movement to the suburbs and increased automobile ownership came at the same time. Living in suburban communities was conducive to a more casual lifestyle. While the mothers of suburban women had tended to wear housedresses (washable cotton frocks of simple designs) for daily home-making tasks, the suburban women of the late 1940s, 1950s, and after wore easy-care washable pants and shorts with blouses or shirts. This change has persisted, making casual dress and sportswear the predominant style for many American women.

Air travel

Although humans' dreams of flying have been enshrined in mythology, and there are examples of many attempts at flight in various parts of the world that met with various degrees of success, it was not until 1783 that a flight safely carried people without injury in a hot air balloon. Hot air balloon rides are still available, but they tend to be taken by balloon owners in shows and competitions or as a novelty experience for paying passengers.

As with automobiles, the seats of planes flown by the pioneers of aviation were in the open and pilots and any passengers were windblown and unprotected from the elements. One item of dress that was absolutely essential was goggles. Skirts were a serious hazard, requiring women to have their skirts tied to their legs. Fashion magazines used planes as a visual prop in promoting fashions, but the practical solution to dress for women aviators was to adopt men's clothing including boots, breeches, leather jackets, and helmets, along with the essential goggles that aided visibility. The most famous female aviator was Amelia Earhart. Her celebrity helped her to market a line of clothing in 1934 in order to support her aviation expeditions. She probably did not do the actual designing. Among the things featured in her fashion line were propeller buttons and aviation themed trimmings. In 2009, couturier Jean Paul Gaultier produced a line inspired by Amelia Earhart and the kinds of dress in which she was photographed for flying. Once planes added enclosed cabins and comfortable seats, women could wear what have been described as "fashionable sports costumes" (Wosk, 2001: 163).

From the earliest flights by the pioneers, aviation moved gradually to include modern airplanes that provide general passenger and freight transport as well as military aviation and private ownership. Passenger travel began in earnest in the 1920s and continued to grow. In order to compete successfully, airlines increased comfort, adding male service personnel called stewards in 1928 and female stewardesses in 1930. The requirements for women flight attendants were strict. They had to be single, 20 to 26 years of age, no taller than 5 feet 4 inches, and weigh less than 118 pounds. In the 1960s, airlines began hiring noted fashion designers such as the Italian Emilio Pucci, Frenchman Pierre Balmain, and American Halston to create uniforms. As countries with distinctive and exotic textile traditions began establishing passenger airlines, the flight attendant uniforms utilized fabrics that reflected the homeland traditions. No-longer-used flight attendant uniforms can be purchased as collectibles on e-Bay. By the 1950s, passenger flights featured formal food service using crystal and fine china. Passengers tended to dress more formally than do twenty-first century travelers.

Motorcycling

A web site offering advice about what to wear to those neophytes invited to go on their first motorcycle ride begins by stressing protection in "the unlikely case of a spill." Recommended are: sturdy footwear (boots especially recommended); durable pants – best are leather or 14 oz denim; an abrasion resistant jacket; leather gloves; and a helmet with eye protection. Leather has become a staple in the motorcycle-rider's wardrobe, and the black leather jacket that became such an important fashion trend clearly derived from the preferred garb of motorcyclists.

As modes of transportation both public and private became an ordinary feature of everyday life, the public ceased to adopt any special form of dress unless the transport required it for safety or comfort or when it was a sport with a customary uniform. Chapter 12 will deal with these latter examples.

Transportation is an area much affected by technology. In this and several subsequent chapters we see that dress can be affected by technologies that have nothing to do with the fabrication of what people wear. In this chapter we have seen how new forms of transportation can clash with what people wear as they move or are moved from one place to another and that fashions may need to undergo changes as a result. Generally to be carried from one place to another requires entering and exiting some kind of conveyance. When dress is simple and practical, this may pose no difficulty, However, fashions in dress may present obstacles making utilizing transportation problematic. The result may require adaptation.

Looking at relationships through illustrations

The illustrations used in this section are chosen to show the changes in women's dress that might be attributed to the advent of the automobile as transportation.

Serge coat 2699   (Skirt 2718, on page 184)

Figure 11.2 Example of women's typical outdoor wear in 1909 (source: author's image)

The woman in Figure 11.2 is dressed to go out of doors in 1909, just one year after the introduction of the Model T Ford. The general public was just beginning to be actively involved with automobiles as practical transportation. Most women had not had to think about how to dress to ride in or drive an automobile. Although women had become more active in the work force and outside of the home, fashionable dress for adult women in 1908 featured ankle length dresses, a fairly slim line and very large hats ornamented with the plumage of whole birds. Muffs appear to have been a popular accessory for keeping the hands warm.

For women who wanted to drive, these styles would not have been very convenient. The skirts could have interfered with the two speed foot pedals located on the floor. Almost any model of the car body was open enough that strong breezes could blow off the hat and also disarrange the coiffure. The hat would have blocked a clear view. Corseting probably played a part in maintaining a slim figure but could have impeded easy movement. In short, the fashions and the auto were not a good match.

A woman taxi driver of 1921 stands beside her car (Figure 11.3). The woman's dress is very different from that of about a decade earlier. The most radical difference is in the length of her skirt, which ends several inches below the knee. She should no longer have any interference from a floor-length skirt. It is also full enough that she would be able to cope with shifting her position while driving if that becomes necessary. One can even see the lower part of her legs, which are

Figure 11.3 A woman taxi driver standing beside her car (source: Getty)

covered with knitted, probably silk, and sheer stockings. Hats are simpler in shape and seem to cover hair that is cut short. Automobiles were not the only factor driving the radical style changes of the 1920s, but they had to have been a significant contributor. And once women got into automobiles as drivers, they rarely ever returned to long skirts.

12

THE EFFECTS OF SPORTS
(19th to the 21st centuries)

One can say a great deal about sports and fashion in dress, but its place in technology is more complex. Sokolowski's (2010) parameters for activities that she classifies as "sports" dress provide a useful definition of a sport. In her view the requirements are physical skill, rules, or customs for the activity and specific dress and environment. She also points out the distinction between recreational sports and professional sports. In the former, individuals with various levels of skill may participate and they may or may not engage in competition, but in professional sports where athletes are selected for and compensated in relation to their prowess in the sport, participants are limited to those who meet the appropriate physical and skill qualifications, and they most definitely engage in competitions! Sports have been a part of most cultures, but how technology relates to the dress assigned to particular sports and even what comprises "dress" is not unique to the sport. In contemporary sport, the relationship to technology is generally present in the high tech textiles that can now be created. Given the many fans that follow favorite teams or players, fashions in dress often originate with dress items used for sports.

Cultures have existed in which athletes may participate undressed or in the ordinary dress of the culture. But where some form of dress is associated with a particular sport, then whatever textile technology is available at that time period plays an important role in creating these fabrics or materials. In this chapter, I am confining the discussion, aside from some historical notes on the origins of the sport, to sports as they developed in the nineteenth to the twenty-first centuries. Over this time sports gained many new participants and/or became professionalized in Euro-American countries. As international sporting competitions multiplied, global participation in certain sports increased. Due to space limitations, professional sports will receive limited attention beyond acknowledging that because of the large audiences of fans who view, support, and follow these sports, professional athletes' dress is likely to influence fashions.

Functional dress, as defined by Watkins (2010), is an integral element of dress for sports. She describes functional dress as presenting a protective barrier between the wearer and some hazard and goes on to say that this may make some activities possible or boost performance in others. It is in this area that the relationships between technology and dress for sports can be seen most clearly. While textiles are an important component of dress for sports, Watkins (2010: 240) reminds us that in functional dress, in this case for sports, some of the elements may be made of hard goods either incorporated into the dress, attached to or supported by the body, or they may be portable. I would argue that some of what might be called the tools of particular sports should also be considered as part of the dress for that sport. For example, a tennis racquet or a pair of skis and poles are as much a part of the dress for tennis and skiing as the footwear and gloves that are worn.

Social attitudes and aspects of sports that affect dress

The attitudes and values of any culture in its specific time period will affect the choices made about appropriate dress for particular activities including sports. Writers who are looking to identify motivations that underlie decisions about dress include modesty as one of the primary reasons for dress. The others are protection, status, and decoration (Horn and Gurel, 1981: 34). However, standards of modesty are far from universal, and as a result the appropriate dress for sports may be governed not only by function but also by where and when it is worn.

In ancient Greece, sports were an important part of the culture, because Greek society valued physical fitness. Athletic competitions were an expression of these values. Sports also had direct connections with religious beliefs and festivals. The Greeks celebrated the first Olympic Games in 776 BCE (McComb, 2004). Participants were male. From Greek art it is clear that men wore no clothing for athletic events and that nudity was not considered immodest, at least in this context. Although athletics were largely a male activity, Greek women also participated in athletic games of their own. Women dressed in short tunics ending above the knee. The right breast was bare. From this one could conclude that standards of modesty varied by gender, although even Greek female dress for sports would be seen as immodest by many twenty-first century Americans, given the furor that arose when Janet Jackson bared a breast on a half-time Super Bowl show in 2004.

Standards of modesty that are associated with religious beliefs may discourage participation in athletic activities, because encumbering dress is required by the faith. The veiling of women associated with many Islamic societies is one example. Among the Old Believers, an Orthodox Russian Christian group with some settlements in the US state of Alaska, young girls and women are expected to wear full length dresses, but in recent years a few of the more liberal of these communities have permitted girls to wear knee-length shorts so they can participate in soccer teams.

Women's dress in the Euro-American regions throughout the nineteenth century covered the upper body beginning somewhere around the neckline, while the lower half of the body was enclosed in a skirt no shorter than the ankles and often extending all the way to the floor. Fashion determined the fit of the upper and lower parts of the garment. Add to this a closely fitting corset that helped to achieve the fashionable silhouette. Many popular sports had their origins in the nineteenth century and gained in popularity in the twentieth. The dress of women served to discourage or limit their early participation, though it did not keep them from trying. Photos show corseted women in full length skirts on mountain trails when mountain climbing became fashionable recreation in the late nineteenth century. Dress was modified for girls who participated in physical education classes. The technologies associated with many sports led to shaping the garb not only for men but also for women, and frequently dress for sports became the stimulus for popular fashions.

A closer look at a few areas of sport

McComb's (2004) excellent and comprehensive illustrated history of sports provides a clear review of the origins and evolution, not only of the sports discussed in the section that follows, but of many other sports as well. It is from this source that much of the historical information that follows was derived.

Horseback riding

Horseback riding is more than a sport. For centuries before motorized travel, riding a horse or sitting in a vehicle pulled by a horse or some other animal had been the chief means of travel on land. This aspect of transportation was discussed in Chapter 11. The Medieval tournament in which knights mounted on horseback engaged in competitions to prove their skills and bravery was a game, an early sport, though it could prove to be a fatal game for some contestants. Its uniform was the armor worn in war, although the armor for jousting was often modified to be more decorative and less protective than that worn in battle.

Other sports on horseback evolved from practical pursuits. Hunting progressed beyond the necessity to find food and in the courts of the powerful became a kind of game testing the abilities of participants in killing various kinds of game. Eventually even the notion of using the object of the hunt for food disappeared altogether as the tradition of fox hunting evolved.

Other horse-related sports included racing of various kinds – some forms are depicted in Greek and Roman art – and polo. Polo was an Indian game brought back to England in 1869 by British military men. These sports each had their own sets of gear and polo brought with it the pants called jodphurs, a style still worn for riding today. Both riding and driving developed as recreational activities, as well as continuing to be a means of transportation. Women could not be excluded from riding in order to get from one place to another. And some powerful women, for example Queen Elizabeth I, whose status gave them the power to make their own rules, participated in hunts. But when women rode, they were expected to ride sidesaddle. The difficulties of managing long skirts on horseback made this necessary in order to observe the standards of modesty.

Swimming

Men in ancient civilizations engaged in swimming as recreation. The art of Greece, Etruria, and Rome depicts young men diving into water and engaging in water play. Whether women also participated is not clear from this art, but given the segregation of the genders in other sporting activities, if they did, it would probably have been in female-only environments. A mosaic in a Roman villa in Sicily depicts women in bikini-like garments, but they are not shown swimming. This was probably a garment used for other sports or exercise (Croom, 2002: 950). In Western Europe and America in the nineteenth century, swimming was seen not so much as an athletic activity but as health-promoting. Those who lived near the sea would immerse themselves in sea water for a short time. Those who were inland might go to a spa where there were opportunities to bathe in mineral springs. In English seaside resorts, men and women bathed separately. Throughout the nineteenth century, bathing was a more descriptive name than swimming for water-based activities for women. The bathing dress they wore had lines similar to women's fashionable dress at the time. It covered their bodies fully and would have been an encumbrance to anyone who wanted to actually swim.

Australian Annette Kellerman was not only an athlete, but also a vaudeville and movie star. She is noted as the first swimmer to wear a one-piece, practical swimsuit. Others followed her lead. Swimming as an athletic competition in Europe and North America did not develop until the last quarter of the nineteenth century. The first US swimming championship was held in New York in 1883. Long distance swimming, especially swimming across the English Channel, publicized swimming to the general public. The English swimmer Matthew Webb made the first crossing in 1875. Using the breast stroke he swam 38 miles. His time was 21 hours and 45 minutes. Gertrude Ederle, an American swimmer, entered the competitions in 1926 and exceeded the men's record by two hours and was rewarded by a ticker tape parade through the streets of New York. She toured the United States giving demonstrations of swimming in a portable tank. Although most women were still wearing fairly encumbering bathing dress, Ederle wore a tank suit of wool similar to Kellerman's that has been described as being "cut high across the leg." Fashion followed Kellerman's and Ederle's lead as women adopted more functional swimming dress (McComb, 2004: 85–6).

Speed is the primary objective in competition swim racing. The textiles used and the cut of the swimsuits had much to contribute to winning a race. Competing swimmers and their coaches therefore based their swimwear choices on the performance of these garments. Recreational swimmers chose styles for their aesthetic and figure enhancing qualities. As Western countries gradually relaxed requirements for "modest" dress on public beaches, fashion became a major determinant of the swimsuit styles that appeared. Both men and women sought to show a handsome figure, and technology came to their aid. By the 1930s, swimsuits could benefit from a form-fitting fabric called Lastex that was made by sheathing a rubber core in another fabric such as wool, cotton, or rayon. Lastex was the choice for competition swimmers who wanted to increase their speed and for those who wanted to look good while tanning (a fashionable thing to do before the dangers of too much sun exposure were known). Motion pictures also helped to reinforce the fashion for women's bathing suits made from Lastex. Esther Williams, formerly a competitive swimmer and then a performer in a water show, became a major movie star who usually appeared in her films in swimming routines and fashionable bathing suits.

The technologies leading to the synthesis of synthetic fibers after World War II contributed to additional changes in bathing suit design. Nylon proved to be especially popular given its elasticity and quick drying qualities. When elastomeric fibers (called spandex in the United States and elastane globally) became available after 1959, they were utilized instead of rubber. Spandex fibers can stretch 500 to 600 per cent without breaking and their recovery from stretching is excellent. Although they can be woven or knitted into fabrics in combination with other yarns, it is more likely that they serve as the core of a yarn that is covered by other fibers. Used in a wide variety of garments, spandex is particularly favored for swimwear as it has excellent resistance to damage from sunlight and chlorine, qualities that rubber does not have (Collier et al., 2009: 197–203).

Competition swimmers saw these close-fitting swimsuits as an advantage and adopted them. Speedo developed a bodysuit they called Fastskin, by using research from physics and analyses of the motions used in swimming as well as the structure of the skin of fast-moving sharks. Although these and later high tech fabric swimsuits had been permitted in earlier Olympic Games, FINA (Federation International de Natation Amateur) ruled that from 2010 on swimsuits

Figure 12.1 Olympic high tech swimwear for the 2004 Olympics (source: Getty)

had to be submitted for approval twelve months in advance of a world championship or Olympic Games and that FINA would publish a list of approved models. FINA was perhaps responding to critics of the high tech suits who argued that "the buoyancy they create amounts to technological doping."

Bicycling

Until the development of high tech fibers in the late twentieth and twenty-first centuries, technology relating to the sport of cycling is most evident in the bicycle and not in the dress worn for the sport. Fashion, however, was clearly present when women started to cycle. After earlier attempts to develop wheeled transport powered by humans, Frenchman Pierre Michaux successfully placed a crank and pedals on the front wheel of a two-wheeled vehicle very similar to a modern bicycle. Improvements followed, so that by 1890 bicycles were comfortable to ride, having air-filled tires and the basic configuration of the vehicle we know as a modern bicycle (Macy, 2011).

Warner (2006) recounts the journey of the bloomer dress starting with its introduction in the 1840s as an unsuccessful attempt by women's rights activists to reform women's dress. To some extent it was used in some women's physical education classes and further attempts were made to promote it as "rational

Figure 12.2 Fashionable bloomer costume for bicycling in 1894. Victorian fashions and costumes from *Harper's Bazaar* 1867 to 1898 (courtesy of Dover Publications, inc.)

dress." When women started to participate in the "bicycle craze" (1887 to 1903), riding a bicycle in a fashionable long full skirt must have made pedaling a bicycle without mishap a challenge. As a result, women began to wear a bloomer dress in public for bicycle riding.

Similar styles were also adopted for physical education. The style appeared in fashion magazines and patterns to make the bloomer costume more available. But the style did not outlast the bicycle craze and women adopted a divided cycling skirt with the appearance, when standing, of a skirt. One longer-lasting effect, however, came from the demands of bicycle riding: a loosening of corsets, necessary in order to take a deep breath. Shorter skirts were another legacy, reinforced by the increase in women entering the work force. Fashion magazines of the first decade of the twentieth century show patterns for skirts with several alternative lengths, a clear indication of interest in shorter skirts.

Over time, as pants and shorts for women became acceptable, recreational bicycling dress for women and men was usually any garb that was practical for riding a bicycle. This tended to be pants of a length that would not catch in the bicycle mechanism, with whatever type of top was fashionable at the time. All this changed with the development of interest in bicycle racing after the Tour de France expanded from a French event to its current international participation. Race T-shirts were sold to onlookers as souvenirs. The synthetic stretch fiber called either spandex or elastane has become an element not only of bicycling dress but of many types of dress for active sports where its stretch qualities allow greater flexibility in movement. Interesting combinations of natural and synthetic fibers have been developed to meet the needs of sports participants. For example, a blend of wool and polyester for cyclists utilized the wicking properties of polyester to carry off and evaporate moisture from perspiration, while the natural stretch of wool provided a close fit.

Tennis

The game of tennis appears to have grown from French ball games in monasteries in which a ball was hit over a rope with bare hands so it bounced off the wall, making it difficult to return. By the fifteenth century, racquets were used and men in European royal courts played the game. Both men and women played recreational tennis in the nineteenth century. In fact, it was a woman who brought tennis to the United States in 1874, after seeing the game being played by British players in Bermuda (McComb, 2004). Photographs generally show male players wearing fairly informal and comfortably fitting versions of the trousers and shirts of the period. By contrast women appear to be tightly corseted (Figure 12.3). While the bustle dress was in vogue, they are seen posing, racquets in hand, in these skirts with their exaggerated back fullness.

Tennis competitions first developed around 1900, with male participants and British and American players competing. After 1903, players from other countries participated. Women entered competition in the 1920s and in 1970–71 they gained professional status, something men had enjoyed since both male

Figure 12.3 Tennis dress c. 1911. Women's long skirts have to be managed for playing tennis while men's trousers did not inhibit their play (source: Shutterstock/Hein Nouwens)

Figure 12.4 Contrast the tennis dress of 2012 with that of Figure 12.3 (source: Shutterstock/dboystudio)

professionals and amateurs had been admitted to the prestigious Wimbledon tournament in 1968.

The evolution of tennis racquets relied in large part on advances in materials technologies. Beginning with wooden framed racquets, steel frames came into use in 1967, aluminum in the 1970s, and fiberglass with graphite soon after. And later still, use of synthetic materials and carbon fiber. The size of racquets increased too (McComb, 2004). By 2000, the International Tennis Federation had placed limits on the size of racquets that can be used in its tournaments.

Technology did not play a major role in creating dress for tennis. The acceptable dress for women evolved gradually from contemporary dress to the point where individual players decided what to wear. On the other hand, tennis dress developed its own styles that changed from year to year.

One of the most obvious examples of the impact of tennis on fashion was the choice made by French designer Jean Paul Gaultier to show his 2010 ready-to-wear Spring-Summer collection for the house of Hermes on a runway simulating a tennis court. Many of the styles shown were clearly inspired by tennis dress past and present. And tennis dress contributed to the popularity of styles such as Bermuda shorts, short shorts, cable knits, V-neck sweaters, and sweatbands.

Protective and performance enhancing dress for sports

Some sports place the players in situations where they may be injured by equipment, conditions encountered, or other players. As a result, protective clothing is used to lessen the likelihood of injury. This protective dress is used in both professional and amateur sport. Some of what is worn protects vulnerable parts of the body. In other situations, the materials from which the dress for sports is made must provide protection from excessive cold or heat. In any case, the protective clothing must not prevent the athlete from performing effectively. At times the dress worn may seek to enhance performance and offer special advantages to the wearer. Use of dress that enhances performance may be banned by organizations governing the particular sport (e.g. swimming). Often both protective and performance enhancing dress rely on what are known as high performance or high tech fabrics or other devices in their dress that require advanced technologies for their production. The range of these fibers and fabrics has become too extensive for a full discussion. The specific applications of such fibers are generally made after careful analysis of the conditions under which they are used, the stresses encountered, and the actions and activities that an athlete must perform, and the conditions he or she will encounter. For example, for a sport such as automobile racing, fire resistant garments would be needed. Other sports would need maximum strength fabrics. Watkins (2010), an expert in functional dress, provides this information about protective equipment components, a rigid plastic plate combined with a shaped combination pad, to conform to the surface of a body part and energy-absorbing material.

Figures 12.5 and 12.6 show the protective clothing worn by high school hockey players. Figure 12.5 shows the layer underneath of what is seen when players are on the ice. In Figure 12.6 the player is dressed for play. One function of the undermost layer is to keep the skater from becoming wet from perspiration and it is therefore made to enclose the trunk and arms of the upper body in polyester or polypropylene, both of which will wick away moisture. Socks may

Figure 12.5 Young ice hockey player displaying the variety of protective devices worn under his hockey uniform (source: author's family photograph)

be of polyester, wool, or even cotton blends. A layer of upper-body body armor is placed over this and consists of a pullover containing segmented sewn-in high-density foam padding over the chest, back, and shoulder. Boxer style garter shorts contain a genital protective cup of polyethylene and polyurethane foam.

Figure 12.6 Young ice hockey player wearing a variety of protective devices with his hockey uniform (source: author's family photograph)

There are Velcro tabs in the shorts to secure the outermost layer of thigh-length over-socks. Elbows are protected by a separate pad made of polyester with a rigid polyethylene cup over the point of the elbow and high density foam padding extending down the forearm. Shin pads of polyester and nylon have a rigid polyethylene cap outside and high-density foam padding inside.

The helmet has a rigid plastic shell, steel mesh face guard, and foam padding lining the helmet. A separate chin protector is attached to the face guard mesh with nylon straps. Aside from goalies who wear a similar full-face steel mesh face guard, professional players have a clear polycarbonate eye shield, but no lower face protection. Heavy synthetic gloves padded with high-density foam extend above the wrist, with an unpadded synthetic leather palm to allow precise handling of the hockey stick. Thick nylon or polyester hockey pants, generally worn with elastic suspenders have rigid plastic segmented pads embedded in sewn-in pockets protecting against impact to the front of the thigh, waist, and base of the spine/sacrum. High-density foam pads the back of the thigh.

Hockey skates are usually heat molded to the skater's skate shoe at the time of purchase. The skate shoe upper is synthetic leather material and has a rigid toe box and synthetic leather lining. Skate blades are stainless steel. Not pictured is a plastic, custom-made, mouth guard heat-molded to the player's mouth. Younger players are often required to wear a thinly padded wrap-around neck guard to protect against accidental skate cuts to a downed player. Goalies at all levels wear rigid plastic neck shields attached to the lower helmet as well as more extensive pads to the legs and arms.

The emergence of sportswear from dress for sports

One of the categories of dress merchandise used by retailers is sportswear. The name would have originally been applied to the clothing worn for participating in one of the amateur sports, but by 1920s and 1930s was more often applied to casual dress worn by those participating as a spectator of some sport, and now is applied to casual dress for daytime or evening or for work.

Warner (2006) makes the emergence of a uniquely American style of dress clear as she describes the development of sportswear relating it as coming out of the rational dress proposed by the dress reform movement that eventually was adopted by female cyclists in the 1890s. One might argue that the bicycle technology was to some extent midwife to a major fashion change that came in the twentieth century. Warner's work describes the effects of additional technologies. The mechanization of knitting had been accomplished after the Industrial Revolution, but it took giant leaps forward in the twentieth century (Chapter 10). The simpler lines and more comfortable fit of the garments for women that were often knitted caught on quickly, especially when French designer Gabrielle Chanel's post World War I collections featured simple, wool knits she had borrowed from French fishermen. Yet another technology was a factor: motion pictures. Warner credits clothes worn by popular actresses such

Figure 12.7 Examples from the 1930s of the type of women's dresses that were beginning to be merchandized as "sportswear." The caption describes the clothes as "sporty" (Courtesy of Dover Publications, inc.)

as Katharine Hepburn and Marlene Dietrich – casual styles, often trousers – as an important influence. More recently, the wide use of spandex in fashionable dress, where it has moved from swimsuits and other sports gear is one example of evolution in textile fiber uses. Sokolowsky (2010: 325) makes the point when she notes how recreational swimwear has influenced styles in areas of sport such as gymnastics, running apparel, speed-skating, and also in general fashion.

For professional and amateur sports

These concluding comments are brief and quite general. Obviously dressing the players in sports teams, either professional or amateur, grows out of the need for players and viewers to be able to recognize the members of their teams. The specific uniform was, of course, adapted to suit the physical requirements of the sport being played, but as time passed not only were the characteristics of the fabrics a practical factor in determining what players would wear, but fans, whose support helped to keep teams going, developed loyalty to the team colors and uniforms so that team traditions played a part in preserving some long-standing styles. Some items, such as baseball caps and tennis shoes, migrated from the sport to become items of classic dress apart from the sport. Others were abandoned or evolved. And some continued, perhaps undergoing modifications to provide greater speed, comfort, or protection.

Recreational sports, as contrasted with professional sports, have been both affected by fashion and have affected fashion. At a time when participation in any kind of sport was a largely male activity and women's participation was just beginning, we can see that women's dress was often a hindrance to full and active play. It required time for women's dress to adapt so that they could fully participate. As the fashion industry in the United States developed, interest in sports had grown to such an extent that dress intended for wear while watching, rather than participating in, sports became so important that an entire segment of the fashion industry was given the name "sportswear." This type of casual dress is seen as a hallmark of fashion originating in the United States in the twentieth century.

Looking at relationships through illustrations

The two garments being compared here (Figures 12.8 and 12.9) are associated with the same sport. They were worn about two decades apart and reflect both social and technological changes.

It is 1916, and the young woman here is on vacation with her family on Staten Island, New York. Dressed for the beach, her conservative immigrant family would have had to approve her bathing dress. She wears a bathing suit of the time. If and when she went into the water it would not have been to swim, but

Figure 12.8 Bathing dress, 1916 (source: author's image)

probably at the most to play in the waves. Most of the bathing dress at this time was made from wool, and was knitted. The stockings were clearly knitted, but it is not possible to see the structure of the rest of the fabric, though it is likely to have been wool.

Figure 12.9 Group of women in bathing suits, 1938 (Every Day Fashions of the Thirties, edited by Stella Blum, courtesy of Dover Publications, inc.)

It is now 1938, and in two decades, much has changed. These swim styles are now intended for the water. And the one second from the left has utilized two new technologies: rayon and Lastex. Rayon was the first manufactured fiber to come into commercial use. It was regenerated from short cotton fibers or wood chips. Lastex combined rubber for stretch with rayon in a lustrous satin weave fabric to make an attractive more form-fitting swimsuit.

13

COMMUNICATIONS TECHNOLOGIES THAT DISSEMINATE FASHION INFORMATION
(19th to the 21st centuries)

In order for fashion in dress to flourish, those ready to adopt new styles must have some way to learn about what is new. When most of the population spent their lives in the same town or village and had little contact with the world beyond their communities, fashion information would have been communicated by personal contact and visual observation of and interaction with others. But once individuals were able to read and see printed descriptions and visual representations of what was being worn, printing technology became an important driver of and influence on fashion trends.

Printed fashion information

As noted in Chapter 4, the printed word accompanied by illustrations was making fashion information available by the late 1600s. Publications, such as the British *Lady's Magazine* of 1770 featured fashion plates in black and white, but by 1790 this included hand-colored or "embellished" printed fashion plates. The *Lady's Museum* 1798–1832 was another early magazine, that stated it was focused on the interests of "the superior class" of women. Beetham (1996), in her study of women's magazines, states that the audience of these early magazines was expected to be mothers and upper class. *The Belle Assemblée* acknowledged its interest in fashion in this rhyme from the magazine:

Every week does modish show
What bonnets are worn and what caps the go (Beetham, 1996: 27).

By 1782 and after, women had access to a variety of fashion magazines published in major European cities. Often the styles depicted were identified as French or English, as readers had greater faith in styles endorsed by these countries.

The first American magazine explicitly directed to a female clientele was a literary magazine, published in 1782. It had no fashion information. The earliest and most successful of the widely read US magazines that carried fashion information was *Godey's Lady's Book*, published from 1830–1898. Others came and went, some such as *Peterson's Magazine* or *Demorest Monthly Magazine*, with relatively long and others with brief lives. Although fashion was featured, articles and fiction thought suitable for ladies made up the majority of the printed pages. By the later 1800s, magazines had gradually begun to be directed to readers with specific interests. *The Delineator* began as a paper pattern catalog and gradually evolved to become well-known for the short stories by some of America's most prominent writers. It did maintain its fashion focus until it ceased publication in the 1930s. Two of the fashion-focused magazines first published in the late nineteenth century, *Vogue* and *Harper's Bazaar*, can be found on news-stands today. Over time, these magazines came to focus almost exclusively on fashion.

At first *Godey's* had few illustrations. The fashion news featured one hand-colored fashion plate described at length in the text of the magazine. Some issues augmented these color illustrations with additional black and white sentimental illustrations and gradually added illustrations of accessories, craft projects, and occasionally, modest undergarments.

The early fashion plates accompanied with descriptions provided some guidance to seamstresses or other women wanting to sew fashionable clothes for themselves. By the 1850s, fashion magazines often included patterns for current styles, but unlike later paper patterns, these consisted of diagrams of pattern pieces drawn with one pattern piece superimposed on another. The seamstress had to painstakingly trace each separate pattern piece and then enlarge it to the correct size. The hand-colored fashion plates of the early 1800s were fashion drawings colored by women hired to add the fashionable colors to the printed plates. If the colorist ran out of the color mentioned in the description of the garment, she might simply substitute a color that remained in her palette. Often the American plates were direct copies of plates that originated in European magazines (Tortora, 1972).

Godey's did not carry advertising until 1847 and then not in every issue. Placed at the back of the magazine, the quantity increased after 1883. In contrast, fashion magazines of the twentieth and twenty-first centuries carried as

Figure 13.1 Fashion magazine cover from 1908. By this date the increased fashion focus of these magazines is evident on the cover (source: Author's collection – out of copyright)

much or more advertising than editorial copy. Hand-colored fashion plates were replaced by printed color drawings in 1883. Photographs became more and more important as the technologies for printing photographs advanced. Color came to these magazines only in the 1930s, and at first only in drawings. Color

Figure 13.2 Runway fashion shows attract many photographers whose fashion shots will appear in print and various other media (source: Alexander Kalina/Shutterstock)

print photography was used in the 1940s, and predominated after the 1950s. Advances in the technologies for printing photographs influenced these changes. Photogravure, in the late nineteenth century, improved the ability to capture subtle variations within photographs. In the mid-nineteenth century, a process called chromolithography for color printing was available, but being quite expensive was not widely used, whereas in the twentieth century offset lithography through its use of chemical processes made color printing cheaper and less time-consuming.

Talented twentieth-century fashion magazine editors developed a symbiotic relationship with the fashion industry and with the *haute couture*. As a result, fashion magazines that featured the designs of the *haute couture* were considered to be the authoritative source for women interested in dressing in the latest high fashions. Fashion journalism expanded beyond the women's magazines and fashion magazines. Newspapers added fashion features and covered the fashion shows at which designers presented their new lines.

The fashion industries came to rely on the publicity provided by these journals as a way of increasing sales. Being featured in a fashion magazine could be the stimulus that helped to create a new fashion trend. One well-known example of this was the radical changes in dress silhouettes after World War II, which came to be known as "The New Look."

Visual media and fashion

Photography

As the technology matured, photography came to have significant influence on the transmission of fashion information. Prior to the early years of the nineteenth century, drawing and painting represented humans and their surroundings, and as a result information about what people wore was gained either from observation of actual garments or from drawings and paintings of dressed individuals. Drawings and paintings could be misleading for a host of reasons, ranging from inaccurate interpretation by viewers to artistic license by the artist producing the images. Even after photographic images appeared in printed publications, drawn images did not totally disappear.

Through photography, an image of what was actually before the photographer was created. Photography grew out of the use of the camera obscura, a device used by artists to aid drawing. A light passed into a darkened compartment produces an inverted image of a scene or object outside of the compartment. Working with this device in France in 1826, Joseph Niépice was able to capture the projected image on a substance sensitive to light. A colleague, Louis-Jacques-Mandé Daguerre, worked with him. Niépice died in 1833. Daguerre continued the work and in 1839 introduced a successful photographic process. The prints he made were known as Daguerreotypes and were soon marketed around the world.

Other types of photographic processes available after the advent of daguerreotypes were ambrotypes, tintypes, and, later, *carte de visite*, and glass plate negatives. All were widely used by amateur and professional photographers. Advances in photography had led from techniques requiring special skills to the ultimate invention of cameras that could be used by amateurs. Once Kodak cameras were available after 1888, most families were likely to own at least one camera. These advances, together with the ability to print photographs in journals and newspapers, enabled merchants who wanted to sell products to display fashions to potential consumers in newspaper advertisements and catalogs.

Although there is no clear evidence that having photographs of what friends and relatives were wearing influenced fashion trends, it is likely that such things as photographs of famous individuals probably did have an impact. These were available on picture postcards and 3-D–stereopticon viewer cards. Disseminated widely, these could have served either to confirm that one was in fashion or provide ideas for the creative seamstress.

Fashion photography, a tool of the fashion industry, should be differentiated from personal, journalistic, and artistic photography. While the photographs appearing in various print media were limited by the available technology, once that technology became mature, the photographs that appeared in fashion magazines can be seen to have a fashion history of their own. Bull (2010: 147) points out that fashion "by definition and in order to exist commercially must always be new" but is also "constantly recycling and drawing on the past for ideas." As a result, while fashion photography always features some type of dress, the style of the photographs varied widely. In the early decades of the twentieth century, photographers often used society and royal women to create an aura of high society and prestige. Later, some were influenced by art (notably abstraction and surrealism). In the 1950s, clothes in photographs were worn by glamorous women, and soon after settings moved outside the studio to faraway places, then switched to action shots in which it was hard to discern the lines of clothes. Sometimes photographers placed models in fantasy locations. Some photographers developed a personal style that made the photographer a sort of super star and their photographs icons of fashion photography that have outlived the periods in which they worked.

With the advent of technologies such as Photoshop, that can edit photographs to add and subtract elements of images, a controversy has arisen among journalists as to the ethics of this practice. The august *New York Times* has followed a policy that forbids manipulation of images, allowing but one exception to this policy: fashion images! In the Public Editor column that examines journalistic issues for the newspaper, Sullivan (2013) quoted the assistant managing editor for photography as saying, "Fashion is fantasy . . . Readers understand this. It is totally manipulated with everything done for aesthetics." Responding to the Public Editor's questions about this practice, the editor of *T*, the *Sunday New York Times* monthly style magazine, confirmed that fashion magazines did, indeed, alter photographs as they saw fit.

Motion pictures

As is clear from the name, motion pictures grew out of still photography. Once it was possible to make photographs, the next step was to add motion to the picture by placing photographs in sequence, each photo slightly different from the previous. These minor differences can simulate motion. For example, a horse is photographed in a series of steps in which each leg position is just slightly different from the previous. When the photos are projected rapidly, one after another, the horse appears to be running. With this ability it was logical to make the now-moving pictures tell a story. Between the years of 1880 and 1927, silent films gained audiences worldwide as plots grew more sophisticated and film-making techniques improved. Sound came to the movies in 1927. As the technology progressed, films were photographed in color (1950s), in three dimensions (1980s), and with ever-increasing sophistication in image quality, sound, and new techniques used for production.

Evans (2011: 110) observes that in the 1890s, fashion shows and motion pictures had their beginnings at much the same time. Early connections include French designer Paul Poiret's use, in 1910 to 1913, of film as a way of showing his current creations. International newsreels included coverage of the French fashion shows. Some films included fashion shows. A few even built the central movie plot around a fashion show.

The impact of motion pictures on fashion was enormous. In the year 1928 the American film industry released more than 500 feature films and many more short subjects. Films shown in 23,000 theaters could boast at least 100 million ticket buyers.

Gundle (2003: 177) points out that the motion picture industry had developed as a style leader in both dress fashions and interior design by the 1930s. Motion picture studios made sure their leading ladies set a standard of beauty that women who wanted to appear glamorous could copy.

Fan magazines and fan photographs available to admirers of specific stars were another way that the public could keep up with make-up, hairstyles, and accessories that actresses were wearing. The clothes worn in pictures could create specific fashion trends. After Clark Gable appeared without an undershirt in *It Happened One Night*, manufacturers of undershirts saw a drop in sales.

Numerous items of dress were named after actors and actresses. There was the Wallace Beery shirt, the Greta Garbo hat, the Veronica Lake peek-a-boo

Figure 13.3 Stars such Jean Harlow made bleached blonde hair fashionable in the 1930s (source: Shutterstock/Bocman1973)

Figure 13.4 Movie stars had such extensive influence that when Clark Gable took off his outer shirt in a film and revealed he was not wearing an undershirt, moviegoers followed his lead and manufacturers complained because sales dropped (source: Shutterstock/ Sergey Goryachev)

hairstyle. Some, such as the Sabrina collar named after the style of a collar on a dress and the Sabrina heel, a low heel on a ballet-type slipper worn by Audrey Hepburn in the film *Sabrina,* were named after films. Actors such as Greta Garbo and Katharine Hepburn made trousers for women glamorous.

The Academy Awards ceremony has provided fashion influences based on what Hollywood was wearing to this event. The Academy of Motion Picture Arts and Sciences, an organization formed in 1927 to deal with issues within the growing American film industry, established the Academy Awards in 1929. Over the years, the award ceremony developed into the major media event it is today. Although an award is given for excellence in costume design in film, an award not established until 1948, the costume award is not a significant influence on fashion. The major influence comes instead from the fashions of the dresses worn to the ceremony, especially after the Academy relaxed its requirement that nominees wear "semiformal dress." By 1951, some actresses wore gowns designed by French *haute couture* designers. Television coverage began with the awards for films of 1952 and the first color transmission was in 1962. A good portion of the televised award ceremony is occupied by video footage of those attending and the designers who provided gowns for the women are usually identified. In the days following the awards, fashion web sites and blogs post their assessment of the best and worst styles worn to the awards.

An example of the importance of the event to fashion merchandising was the subject of an article in the Sunday fashion section of the *New York Times.* An article in Spring 2013 described how Academy Award dresses shown on television that year inspired high school girls' choices of gowns for high school proms. The influences varied, including color choices, necklines, and ornamentation, as well as silhouette (Meltzer, 2013).

Television

Although television was introduced to the American public in the late 1930s before World War II began, its development and wide acceptance had to wait until after the war ended. Nine commercial television stations grew to forty-eight from 1945 to 1948. Growth accelerated and by 1960 television sets were to be found in 85 per cent of households in the United States. Color television became available in the 1960s and by 1967 color predominated in network programming.

Clearly such a visual medium watched by so many viewers would have an influence on fashion choices made by viewers. Until they appeared on the Ed Sullivan show three times in 1964, the Beatles' suits, hairstyles, and shoes were not known or popular in the United States. Their TV exposure changed that. Looking back at past styles, one Internet web site blog mentioned popular styles such as the cut off denim shorts worn by the star of the *Dukes of Hazard* (on air from 1979 to 1985), after whom these pants were called, in fashion terminology, Daisy Dukes. Shows set in past historic periods such as the Tudor era influenced fashionable colors shown by fashion designers and Ancient Rome-based series inspired draped styles. The leading actresses and actors of TV series, singers, or performers displaying other talents were also imitated.

The television program *Project Runway*, in which designers competed to present designs that satisfied criteria presented by the judges, premiered in December, 2004. It quickly developed a loyal following. There is no firm evidence that the fashion designs shown on the show actually influenced fashions, although some of the winners were able to establish businesses that achieved various levels of success. However, anecdotal evidence indicates that enrollment in higher education fashion design programs did increase.

In 2010, the style pages of the *New York Times* announced that television had surpassed motion pictures in the ability to serve as a fashion trend setter. Nevertheless, the gowns worn at the annual Academy Awards ceremony capture the fashion spotlight, an example of an amalgamation of the influences of cinema and television.

Computers for consumers

The origins of electronic computers lie in the search for calculating machines. They were first put to use in support of the war efforts of both the Germans and the US military during World War II. The first post-war applications using a stored-program computer were in support of research and in 1950 the first computer for business use was available for purchase. The results of the US presidential election were correctly forecast in 1952 by computer (Williams *et al.*, 2000: 306–10). Additional landmarks along the road to twenty-first century personal computers and the World Wide Web included the following events identified by: *networkinghttp://www.internetsociety.org/internet/what-internet/history-internet/brief-history-internet*:

- 1962 The first recorded description of the social interactions that could be enabled through networking;
- first host-to-host message sent;
- first public demonstration of new network technology.

Extensive development work from 1972 to 1985 made this technology an effective tool for researchers and scholars and was already being used by others for daily communication. Commercial interests entered, providing private network services and products. As personal computers became available, commercial interests increased their participation and it was not long before the Internet, dress, and fashion began to connect, so that by the second decade of the twenty-first century, the Internet was a place that consumers could see what was being shown by designers around the world, could follow a favorite fashion blog, or shop online for dress items chosen from online catalogs at the web site of their favorite retailer.

Fashion web sites abound on the Internet, as do fashion blogs. Fashion blogs first appeared in 1990. Rocamora (2013) examines this offspring of the Internet in "How new are new media – the case of fashion blogs." By 2011, there were 18 million. Rocamora sees these blogs as constantly changing. They range from individual to corporate sponsored sites. How influential these sites are is hard to assess. It is likely that the site hosts may serve as tastemakers in unusual ways, especially if they develop a loyal following in some niche or specialized areas.

Participatory web sites, beginning early in the twenty-first century, were an important computer development that has come to include a substantial fashion focus. Watstein and Czarnecki (2010) succinctly summarize this development of the first decade of the twenty-first century as a new category of Internet sites known as "virtual worlds or immersive environments." The vocabulary of these sites uses terms such as participant (the computer user who enters this virtual world), and actor or avatar (the participant's visual presence in the immersive

Figure 13.5 Second Life Avatar shows T-shirts on sale in the virtual world to support her college, Virginia Tech (source: STR/Reuters Corbis)

environment or virtual space). The participant can construct the virtual world environment, choose a personal appearance, and design or purchase items of dress. Over time, with greater participation in the virtual world, commercial interests entered and made virtual versions of their products available for virtual purchase as a means of advertising or dissemination of information.

Colleges and universities offering degrees in fashion studies have had students participate in virtual projects and some fashion designers have shown their new lines in virtual fashion shows that eliminate the traditional runway shows.

Some final thoughts about technology, communication, and fashion

The illustrations in this chapter all relate to the technologies that grease the wheels of fashion change and therefore the chapter does not need an illustration through which the focus is on relationships between technology, dress, and fashion. When means of communication in the nineteenth to the twenty-first centuries are compared to those of earlier centuries, the proliferation of technology-supported communication options is striking. The globalization of fashion described in Chapter 14 is one outgrowth of these developments. But could a fashion industry have developed without these technologies? Of course the manufacturing technology for fabrics and mass fashion were also essential to the production of garments for sale, but suppose there had never been photography, motion pictures, print media, television, or the Internet. Certainly fashion as a social phenomenon pre-dates these technologies, but it also pre-dates the fashion industry. Compare the speed of fashion change before the nineteenth century to the speed and diversity of fashions adopted by various "style tribes," a name given by Polhemus (1994) to the tendency of some young people to affiliate with a particular group (e.g. hippies, punks) and to adopt the fashions associated with that group or the speed with which the fashionista who follows the semi-annual runway shows of high fashion acquires current fashionable dress. This segmentation of the fashion industry's market has certainly been dependent on the many communication technologies.

PART FOUR

HIGH TECH ENTERS

14
TECHNOLOGY CONTRIBUTES TO THE GLOBALIZATION OF FASHION
(20th and 21st centuries)

Many writers have seen globalization as a recent phenomenon and a product of modern technology. The term was first used in relation to economics in the 1980s. However, Mann (2011) in his book *1493* makes a convincing case for the beginning of true globalization as coming with the first voyage of Christopher Columbus to the American continent. From this time on, Mann insists, international trade involving all the world surged forward. In the Fall of 2013, New York's Metropolitan Museum of Art provided visible support for this argument. "Interwoven Globe" was an exhibition of textiles from this burgeoning trade with its inclusion of European owned textiles from the Americas, Southeast Asia, the Indian sub-continent, and the Middle East. Huge silver deposits in South America were rapidly exploited by the Spanish and the silver from those deposits moved not only east to the European countries, especially Spain, but also west to the Philippines where the Chinese, eager for silver, the basis of their coinage, traded silk for the precious metal. That silk, in turn, was carried into the American colonies and also moved on to Europe. The silk that flooded the European market directly competed with European silk industries in ways familiar to the modern world. Textiles and apparel manufactured in the newly industrializing countries of the late twentieth century now compete with the more costly products of the industrialized nations of North America and Europe. Many technologies played a role in this sixteenth century exchange as sea-going vessels and mining improved, and meanwhile the technologies mastered by silk weavers in China, and the highly fashionable Asian embroidered, printed, and painted fabrics set a high standard at low prices that the European industries could not match.

In a sense, globalization has been going on in every era touched on in this book. In the twentieth and twenty-first centuries, globalization has had a marked impact in areas closely related to dress and fashion and is made easier by technology. Another important factor has been the loosening of trade barriers through trade agreements and the elimination of trade quotas that came after 2005.

Ellwood (2011: 14) credits the acceleration in globalization to "computer technology, dismantling of barriers to the movement of goods and capital, and the expanding political and economic power of transnational corporations." Steger (2009: 17) lists the new technological elements most often credited for facilitating globalization: personal computers, the Internet, cellular telephones, digital cameras, high definition television, satellites, jet planes, and more. In the fashion industry, computerized design and automated manufacturing techniques have enabled international connections.

Manufacturing

The stages through which apparel moves from conception to acquisition by a consumer are these: the creation of a design concept, the acquisition of fabric or other material from which to make the garment, the cutting of the pieces that will be assembled, putting together the pieces and incorporating any needed "findings" (i.e. closures, trimmings, linings, etc.). And, finally, if a retailer has not commissioned the product, a retailer must take it to the point where a customer can buy the merchandise. Dickerson (2010) points out that for many years in individual countries, particularly in the United States, the fashion industry had a "nearly captive domestic market." Local employees carried out all the aforementioned steps in the home country. In the 1950s and 1960s, she says, the changes leading to globalization began to erode the domestic fashion industry, especially the construction of garments. As the industry is now organized, the countries that are the primary markets for the end product tend to handle the aspects of design, branding, and retailing, while outsourcing the manufacturing.

Information Technology (IT) has played an essential role in the manufacture of dress in the late twentieth and early twenty-first centuries. It begins when the product is designed, even before the manufacture of an item of dress can commence. The computer may be, but is not always, the first tool used by a designer as he or she conceives the design. Many designers are constantly on the lookout for creative ideas and will sketch ideas, take photos with their telephones, and stay constantly aware of what is going on around them. Manufacturers may encourage the early use of computer-aided design and

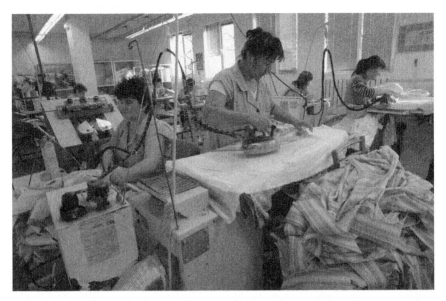

Figure 14.1 This example of off-shore manufacturing shows Pazardjik Bulgarian women ironing shirts in a clothing factory (source: Shutterstock/Anton Chalakov)

manufacturing (CAD/CAM) computer software that can shorten the process. The software not only produces a visual image of the design but also is able to create a pattern in a variety of sizes. The process can then go on through electric data interchange (EDI) to accomplish the tasks required for manufacture of the product. These various operations can be performed at one or at different locations. This kind of interactive manufacturing is enabled by EDI, another of the tools of globalization (Abecassis-Moedas, 2010: 110).

The easiest and first steps came with the cutting and assembly of apparel. In low-wage countries, cutting machines could be acquired, sewing machines could be purchased, and workers, either skilled or unskilled, could quickly learn or be trained to sew pieces of garments or apply findings. As the aforementioned communications and shipping technologies developed, manufacturers striving to lower costs closed their domestic factories and moved overseas. For a time the textile industry, dependent as it was on a sophisticated technology, seemed to be unaffected. But gradually other countries, especially those in East Asia, acquired the needed technologies and skills to compete in this area as well.

As a means of competing, domestic industries mounted efforts based on electronic communication technology to capitalize on the ability to deliver goods quickly and in a timely manner and to exchange data electronically. Even with these efforts and campaigns stressing the desirability of buying American products, globalization continued to take its toll on the once dominant domestic fashion and textile manufacturing industries.

Economist Rivoli (2005) traced the journey of an inexpensive T-shirt in a globalized economy. The fiber was produced in Texas, sold to a manufacturer in China where the yarn was spun, the fabric knit, and the T-shirt sewn. The T-shirt was then printed with a design that would appeal to tourists in Florida, and thanks to then current labeling legislation (this is no longer possible) this final step, the printing, having been done in the United States, the seller could say it had been "manufactured in Florida." What technologies would have made this possible? These are highlighted in the text below. The cotton fiber would have been cultivated with machinery for growing, harvesting, and removing the fibers from the seeds. Then the fiber would be packaged and shipped by air or by sea to China.

Rivoli describes one of the factors leading to globalization of the fashion industry as being based on the character of the American textile industry (and I would add the domestic fashion manufacturing industry as well) as being an industry based on low wages and poor working conditions. In the United States, these industries constantly moved to escape unions that worked for higher wages and improved working conditions. The workers who performed these tasks in China would have been paid wages far lower than their American counterparts. China used equipment, probably bought from textile manufacturers in one of the industrialized countries such as the United States that no longer found it profitable to pay employees the prevailing wages to spin the yarn, knit the fabric, or cut the garment. By 2013, those workers would probably not have been in China, but in a country such as Bangladesh where wages were even lower.

The completed T-shirt was shipped to a company in Florida that had a high tech printing machine that completed the decoration of the garment. Finally the T-shirt then went to a tourist shop in a Florida resort. Throughout the process, the cooperating businesses would have kept in touch by electronic communications and funds would have been transferred though banks equipped to make and receive those bank exchanges electronically. When sold, the place of manufacture of the shirt was said to have been a company in Miami, Florida, which was responsible only for the final step in its manufacture: application of the printed design! Since Rivoli's book was written, this misleading labeling has become illegal and the garment would have been labeled as the product of the country where the steps preceding the addition of the embroidery were done.

The travels of the T-shirt may not have ended with its purchase in a drugstore in Fort Lauderdale. When its owner tired of the shirt it was probably donated to a thrift shop or charity where it may have been resold to American consumers or to the textile recycling industry where its ultimate fate could range from being made into wiping cloths or, if its quality was good enough, it could be shipped to a third world country for resale where it became a part of "world dress."

Global fashions

In her comprehensive exploration of "Globalization and Dress" in the *Berg Encyclopedia of World Dress and Fashion* (vol. 10, 252–63), Margaret Maynard (2010) identifies the factors that have created a climate that encourages the development of global trends: advertising, convenience and time saving, improved transport, free trade agreements, world media networks, and the Internet. Many of these factors are technological in nature or rely on technology for their success. Most have been discussed elsewhere in this book.

What began as a Paris-centered *haute couture* establishment spread to a multitude of worldwide centers from which contributions to fashion trends can be made. New designs are now shown in fashion shows or fashion weeks in almost all major metropolitan areas around the world. A search on the Internet for locations of fashion shows reveals not only how fashion has become a major economic factor worldwide, but also how those interested in fashion can follow the fashion news not only in Paris but also on a tablet or an I-phone in places such as Jakarta. Technology has facilitated the globalization of a fashion industry in which dress can be manufactured far from where it was designed. It can be purchased and worn in equally distant locations. Fashion ideas had once emerged from a few fashion centers that told the rest of the world what the next fashion trend was going to be. Electronic media technologies have made access to information about fashion trends worldwide.

Looking at relationships through illustrations

Traditional dress

Instances of local and traditional dress can be found Figure 14.2. Often they are used for special celebrations, such as this group of Indian women celebrating the Desert Festival. Although more modern technologies such as contemporary looms, sewing machines, and the like can be used to create traditional dress, the form and certain ornamentation would continue long-standing traditions.

World dress

What dress scholar Eicher *et al.* (2010: 52) calls world dress is seen in the example in Figure 14.3. Her definition of world dress is dress that is "commonly worn, high volume, for both men and women, some of which is gender and age

Figure 14.2 These Jaisalmer Indian women show examples of local and traditional dress (source: Shutterstock/gnomeandi)

Figure 14.3 Kenyan street child showing example of world dress (source: Andrew Aitchison/In Pictures/Corbis)

neutral." Some examples that she offers are business suits, long-sleeved shirts, jeans, trousers, T-shirts, and such accessories as baseball caps, athletic training shoes, and sandals. The example offered here is the ubiquitous blue jeans and T-shirt. What are the technologies required to create this example of dress worn by a young African boy?

Chapter 9 introduces synthetic dyes and cites the difficulties of synthesizing indigo dyestuffs. The denim jeans shown in this illustration have, thanks to globalization, become Eicher's world fashion. These jeans are blue in color. The first such garment came out of the California gold rush of 1849. Over its history this garment has been called "jeans," after a fabric very similar to the denim of which they were made, or "Levis" after their first manufacturer Levi Strauss, or "blue jeans" after the color they were usually dyed. In the beginning they were dyed blue with the natural dye indigo. Synthetic indigo was not available until 1897. Blue jeans became fashionable when they were adopted by young protesters against the Vietnam War and moved on to include high fashion designer jeans. By the 1970s they were an international fashion. Although natural indigo made a brief reappearance when some of the jeans dyed with synthetic indigo and other blue dyes did not perform well, because manufacturers had not yet learned the dyeing techniques to produce the best product, Balfour-Paul (2011: 87) points out that once this problem was resolved, this continuing universal fashion has assured the dominance of synthetic indigo and its importance in continuing this fashion.

What other technologies were required to produce this dress? The fabric of the jeans had to be woven and the T-shirt knitted. Both would have utilized technologies for spinning of yarns, perhaps from technologically produced synthetic fibers, such as polyester blended with natural fibers such as cotton. Weaving of the jeans fabric could have been done by any of a number of advanced loom technologies that carry the yarn across the loom with shuttles, gripers, rapiers, or jets of air. The aforementioned synthetic dyes most likely colored the finished fabric. The dyes could have been applied through any of a number of dyeing processes, the specific one chosen for its suitability for the fibers in the cloth and the construction of the fabric. After the denim fabric was woven, it could have been given some kind of special finish to enhance its performance, such as durable press, in order to make it resist wrinkling. This process could be applied either to the fabric or to the garment after its completion. The fabric, with or without the finish, next moved to a factory, where a pattern for the jeans would be used to guide the cutting of fabric pieces. The elements of the pattern would have been chosen, depending on the current fashionable lines for jeans – they might have narrow legs, a bell-bottom shape, or some other current style. Many layers of fabric would be cut at the same time and then move on to an assembly line in which not only the garment pieces but any other elements such as zipper closures, labels, or ornamental buttons, snaps, or rivets would be added. Each operator would have performed one operation then passed that piece along to the next. Sewing was done on powerful electric sewing machines. Finished garments were pressed with electric irons as needed.

The T-shirt fabrics would have been knitted on a weft knit jersey knitting machine, possibly from a yarn blended from cotton and polyester fibers or from 100 per cent cotton. The result would have been in the form of a fabric tube. If a color product is wanted, either the yarn or fabric would have been dyed. The sewing is minimal but does have to be used to attach sleeves, a neckband, and close up the shoulders. Other decorative or functional elements might be added such as pockets, decals, or embroidery, the latter two requiring their own specific technologies to be produced and applied to the garment.

15
ENVIRONMENTS INTERACT WITH TECHNOLOGIES
(20th and 21st centuries)

Chapters 15 and 16 can provide only a glimpse into the roles played by textiles introduced in the late twentieth and the twenty-first centuries. An enormous variety of new manufactured textiles came into being as a result of advances in the technologies for making fabrics in new ways. References that explore these fibers, fabrics, and fashions in depth are included in the Bibliography. The focus here will be on environments that affect dress and fashion. In some cases the environment is produced by technology. In other situations the environment motivates a response through dress that is technologically based. Nor can we ignore fashion and its connections to the technologies that flow from some of these technologically driven forms of dress.

Technologies that produce alterations in natural environments

While outer space technologies may engage the imagination, the more mundane technologies related to work and household space can change consumer dress preferences even more directly than space walks. Central heating, which eliminates the need for warmer clothes in winter, and air conditioning, which may negate the requirement for lighter-weight summer dress, are examples of influential technologies. After the widespread adoption of computers and cellular telephones, designers of handbags and briefcases felt obliged to create storage areas for these mobile devices.

People work and play in a variety of environments. Individuals may have to adapt to the natural environment or to working conditions that have been created through technologies that change environmental factors such as temperature, humidity, and lighting. In the twenty-first century, in developed countries in temperate climate zones, it is hard to envision a time when the entrance of winter cold and summer heat into homes cannot be eliminated. However, as Bryson (2011: 146) points out, "Keeping warm remained a challenge for most people right through the nineteenth century." The open fireplaces used in homes in earlier centuries were not very efficient providers of heat. Although various types of stoves that radiated heat inside buildings had been in use in some parts of the world, the replacement of open fireplaces by stoves, such as the cast iron Franklin stove of 1742, were major advances in the technology of home heating. This stove would have been heated with wood. But it only heated the room in which it was located and perhaps another room through which the stovepipe passed. It was only when coal-fueled boilers in house basements heated water that circulated through radiators throughout the buildings that central heating was possible. Although we might note that the Romans built indoor heating systems for warming the water in their community baths, they did not seem to heat their houses. Subsequently the central heating technologies improved, using fuels that were fed automatically to the burners or that forced hot air through ducts. We now take central heating for granted and rarely think about just how it is achieved unless we experience lengthy power interruptions.

In the 1920s, the popularity of motion pictures waned in the heat of summer, because hot stuffy theaters did not appeal to audiences. In 1925, Willis Carrier, who developed the first air conditioning system for business, convinced a Times Square movie theater to install air conditioning. Other theaters followed and many Americans first experienced air conditioning in movie theaters. Hotels, department stores, and business offices found air conditioning was good for business and increased productivity, but the air conditioned home arrived only after World War II. Initially the units were placed in windows in each room until technology for central air conditioning made cooling the entire house possible beginning in the 1970s.

Ubiquitous heated or cooled interior climates meant that it was no longer necessary to dress for indoor temperatures in the same way. No longer were cotton and linen banished in winter, because such fibers conducted heat away from the body, nor was wool relegated to moth repellent storage in summer and taken out when the temperatures fell, because wool is a poor conductor of heat and therefore provided better insulation to maintain body heat. Such issues were no longer a concern in those parts of the world where central heating and air conditioning were all but universal. Winter still required warmer clothing and summer cooler clothing when going out of doors, but wholesale changes of wardrobes from season to season were no longer obligatory. Furthermore, the availability of manufactured fibers made it possible to use fibers with specific characteristics that made them good or poor conductors of heat or that served to insulate against cold. See Table 10.1 in Chapter 10 for a summary of manufactured fibers and their most significant characteristics. Watkins (1995: 26) points out that thermal characteristics of dress can be altered, not only by choice of fiber but also by "yarn type, fabric type, fabric finish, garment design, and the way a garment is worn."

Natural environments motivate technological responses

Manufacturers of clothing for winter sports utilize the aforementioned textile characteristics to design and produce items of suitable dress. At the same time, fashion is never absent from what is worn. In snow boarding, for example, loosely fitted clothing had been favored, but by 2013 was being replaced by some snowboarders with more closely fitted styles. Proponents of each style engaged in heated debates online about which type of outfit was more "cool," a comment related not to climate but to fashion.

Outdoor activities that expose individuals to the sun can result in skin damage. Dress that provides protection against ultraviolet radiation is available, usually with an indication of Sun Protective Factor (SPF) rating. In these garments, fabric structure plays a major role. Fabrics are created in which the yarns are placed close together so that the ultraviolet light cannot pass through the cloth. Such garments are generally designed to prevent the sun from reaching skin. Most have long sleeves, high necks, and collars that can stand up to protect the back of the neck. Hats of various sizes and shapes that keep sun from the face have long been used to avoid sun exposure, as have eyeglasses treated with ultraviolet light shielding materials.

Some environments provide conditions conducive to growth of insect populations that can carry serious diseases. When work or recreation requires being outdoors, individuals have chosen to use a variety of textile protections against insect bites. This protection can come from fabric shields that are made into fine net structures that keep insects away from the skin. In this case, the shape of the garment has to be such that the fabric is far enough away from skin or the net fine enough that insects cannot manage to reach any bare skin to bite through it. Other dress for insect infested environments is sold that is made with fabrics treated with either insecticides that kill the insect or insect repellents that discourage insects from approaching. Many people who are active outdoors apply these products to their clothing by spraying them with an insecticide or repellent. Some of these spray applications claim to last through a number of launderings. Increasing numbers of retail merchants are selling apparel that has already been treated. Some Internet advertisements for such clothing indicate the treatment is effective for seventy launderings. As the range of some disease-carrying insects seems to be expanding as a result of climate change, interest in these types of dress is likely to grow.

Climate change motivates the fashion industry
to look at sustainability

Fletcher and Grose (2012) raise issues that anyone concerned about threats to
the environment cannot ignore. The authors see the need for transformation of
fashion products, fashion systems, and fashion design. Technology is involved in
all of these areas, either as a positive force or a contributor to problems related
to climate change. It is not possible to go beyond a few of the larger points that
bear consideration. In each of the aforementioned areas, having a positive impact
will require working toward less polluting, more efficient, and more respectful
solutions. The authors provide significant helpings of food for thought and
motivations for action throughout this book.

New technologies stimulate
designer adaptations

Consumers constantly carry electronic technology devices as they go about their
daily activities. Designers have recognized the need for providing ways to make
such personal items as cellular telephones, personal computers, iPads, and the
like both portable and usable. As a result, many utilitarian items of dress such as
handbags, backpacks, briefcases, and garments are now designed with space
for carrying and using these devices. Chapter 16 will examine the present and
potential future developments in dress that go beyond making carrying a personal
device convenient, but a search online in early 2014 for garments and accessories
that allow the user to have the device close at hand reveals some interesting
developments. Often handbags have specific compartments for cellular
telephones, but even more often the bag is advertised as having plenty of space
for the customer's cell phone without providing a designated space. By
comparison, larger devices such as I-pads of various sizes tend to have their
own space and the precise amount of space is advertised.

Space exploration

The development of dress for the exploration of space provides an excellent
example of the interaction of technology, dress, and fashion. The success of the
novels of Jules Verne in the second half of the nineteenth century was an
indication of the desire of humans to venture beyond the earth and into space.
The scientific and technological advances of the next century made the first
manned space flights and landing on the moon a reality in the 1960s. While the

vehicles in which the astronauts journeyed were made possible by one sort of technology, the dress of these men and women was the result of technologies developed by those working in an area that dress scholars call functional dress.

Watkins (2010) enumerates the hazards space travelers face: extreme temperatures; lack of atmospheric pressure that keeps tissues intact; and space debris and micro-meteoroids, which are small particles of rock traveling at rapid speeds. The astronauts also need to be prepared for internal cabin life, space walks outside the vehicle, and once the delivery technology permitted it, walking on the moon. Clearly this was an instance of new environments dictating the need for a completely new kind of dress based on an analysis of the conditions they would have to survive. The results drew on what was known about space in combination with skill in engineering textiles that have since been given the name high-performance or high-technology fabrics. Hongū and Phillips (1990) defined high-tech fibers as "those fibers produced using high technology processes and super fibers," as those that possess at least one or more outstanding properties. The former may be used in a wide variety of products including the new fibers as defined by the authors, which include both "high-tech" fibers and "super-fibers." High-tech fibers are produced using high technology processes – the term has nothing to do with their ultimate use but relates to their production. Super-fibers, on the other hand, have one or more outstanding properties (i.e. tensile strength). These properties determine where their use is most suitable for a variety of hazardous occupations. She explores important concepts that drive the protection of firefighters from extreme heat or scientists working in the Antarctic in extreme cold. Those who apply or clean up toxic chemicals must be provided with dress that prevents the workers' exposure to these materials. Much research and adaptation has led to changes in protective clothing worn by athletes participating in sports that include impacts on one or more parts of the body (Figures 12.5 and 12.6).

Susan Watkins (1995) leads the design student through the steps necessary in order to reach successful final garments that will provide the needed protections and allow the garments to function so that the ultimate wearers can accomplish the assigned tasks, whether it be to score a goal in a hockey game, or fight a fire. The body of that firefighter needs to be protected in extreme fire conditions, while his or her suit is flexible enough to permit that firefighter to climb a ladder. In some cases, technology provides answers to such problems through high-tech heat-resistant textile or high-strength fibers. But in all cases the thorough preliminary research and analyses are crucial to a successful design. Figure 15.1 provides an illustration of a space suit with the various parts and their functions labeled.

Fashion designers are said to be especially sensitive to the *Zeit geist* or spirit of the times as they create designs that seem especially appropriate for the era in which they are working. Often this sensitivity appears in reflections of current

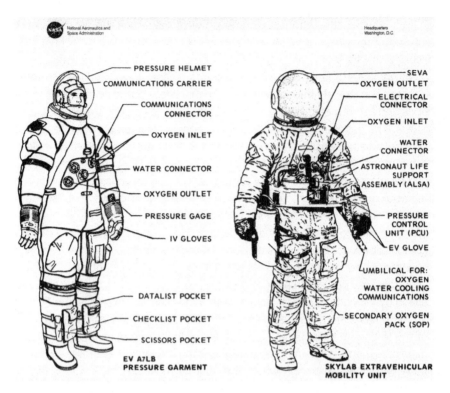

Figure 15.1 The various functions of this space suit are described by the labels indicating various parts of the garment (source: NASA)

events. This was true of those designers who drew inspiration from the space race of the 1960s, as they produced designs ranging from headwear that derived from plastic space helmets to metallic fiber fabric dresses and accessories, and the simplified ornamentation and straight, clean lines of short mini dresses.

The space suit is the ultimate example of dress designed to adapt to environmental conditions. The reader who looks at this illustration (provided by NASA (National Aeronautics and Space Administration)) and reads the printed text that describes the functions of each portion of the garment, will come away with a clearer understanding of how the garment creates its own environment that allows the wearer to function, indeed to survive, in space, a place in which humans have not yet evolved to live and work.

16
NEW TECHNOLOGICAL FRONTIERS FOR DRESS AND FASHION
(21st century)

For the most part, the associations among dress, fashion, and technology prior to the twenty-first century have been related either to the textiles from which dress is made or the techniques used to obtain or construct functional or fashionable dress. Both textiles and methods of fabrication of dress will continue to be related to dress and fashion in the future and appear to some extent in this chapter. Only rarely, though, can new technology itself be said to have served as an obvious inspiration to those who design and/or sell functional or fashionable dress.

Technology incorporated into dress

Fitted dress styles follow the contours of the body, and must have openings that allow the garment to cross over at least some areas of the body. But to achieve the desired appearance, open areas must include a device that closes as well as opens the area. Throughout history, closures have evolved as styles required them or as technologies were invented. What appear to be buttons used as closures can be found in well-documented archeological sites from the Middle Ages. Metal hooks and eyes came later and are still in use.

Other closures such as zippers and Velcro© developed as the technologies behind their design became available. Zippers began as metal teeth mounted on fabric strips that could be opened and closed by a sliding device that brought the teeth together.

Trousers with a zippered fly were adopted in the mid-1930s when the British Prince of Wales, a fashion leader, took up the style. In the 1930s, designers Charles James and Elsa Schiaparelli incorporated these devices, James in a

Figure 16.1 The earliest zipper manufacturers provided information to their customers on how to install this new device (source: author's image)

spiral effect around one of his gowns and Schiaparelli in some of her couture dresses and accessories. Both placed them in locations that made them a design focus. Since then other designers have also made zippers a design feature. As synthetic materials became available, nylon replaced the metal teeth in zippers, making a closure that is smaller and more easily hidden.

Velcro is an example of a technology that comes from bio-mimicry, the copying of something found in nature. This closure is based on the structure of burrs caught in the clothing of Swiss engineer George de Mestral, who patented the product in 1955. The closure is made of two pieces, one with strong fiber hooks and the other with equally strong fiber loops. When one piece is placed over the other, the hooks and loops cling together, the hooks catching the loops. If very strong fibers, such as nylon or polyester, are used the attachment is very strong. Use of Velcro in space flights helped to bring it to public attention and it now appears in a wide variety of types of dress such as shoes, handbags, and garments.

Two examples of technologically supported fashion that became fads are mood rings or other similar jewelry, and shoes with LED (Light-Emitting Diodes) lights. Mood rings were popular in the 1970s when the ring was supposed to be able to diagnose the mood or emotions of the wearer by changes in color. This jewelry is made of a clear glass or quartz shell filled with thermotropic liquid crystals held against the body. This liquid changes color in response to changes in temperature. The crystals reflect different light wavelengths at different temperatures. At normal resting body temperature, the ring appears to be blue or green. When the wearer becomes excited or tense, blood flow from the skin moves to internal organs causing cooling that changes the color to yellow. The manufacturers provided customers with a list of colors to which the ring may change and the mood state each color reflects. For example, blue-violet was described as happy and romantic, blue as calm and relaxed, and yellow as tense and excited. Black indicated cold temperature or a damaged ring.

Another example of technology being incorporated into an item of dress is a type of athletic shoe first marketed for children in 1992. The shoes had LED lights incorporated into the soles. The lights are produced by the movement of electrons in a semiconductor, which is a substance able to conduct electricity under certain conditions. A switch activated the lights. LA Gear introduced these shoes, which quickly became tremendously popular among children, the company selling over five million pairs a year of the "LA Lights" in the 1990s. After making shoes for children, the company followed with those for runners. This made those running after dark more visible – a safety feature. Every time the heel hit the ground, the shoe lighted. Basketball players could buy shoes that lighted when the player left the ground. Although they can still be bought, the fad for such shoes passed. Now LED lights have become a tool for many of the designers who are interested in enhanced fashion.

Seymour's analysis of "Fashionable Technology"

Sabine Seymour, CEO and Chief Creative Officer of Moondial, a company that consults on fashionable technology, analyses fashionable technology in a book

Figure 16.2 Some designers using new technologies creatively incorporated LED lights into their designs (source: Boris Roessler/dpa/Corbis)

of the same title. Her definition of fashionable technology is ". . . the intersection of design, fashion, science, and technology" (Seymour, 2009: 12). She argues that through fashionable technology, the functions of clothing can be enhanced and new functions defined. Her insightful analysis provides a useful framework for viewing these developments.

Seymour assigns items of dress that incorporate technology a place on a range, extending from expressiveness at one end to functionality at the other. For example, high fashion items may be placed at the expressive end of the range, while dress for specific types of work may rest at the functionality end of the scale. Other items may occupy a place where expressiveness and functionality overlap. How technology is incorporated into dress can vary also, with some items being held in the hand, some being integrated into dress or into its elements such as textiles, and some can even be implanted into the wearer's body. In many of the technologies that are part of dress in the twenty-first century, information must be gathered from the wearer or from the environment. Seymour calls this "input." In order to obtain the needed information, sensing devices do the gathering. Some are part of textiles, while others are sensors placed so as to gather data from the body of the wearer or from the environment. Most often, microprocessors analyze the data. "Output" results from the five senses: touch, sound, vision, scent, and taste and can be expressed through such means as heat sensitive inks that become visible or scent capsules that present an aroma (Seymour, 2009).

The kinds of materials used include electronic textiles with embedded electronic connectors, very fine microfibers, nanofiber technology that utilizes even finer fibers with a diameter of less than one micron, and biomimetry. Energy sources may be required, and those commonly used are batteries or alternative power generation such as solar energy.

Recent developments in a wide range of technical fields have emerged as stimuli to new styles. Computers are built into jackets, solar panels mounted on outerwear can store energy to recharge a mobile phone, or clothes for outdoor sports can adapt to rising or falling temperatures.

Further technological advances in functional dress

Functional dress has been discussed in Chapters 12, 13, and 15 in relation to sports, space, and protective dress. To these examples, one can add dress that plays a role in health care. Dress scholar Bradley Quinn has explored the potential directions of textiles and advanced technology in a number of books and articles. Quinn (2012: 6–9) summarizes present and potential uses of textiles with medical applications in a chapter he titles "Vital Signs." Not only do these textiles function to deliver medications, monitor vital signs, promote healing, and replace damaged tissue, but they are designed to provide patients with positive feelings through products that "look normal . . . and allow them to see themselves as well rather than sick." Quinn (2010: 85) also calls attention to products widely used that are textile based, but that the public often does not think of as either medical or textile (e.g. the nicotine patch). Transdermal (through the skin) application of medication is widely used and often is applied via a textile patch. All of these items of dress and others would fall at the functionality end of Seymour's range of fashionable technology.

A number of accessories with technological capabilities have been successfully marketed, are being tested, or are under development. Accessories that serve one or more purposes may be adopted more quickly than garments with imbedded technology. When a customer buys a garment, he or she is not likely to wear it every day. Accessories are often worn frequently if not daily, so the cost of the investment in the item may seem more reasonable. Garments generally have to be cleaned regularly; accessories rarely require the same level of maintenance as garments.

For example, the Casio watch incorporates the technology necessary to make one model "the world's smallest MP player" and another will display

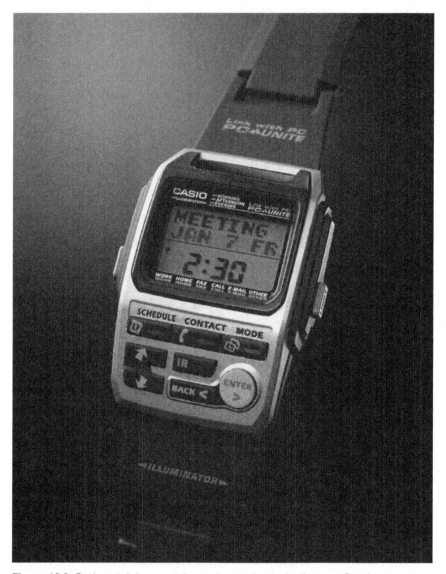

Figure 16.3 Casio watch incorporating various technologies (source: Getty)

contacts, calendars, and other data that has been downloaded from the wearer's computer with infrared technology. Google glass, under development and trial, is "a wearable Android-powered computer built into spectacle frames." It can take photographs, send messages from dictation, and check out directions.

High-tech bracelets, smart phone bracelets, bracelet mobile phones, and smart watches can all be found on the Internet.

Figure 16.4 The Google Glass platform is worn on a device placed as eyeglasses but without lenses. Described variously as a wearable computer or smart phone, its functions, sure to be expanded in the future, are accomplished through a small glass screen. The device allows voice-controlled photography, provides digital information, pairs with smart phones, and continues to develop a line of apps for use on the device (source: Shutterstock/ Helga Esteb)

The expressive end of the range

As he was writing in 2012, Quinn acknowledged that only a few of the innovations he describes had, at that point, been embraced by the fashion industry. Nevertheless, his expectation is that there will be a time when fashion and wearable technology will merge. The picture he and other authors paint of the potential for technologically sophisticated textiles, dress, and fashion is worth examining. At the same time there are cautionary voices, uncertain about the ability of the fashion industry to adapt to what Gale and Kaur (2004: 188–91) see as "a new context for textiles and fashion." Questions can be raised about the fashion industry with its business model of the celebration of creative new products accepted broadly, but then put aside in order to follow a new design. In the past, the technologies associated with fashion products have been tools to enable manufacture of the raw material. In what ways can the incorporation of technology into dress conform to the fashion model? Or is the result destined to be a separation between functional dress and expressive dress? Will those technologies that serve the aesthetics of dress and those that make it possible for dress to perform a practical function merge or go their separate ways?

Past, present, and future technologies have and will serve to assist the creator of dress, whether that creator is using the simplest of tools or the most complex. It may expand his or her options or limit them. Technology has enabled the accomplishment of specific objectives – for example, the creation of a flame resistant garment for a sleeping child or the metal structure of the hoop that supported the lavish ball gowns conspicuously displaying the wealth of Victorian families. Over the centuries in many parts of the world the production of dress has moved from the home to production in a factory setting. Often that factory may be far from the store in which it will be purchased.

One result of the changes in the construction of the dress we buy and wear is the development of the career of the fashion designer and the ways that role was incorporated into the manufacturing process. With the enormous advances in technology taking place in the twenty-first century, technology can be a tool for the designer. Will technology also serve to lead designers in new creative directions? Technology in 2014 is not just a tool to accomplish work such as pattern drafting. Its partisans see the new technologies as a potential source of inspiration.

A number of authors have introduced some of the pioneering work and the designers doing that work to readers in books that focus on these new directions in fashion design. Among the fashion designers and design firms often singled out for attention, are those whose names would be familiar to followers of international fashion. Whenever fashionable technology is discussed, the name of British designer Hussein Chalayan is sure to come up. One of the earliest designers to embrace the potential of wearable technology, he collaborated with

Moritz Waldemeyer (interactive design expert) in 2008 to create dresses that can, and did when shown, project a moving image. Subsequently, the same team projected laser beams in such a way as to create the illusion that the wearer was dressed in "a starburst of radiating lights" (Quinn, 2012: 42).

Famed Japanese designer Issey Miyake is described as "passionate about technology" (Clarke and Harris, 2010: 94–5). He is known for his collaborations with experts with highly developed technological skills in textile design. He has utilized advanced computerized textile equipment for knitting. One example of the results of his experimentation in the 2001/2002 season was a garment in which the wearer could choose to put her arms or legs through any of a number of different openings placed at different locations on a garment, thereby creating any of a number of different effects.

The technologies utilized in collections by Maison Martin Margiela, a Belgian fashion house known for its deconstructionist styles, are not electronic, but instead utilize craft techniques in their construction while relying on recycling methods that allow the deconstruction of diverse objects such as soccer balls, rubber bands, and umbrellas. According to San Martin (2010: 102), the resulting pieces from 2008 are as high quality as the conventional fabric pieces of the rest of the collection.

Fashion label Prada has consistently produced a number of designs utilizing new technology that would fall at the expressiveness end of Seymour's range of fashionable technology. Among the tools used to achieve the characteristically exciting and wearable Prada designs are digital printing, laser cutting, and computer animation. Digital-printed designs in some models derived from feather patterns. Yet another reproduced the pattern of python skin.

Searching on the Internet for technologically enhanced products would tend to indicate that many of the items featured are special occasion or special use items. An interested web browser can find wedding dresses, children's costumes, footwear for athletes, and accessories that complement the electronic gear so many now carry with them.

One of the areas that has been getting a great deal of attention in the fashion world in 2014 is 3-D printing, a technology in which the printing machine is programmed to produce a particular design of some actual item of dress. One contestant on the Project Runway show produced belts to use with his design. Shoes were one of the first 3-D printed items to be publicized. A fashion show in early 2014 showed only garments made with 3-D printing and the underwear worn by models was also created with the 3-D printer. The items made at that time were described as "not super thin" and the resulting products are not delicate or soft. Discussion among those enthusiastic about the future of this technology tends to make the point that its speed and ability to change rapidly from one style or form to another is just what fashion is all about.

Figure 16.5 A variety of dress products have been produced using 3-D printing technology. Opportunities to see what is being done come through shows such as this 3-D Print Show in Paris in November 2013 (source: Getty)

The issues that will determine whether technology becomes a driving force in fashion are many and complex. Economic factors will play a role. High-tech fibers have high development costs, so for those costs to be justified these materials must go into mass production. If their price is high, will consumers be willing to pay for innovations of this kind? How resistant will consumers used to dress produced in low wage countries and sold for relatively low cost be to paying the costs of technologically enhanced products? Is the manufacturing complex agile enough to adapt to needed changes quickly and easily enough to satisfy a public hungry for fashion change?

In the end, the designers of the future will probably be instrumental in deciding the directions in which mainstream fashion will move. But these designers are likely to develop attitudes they encounter and use skills acquired during their training. Some informal inquiries addressed to colleagues teaching in design-related programs have indicated that the level of study and experience provided for undergraduate design students is highly variable. Some institutions where designers are educated are already incorporating work with advanced technology, while others do not even introduce design students to advanced technologies in basic textile classes.

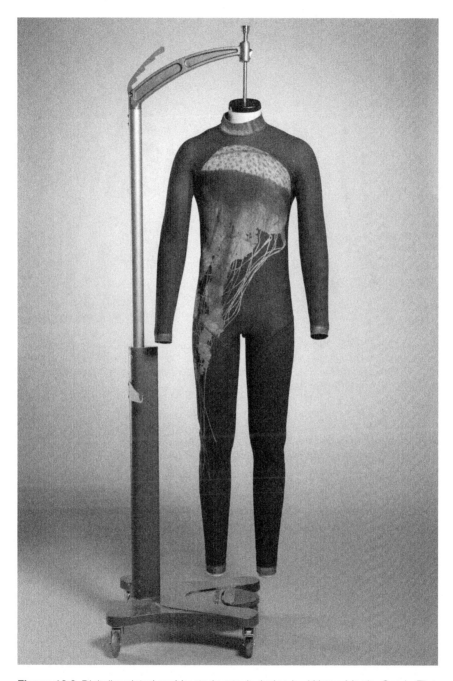

Figure 16.6 Digitally printed and heated wetsuit design by Kristen Morris, Sandy Flint, and Huiju Park at Cornell University (photograph by Shai Eynav)

Figure 16.7 Fashion design students are introduced to new technologies that can stimulate students' creativity, as can be seen in this Cornell University Fashion Design Student Exhibition: *Laser Cut Surfaces for Fashion Design* (photograph provided by and photographed by Professor Anita Racine)

It is frustrating to end this exploration of the interweaving of technology, dress, and fashion at a time when so much is yet to come. Sara Fishco, in an interview about a radio documentary she did for Studio 360 on National Public Radio that she called Culture shock: 1913, suggested that the present time might be comparable to the birth of Modernism in the arts and public life in 1913. Just as it was difficult for the consumers of culture to adapt to the advent of Modernism in the graphic arts, in music, dance, literature, and the theater, it may also be a challenge for consumers and producers of fashion to adapt to a new era that is coming through technology. But as we look back today to the shocking new developments in the arts in 1913, adapt we did!

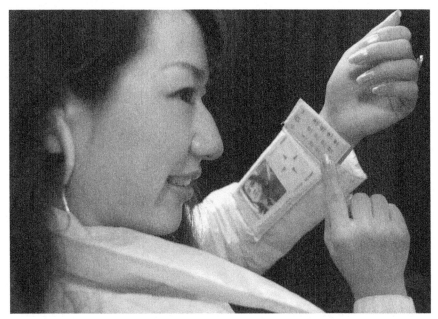

Figure 16.8 Incorporation of technology into dress is exemplified by this "Wearable PC" from Japan, produced by the Pioneer Corporation (source: Eynav)

BIBLIOGRAPHY

Abecassis-Moedas, Céline (2010) 'Snapshot: IT in the clothing industry', in Joanne
   Eicher (ed.), *Berg Encyclopedia of World Dress and Fashion*, vol. 8, The United States
   and Canada, Oxford: Berg Publishers, p. 110.
AF Encyclopedia of Textiles (1972) 2nd edition, Englewood Cliffs NJ, Prentice-Hall Inc.
Allgrove-McDowell, Joan (2003) 'Ancient Egypt, 5000–322 BC', in David Jenkins (ed.),
   The Cambridge History of Western Textiles, vol. 1, Cambridge: Cambridge University
   Press, pp. 30–6.
American Heritage Dictionary (1992) New York: Houghton Mifflin Company.
Anawalt, Patricia (2007) *The World Wide History of Dress*, New York: Thames & Hudson,
   pp. 81–6.
Angeloglou, Maggie (1970) *A History of Make-up*, New York: The Macmillan Company.
Anspach, Karlyne (1967) *The Why of Fashion*, Ames IA: Iowa State University Press,
   p. xiii.
Armstrong, Nancy (1978) *The Book of Fans*, New York: Mayflower Books Inc.
Arnold, Janet (1988) *Queen Elizabeth's Wardrobe Unlock'd: The inventories of the
   wardrobe prepared in July 1600*, Leeds: Maney.
Ashton, T S (1968) *The Industrial Revolution: 1760–1830*, Oxford: Oxford University
   Press.
Bailey, Brian (1998) *The Luddite Rebellion*, New York: New York University Press.
Balfour-Paul, Jenny (2011) *Indigo: Egyptian mummies to blue jeans*, London: British
   Museum Press.
Bandi, Hans-Georg *et al.* (1961) *The Art of the Stone Age*, New York: Crown Publishers
   Inc.
Barber, Elizabeth (1991) *Prehistoric Textiles*, Princeton NJ: Princeton University Press.
Barber, Elizabeth (1994) *Women's Work: The first 20,000 years*, New York and London:
   W W Norton & Co Inc.
Basinger, Jeanine (1993) *A Woman's View: How Hollywood spoke to women,
   1930–1960*, New York: Alfred A. Knopf.
Baumgarten, Linda (2002) *What Clothes Reveal*, Williamsburg VA: The Colonial
   Williamsburg Foundation.
Beaton, C and Buckland, G (1975) *The Magic Image: The genius of photography from
   1839 to the present day*, New York: Oxford University Press.
Beetham, Margaret (1996) *A Magazine of her Own? Domesticity and desire in the
   woman's magazine, 1800–1914*, London and New York: Routledge.
Belfanti, Carlos (2008) 'Was fashion a European invention?' *Journal of Global History*,
   3: 3.
Bellenir, Karen, ed. (2007) *Cosmetic and Reconstructive Surgery Sourcebook*, 2nd
   edition, Detroit MI: Omnographics.

Benn, Charles (2002) *China's Golden Age: Everyday life in the Tang Dynasty*, New York: Oxford University Press, pp. 97–118.

Berg, Maxine and Hudson, Pat (1992) 'Rehabilitating the Industrial Revolution', *Economic History Review*, 45: 1.

Bernstein, William J (2008) *A Splendid Exchange: How trade shaped the world*, New York: Atlantic Monthly Press.

Blumin, S M (1994) *The Emergence of the Middle Class: Social experience in the American city, 1960–1900*, Cambridge: Cambridge University Press.

Boulnois, Luce (2004) *Silk Road: Monks, warriors and merchants on the Silk Road*, Helen Loveday (trans.), New York: W W Norton & Co Inc.

Braddock Clarke, Sarah E and Harris, Jane (2008) *Digital Visions for Fashion + Textiles*, New York: Thames & Hudson.

Braddock Clarke, Sarah E and Harris, Jane (2012) *Digital Visions for Fashion + Textiles: Made in code*, New York: Thames & Hudson.

Brydon, Anne and Neissen, Sandra (eds) (1998) *Consuming Fashion*, New York: Oxford University Press.

Bryson, Bill (2011) *At Home: A short history of private life*, New York: Anchor Books, pp. 146–8.

Bull, Stephen (2010) *Photography*, New York: Routledge.

Bumke, Joachim (1991) *Courtly Culture and Society in the High Middle Ages*, Thomas Dunlap (trans.), Berkeley CA: University of California Press.

Burke, James (1978) *Connections*, Boston MA: Little, Brown & Company.

Bushman, Richard L (1992) *The Refinement of America*, New York: Alfred A. Knopf.

Cahill, Suzanne E (1999) 'Our women are acting like foreigners' wives', in Valerie Steele and John S. Major (eds), *China Chic: East meets West*, New Haven CT: Yale University Press, pp. 103–17.

Cannon, Aubrey (1998) 'The cultural and historical contexts of fashion', in Anne Brydon and Sandra Neisson (eds), *Consuming Fashion: Adorning the transnational body*, United States and Canada, Oxford: Berg Publishers.

Carcopino, Jerome (1940) *Daily Life in Ancient Rome*, New Haven CT: Yale University Press.

Chapman, Stanley (2003) 'Hosiery and knitwear in the twentieth century', in David Jenkins (ed.), *The Cambridge History of Western Textiles*, vol. II, Cambridge: Cambridge University Press, p. 1028.

Clarkson, Leslie (2003) 'The linen industry in early modern Europe', in David Jenkins (ed.), *The Cambridge History of Western Textiles*, vol. I, Cambridge: Cambridge University Press, pp. 473–92.

Coe, Brian (1977) *The Birth of Photography*, New York: Taplinger Publishing Co.

Collier, Billie, Bide, Martin, and Tortora, Phyllis (2009) *Understanding Textiles*, Saddle River NJ: Pearson/Prentice Hall.

Cosgrove, Bronwyn (2007) *Made for Each Other: Fashion and the Academy Awards*, New York: Bloomsbury USA.

Craik, Jennifer (1944) *The Face of Fashion*, London and New York: Routledge.

Croom, A T (2002) *Roman Clothing and Fashion*, Charleston, SC: Tempus.

Crouch, Tom D (2003) *Wings*, New York: W W Norton & Co Inc.

Cumming, Valerie, Cunnington, C W, and Cunnington, P E (2010) *The Dictionary of Fashion History*, United States and Canada, Oxford: Berg Publishers.

Cunnington, C Willett and Cunnington, Phillis (1970) *Handbook of English Costume in the 19th Century*, Boston MA: Plays Inc.

Cunnington, C Willett, Cunnington, Phillis, and Beard, Charles (1972) *A Dictionary of English Costume*, London: Adam & Charles Black.

Cunnington, C Willett and Cunnington, Phillis (1992) *The History of Underclothes*, New York: Dover Publications Inc.

Cunnington, Phillis and Mansfield, Alan (1969) *English Costume for Sport and Outdoor Recreation: From the sixteenth to the nineteenth centuries*, New York: Barnes & Noble.

Curry, A (2012) 'Caesar's Gallic outpost', *Archeology*, 12 February.

Curtin, Philip D (1984) *Cross Cultural Trade in World History*, New York: Cambridge University Press.

Davenport, Millia (1948) *The Book of Costume*, New York: Crown Publishers Inc.

Dhamija, Jasleen (1989) *Handwoven Fabrics of India*, Middletown NJ: Grantha Corp.

Dhamija, Jasleen (2005) 'Asia, Central, history of dress', in Valerie Steel (ed.), *Encyclopedia of Clothing and Fashion,* vol. 1, New York: Thomson Gale, pp. 85–92.

Diamanti, Joyce (2003) 'Beads, trade, and cultural change', in James W. Lanktom, *A Bead Timeline*, vol. 1, Prehistory to 1200 CE, Washington DC: The Bead Society of Greater Washington, p. 13.

Dickerson, Kitty (2010) 'Textile and apparel industries at the turn of the millennium', in Joanne Eicher (ed.), *Berg Encyclopedia of World Dress and Fashion*, vol. 3, United States and Canada, Oxford: Berg Publishers, pp. 104–9.

Dickson, Carol Anne (2010), 'The pattern industry', in Joanne Eicher (ed.), *Berg Encyclopedia of World Dress and Fashion*, vol. 3, United States and Canada, Oxford: Berg Publishers, pp. 80–6.

Dixon, Wheeler Winston and Foster, Gwendolyn Audry (2008) *A Short History of Film*, New Brunswick NJ: Rutgers University Press.

Dreusedow, Jean (1965) 'Aside and astride: A history of ladies' riding apparel', in Alexander Mackay Smith, Jean Druesedow, and Thomas Ryder (eds), *Man and the Horse*, New York: Metropolitan Museum of Art, pp. 58–92.

Dubin, Lois Sherr (2009), *The History of Beads*, New York: Abrams.

Earnshaw, Pat (1994) *The Identification of Lace*, Princes Risborough UK: Shire Publications, pp. 7–25.

Egan, Geoff and Pritchard, Frances (2002) *Dress Accessories: Medieval finds from excavations in London*, London: Stationary Office Books.

Eicher, J B and Roach-Higgins, M E (1992) 'Describing dress: A system of classifying and defining', in R Barnes and Joanne Eicher (eds.), *Dress and Gender: Making and Meaning in Cultural Context*, United States and Canada, Oxford: Berg Publishers, reprinted in 1993 paperback, pp. 8–28.

Eicher, Joanne B, Evenson, Sandra Lee, and Lutz, Hazel A (2010) *The Visible Self: Global perspectives on dress, culture, and society*, 3rd edition, New York: Fairchild Publications Inc.

Ellwood, Wayne (2011) *The No-nonsense Guide to Globalization*, 3rd edition, UK: New Internationalist™ Publications Ltd.

Encyclopedia of American Fabrics (eds) (1972) Englewood Cliffs NJ: Prentice Hall, Inc.

Encyclopedia of Textiles, see *AF Encyclopedia of Textiles*.

Evans, Caroline (2011) 'The Walkies: Early French fashion shows as a cinema of attractions', in Adrienne Munich (ed.), *Fashion in Film*, Bloomington IN: Bloomington University Press, pp. 110–34.

Fagan, Brian (2010) *Cro-Magnon*, New York: Bloomsbury Press.

Fairservis, Walter A (1971) *Costumes of the East*, Riverside CT: Chatham Press Inc.

Feder, Kenneth L (2010) *The Past in Perspective*, New York: Oxford University Press, p. 195.

Feltwell, John (1990) *The Story of Silk*, New York: St Martin's Press.

Fenichell, Stephen (1996) *Plastic: The making of a synthetic century*, New York: Harper Collins Publishers.

Finkelstein, Norman H (2008) *Plastics*, New York: Marshall Cavendish.

Fletcher, Kate and Grosem, Lynda (2012) *Fashion and Sustainability*, London: Lawrence King Publishing Ltd.

Fowler, Brenda (2000) *ICEMAN: Uncovering the life and times of a prehistoric man found in an Alpine Glacier*, New York: Random House.

Freedman, Russell (1965) *Jules Verne: Portrait of a prophet*, Harrison NY: Holiday House.

Gale, Colin and Kaur, Jasbir (2004) *Fashion and Textiles: An overview*, United States and Canada, Oxford: Berg Publishers.

Genova, Aneta (2012) *Accessory Design*, New York: Fairchild Publications Inc.

Gernsheimer, T R (1984) 'The role of shell in Mesopotamia: Evidence for trade exchange with Oman and the Indus Valley', *Paleorient*, 10: 61.

Gies, Frances (1990) *Life in a Medieval Village*, New York: Harper & Row.

Gies, Frances (1994) *Cathedral, Forge, and Medieval Technology and Invention in the Middle Ages*, New York: Harper Collins Publishers.

Gilman, Sander L (1999) *Making the Body Beautiful: A cultural history of aesthetic surgery*, Princeton NJ: Princeton University Press.

Ginsburg, Madeleine (1990) *The Hat: Trends and Traditions*, New York: Barron's, pp. 64–71.

Green, Nancy L (1997) *Ready to Wear Ready to Work: A century of industry and immigrants in Paris and New York*, Durham NC: Duke University Press.

Greenfield, Amy Butler (2005) *A Perfect Red*, New York: Harper Collins Publishers.

Gundle, Stephen (2003) *Glamour*, Oxford: Oxford University Press.

Gustavson, Todd (2009) *Camera: A History of photography from daguerrotype to digital*, New York: Sterling Publishing Co Inc.

Haiken, Elizabeth (1999) *Venus Envy: A history of cosmetic surgery*, Baltimore MD: Johns Hopkins University Press.

Hall-Duncan, N (1979) *The History of Fashion Photography*, Grand Rapids MI: Alpine Book Company.

Hansen, Waldemar (1972) *The Peacock Throne: The drama of Mogul India*, New York: Holt, Rinehart & Winston.

Harmsworth, Alfred Charles William (1904) *Automobiles and Automobile Driving*, London: Longmans Green & Co.

Harrison, Martin (1991) *Appearances: Fashion photography since 1915*, London: Cape.

Heller, Sarah-Grace (2007) *Fashion in Medieval France*, Rochester NY: D S Brewer.

Herlihy, David (1990) *Opera Muliebria: Women and work in Medieval Europe*, Philadelphia: Temple University Press.

Hibbert, C (1975) *Daily Life in Victorian England*, New York: American Heritage Publishing Co.

Hicks, Peter (2010) *Documenting the Industrial Revolution*, New York: Rosen Publishing Group Inc.

Hollander, Anne (1994) *Sex and Suits*, New York: Alfred Knopf, p. 72.

Hongu, Tatsuya and Phillips, Glyn O (1990) *New Fibers*, New York: Ellis Horwood.

Horn, Marilyn J and Gurel, Lois M (1881) *The Second Skin: An interdisciplinary study of Clothing*, Boston MA: Houghton Mifflin Company.

Jackson, Kenneth T (1985) *Crabgrass Frontier: The suburbanization of the United States*, New York: Oxford University Press.

Kawamura, Yuniya (2005) *Fashion-ology*, United States and Canada, Oxford: Berg Publishers, pp 26–37.

Kelly, Francis M and Schwabe, Randolph (2002) *European Costume and Fashion: 1490–1790*, New York: Dover Publications Inc.

Kratz, Anne (1989) *Lace: History and fashion*, New York: Rizzoli.

Lee, Suzanne (2005) *Fashioning the Future: Tomorrow's wardrobe*, London: Thames & Hudson.

Lemire, Beverly (2003) 'Fashioning cottons: Asian trade, domestic industry and consumer demand', in David Jenkins (ed.), The *Cambridge History of Western Textiles*, Cambridge: Cambridge University Press, p. 493.

Levey, Santina (2003) 'Machine-made lace: The industrial revolution and after', in David Jenkins (ed.), *The Cambridge History of Western Textiles*, Cambridge: Cambridge University Press, pp. 846–59.

Levin, Eric (ed.) (2001) *Styles of the Stars*, New York: People Books.

Lloyd, J D (ed.) (2003) *Body Piercing and Tattoos*, Farmington Hills MI: Greenhaven Press.

Lord, Walter (1965) *The Good Years*, New York: Bantam Pathfinder Edition, p. 108.

Loveday, Helen, Wannell, Bruce, Baumer, Christoph, and Omrsni, Bijan (2005), *Iran: Persia: Ancient and Modern*, New York: W W Norton and Co Inc.

Lyons, Martyn (2011) *Books: A living history*, Los Angeles CA: J. Paul Getty Museum.

Macy, Sue (2011) *Wheels of Change*, Washington DC: National Geographic Society.

Mann, Charles C (2011) *1493: Uncovering the New World Columbus created*, New York: Alfred Knopf.

Maskiell, Michelle (2002) 'Consuming Kashmir: Shawls and Empire, 1500–2000', *Journal of World History*, 3: 1.

Mastai, Marie-Louise d'Orange (1981) *Jewelry*, Washington DC: Smithsonian Institution.

Maynard, Margaret (2010) 'Globalization and dress', in Joanne Eicher (ed.), *Berg Encyclopedia of World Dress and Fashion*, vol. 10, United States and Canada, Oxford: Berg Publishers, pp. 252–63.

McCaulay, David (1983) *The Mill*, Boston MA: Houghton Mifflin Company.

McComb, David G (2004) *Sports: An illustrated history*, New York: Oxford University Press.

McCracken, David (1988) *Culture and Consumption*, Bloomington IN: Indiana University Press.

McKay Smith, Alexander (1965) 'The evolution of riding and its influence on equestrian costume', in Alexander McKay Smith, Jean R. Dreusedow, and Thomas Ryder (eds), *Man and the Horse: An illustrated history of equestrian apparel*, New York and Oxford: Oxford University Press, pp. 11–55.

McKendrick, Neil, Brewer, John, and Plumb, J H (1982) *The Birth of Consumer Society: The commercialization of eighteenth-century England*, Bloomington IN: Indiana University Press.

Meikle, Jeffrey I (1995) *American Plastic: Cultural history*, New Brunswick NJ: Rutgers University Press.

Mellars, Paul (1994) 'The Upper Paleolithic Revolution', in Barry Cunliffe (ed.), *The Oxford Illustrated History of Prehistoric Europe*, New York and Oxford: Oxford University Press, pp. 50–66.

Meltzer, Marisa (2013) 'A Prom Night Inspired by Oscar', *New York Times,* April 14, 2013, http://www.nytimes.com/ref/membercenter/nytarchive.html [accessed: 14 November, 2014].

Mills, Wright C (1956) *White Collar: The American middle classes*, New York: Oxford University Press.

Mithen, Steven J (1994) 'The Mesolithic Era', in Barry Cunliffe (ed.), *The Oxford Illustrated History of Prehistoric Europe*, Oxford: Oxford University Press, pp. 88–9.

Mott, Frank L (1930) *American Magazines, 1745–1860*, vol. I, Cambridge MA: Harvard University Press.

Munich, Adrienne (2011) *Fashion in Film*, Bloomington IN: Bloomington University Press.

Munro, John H (2003) 'Medieval woolens', in David Jenkins (ed.), *The Cambridge History of Western Textiles*, vol. I, Cambridge: Cambridge University Press.

Munro, John H (2010) 'Medieval woolens: Textiles, textile technology and industrial organization, c. 800–1500', in David Jenkins (ed.), *The Cambridge History of Western Textiles*, vol. 1, Cambridge: Cambridge University Press.

Mussarelli, Maria Giuseppina (2011) 'Sumptuous shoes', in Giorgio Riello and Peter McNeil (eds), *Shoes: A history from sandals to sneakers*, New York: Berg Bloomsbury, pp. 50–75.

Muthesius, Anna (2003) 'Silk in the medieval world', in David Jenkins (ed.), *The Cambridge History of Western Textiles*, vol. I, Cambridge: Cambridge University Press.

Neissen, Sandra and Leshkowich, Ann Marie (eds) (2005) *Re-Orienting Fashion*, New York: Oxford University Press.

Nevenson, J L (1967) 'Origin and early history of the fashion plate', *Museum and Technology Bulletin*, No. 250, Pater 60, Washington DC: Smithsonian Press.

Newton, Stella Mary (1980) *Fashion in the Age of the Black Prince*, Woodbridge UK: Boydell Press.

O'Connor, Kaori (2005) 'The other half: The material culture of new fibres', in Susanne Kuchler and Daniel Miller (eds), *Clothing as Material Culture*, United States and Canada, Oxford: Berg Publishers, pp. 41–59.

Olian, Jo Anne (1977) 'Sixteenth-century costume books', *Dress*, 3: 20–48.

O'Mahony, Marie and Braddock, Sarah E (2002) *Sportstech: Revolutionary fabrics, fashion and design*, New York: Thames & Hudson.

Pacey, Arnold (1990) *Technology in World Civilization: A thousand year history*, Cambridge MA: The MIT Press.

Palliser, Bury (1971) *A History of Lace*, 3rd edition, Detroit MI: Tower Books.

Phillips, Clare (1996) *Jewelry: From Antiquity to the present*, London: Thames & Hudson.

Polhemus, Ted (1994) *Street Style*, New York: Thames & Hudson.

Pritchard, Frances (2003) 'The uses of textiles, c. 1000–1500', in David Jenkins (ed.), *The Cambridge History of Western Textiles*, vol. I, Cambridge: Cambridge University Press.

Quinn, Bradley (2002) *Techno Fashion*, United States and Canada, Oxford: Berg Publishers.

Quinn, Bradley (2010) *Textile Futures: Fashion, design, and technology*, United States and Canada, Oxford: Berg Publishers.

Quinn, Bradley (2012) *Fashion Futures: Fashion, design, and technology*, London, New York: Merrell.

Rabine, Leslie (2005) 'Globalization', in Valerie Steele (ed.), *Encyclopedia of Clothing and Fashion*, vol. 2, New York: Charles Scribner's Sons, pp. 143–5.

Reilly, Valerie (1987) *The Paisley Pattern: The official illustrated history*, Salt Lake City UT: Peregrine Smith Books.

Rexford, Nancy E (2000) *Women's Shoes in America, 1795–1930*, Kent OH and London: Kent State University Press.

Ribeiro, Aileen (2002) *Dress in Eighteenth Century Europe, 1715–1789*, New Haven CT: Yale University Press.

Ricci, Stefana (2006) 'Made in Italy: Salvatore Ferragamo and twentieth-century fashion', in Giorgio Riello and Peter McNeil (eds), *Shoes: A history from sandals to sneakers*, New York: Berg Bloomsbury, pp. 306–30.

Riello, Giorgio and McNeil, Peter (eds) (2011) *Shoes: A history from sandals to sneakers*, New York: Berg Bloomsbury.

Rivoli, Pietra (2005) *The Travels of a T-Shirt in the Global Economy*, Hoboken NJ: John Wiley & Sons Inc.

Rocamora, Agnès (2013) 'New Fashion Times: Fashion and digital media', in *The Handbook of Fashion Studies*, London: Bloomsbury.

Rothstein, Natalie (2003a) 'Silk: The Industrial Revolution and after', in David Jenkins (ed.), *The Cambridge History of Western Textiles*, vol. 1, Cambridge: Cambridge University Press, p. 793.

Rothstein, Natalie (2003b) 'Silk in the Early Modern Period: c. 1500–1780', in David Jenkins (ed.). *The Cambridge History of Western Textiles*, vol. 1, Cambridge: Cambridge University Press, pp. 528–61.

San Martin, Macarena (2010) *Future Fashion*, Barcelona: Promopress.

Scarre, Chris (ed.) (1993) *Smithsonian Timelines of the Ancient World*, New York: Dorling Kindersley Books.

Scarre, Chris (ed.) (2005) *The World Transformed: From foragers and farmers to states and empires. The Human Past: World prehistory and the development of human societies*, London: Thames & Hudson, pp. 1–4.

Schafer, Edward H (1963) *The Golden Peaches of Samarkand*, Berkeley CA: University of California Press.

Schimmel, Anne Marie (2000) *The Empire of the Great Mughals: History, art and culture*, London: Beakton Books.

Schlereth, Thomas J (1991) *Victorian America: Transformations in everyday life, 1876–1915*, New York: Harper Collins Publishers.

Schoeser, Mary (2003) *World Textiles: A concise history*, London: Thames & Hudson.

Schorman, Rob (2010) 'The garment industry and retailing in the United States', in Joanne Eicher (ed.), *Berg Encyclopedia of World Dress and Fashion*, vol. 3, United States and Canada, Oxford: Berg Publishers, pp. 87–96.

Schulberg, Lucille (1968) *Historic India*, New York: Time Inc.

Sebesta, Judith Lynn and Bonfante, Larissa (eds) (1994) *The World of Roman Costume*, Madison WI: University of Wisconsin Press.

Seymour, Sabine (2009) *Fashionable Technology*, New York: Springer Wien.

Seymour, Sabine (2010) *Functional Aesthetics: Visions in fashionable technology*, New York: Springer Wein.

Smith, Bradley and Wen, Wan-go (1973) *China: A History in Art*, New York: Harper & Row.

Soffer, O J M, Adovasio, J M, and Hyland, D C (2000) 'Venus figurines', *Current Anthropology*, 41(4): 511–37.

Sokolowski, Susan (2010) 'Dress for recreational sports and professional sports', in Joanne Eicher (ed.), *Berg Encyclopedia of World Dress and Fashion*, vol. 3, United States and Canada, Oxford: Berg Publishers, pp. 322–8.

Spindler, Konrad (1994) *The Man in the Ice*, New York: Harmony Books.

Steele, Valerie and Major, John (1999) *China Chic: East meets West*, New Haven CT and London: Yale University Press.

Steger, Manfred B (2009) *Globalization: A very short introduction*, Oxford: Oxford University Press.

Stott, Carole (1997) *Space Exploration*, London: Dorling Kindersley.

Sullivan, Margaret (2013) 'Tattoo removal on the photo desk', *New York Times*, May 18.

Swan, June (1982) 'Shoes', in Aileen Ribeiro (ed.), *Shoes*, London: B T Batsford Ltd.

Temple, Robert (1986) *The Genius of China: 3000 years of science, discovery and invention*, New York: Simon & Schuster, pp. 82–3, 120.

Thirsk, Joan (2003) 'Knitting and Knitwear c. 1500–1780', in David Jenkins (ed.), *The Cambridge History of Western Textiles*, vol. I, Cambridge: Cambridge University Press, pp. 562–84.

Thompson, F M L (1988) *The Rise of Respectable Society: A social history of Victorian Britain 1830–1900*, Cambridge MA: Harvard University Press.

Tortora, Phyllis (1972) 'The evolution of the American fashion magazine as exemplified in selected fashion journals: 1830–1969', Unpublished Doctoral Dissertation, New York University.

Tortora, Phyllis and Merkel, Robert (1996) *Fairchild's Dictionary of Textiles*, 7th edition, New York: Fairchild Publications Inc, p. 214.

Tortora, Phyllis and Eubank, Keith (2010) *Survey of Historic Costume*, New York: Fairchild Publications Inc.

Vainker, Shelagh (2004) *Chinese Silk: A cultural history*, New Brunswick NJ: Rutgers University Press.

van Buren, Anne H (2011) *Illuminating Fashion: Dress in the art of Medieval France and the Netherlands: 1325–1515*, New York: The Morgan Library.

Van Der Wee, Herman and Munro, John (2003) 'The Western European woolen industries, 1500–1700', in David Jenkins (ed.), *The Cambridge History of Western Textiles*, vol. I, Cambridge: Cambridge University Press' pp. 397–492.

Veblen, Thorstein (1899) *The Theory of the Leisure Class*, New York: Macmillan & Co.

Vincent, Susan J (2009) *The Anatomy of Fashion: Dressing the body from the Renaissance to today*, United States and Canada, Oxford: Berg Publishers.

Vogelsang-Eastwood, Gillian (2003) 'The Arabs, AD 600 to 1000', in David Jenkins (ed.), *Cambridge History of Western Textiles*, Cambridge: Cambridge University Press, pp. 158–65, 493.

Volti, Rudi (2004) *Cars and Culture: The life story of a technology*, Baltimore MD: Johns Hopkins University Press.

Waateringe, W, Groenman-Van, M, and Van Londen, Filian H (1999) 'Curing of hides and skins in prehistory', *Antiquity*, 1(73): 884–90.

Warner, Patricia Campbell (2006) 'When the Girls Came Out to Play: *The Birth of American Sportswear*, Amherst and Boston: University of Massachusetts Press.

Warner, Patricia Campbell (2010) 'Film', in Joanne Eicher (ed.), *Berg Encyclopedia of World Dress and Fashion*, vol. 3, United States and Canada, Oxford: Berg Publishers, pp. 267–72.

Watkins, Susan M (1995) 'Clothing: The portable environment', in *The Design Process*, Ames IA: Iowa State University Press.

Watkins, Susan M (2010) 'Functional dress', in Joanne Eicher (ed.), *Berg Encyclopedia of World Dress and Fashion*, vol. 3, United States and Canada, Oxford: Berg Publishers, pp. 241–8.

Watstein, Sarah Barbara and Czarnecki, Kelly (2010) 'Virtual worlds, dress, and fashion', in Joanne Eicher (ed.), *Berg Encyclopedia of World Dress and Fashion: Global perspectives*, vol. 10, pp. 276–82, vol. 3, United States and Canada, Oxford: Berg Publishers, p. 240.

Weibel, Adele Coulin (1972) *Two Thousand Years of Textiles*, New York: Hacker Art Books.

White, Randall (1986) *Dark Caves, Bright Visions: Life in Ice Age Europe*, New York: American Museum of Natural History in association with W W Norton & Co Inc.

White, Randall (2007) 'Systems of personal ornamentation in the Early Upper Paleolithic: Methodological challenges and new observations', in Paul Mellars, Katie Boyle, Ofer Bar-Yosef, and Chris Stringer (eds), *Rethinking the Human Revolution: New behavioural and biological perspectives on the origin and dispersal of modern humans*, Cambridge: McDonald Institute for Archaeological Research, pp. 287–302.

Whitehouse, Ruth (1994) 'Early farming communities in Europe', in Desmond Collins, (ed.), 1976, *The Origins of Europe*, New York: Thomas Crowell, pp. 143–68.

Whittle, Alasdair (1994) 'The first farmers', in Barry Cunliffe (ed.), *Oxford Illustrated History of Prehistoric Europe*, New York: Oxford University Press.

Wild, Anthony (1999) *The East India Company: Trade and conquest from 1600*, New York: Harper Collins Publishers.

Wild, John Peter (2003) 'Anatolia, Mesopotamia and the Levant in the Bronze Age, c. 3500–1100 BCE', in David Jenkins (ed.), *The Cambridge History of Western Textiles*, vol. 1, Cambridge: Cambridge University Press, pp. 43–6.

Williams, Trevor and Schaaf, William E Jr. (2000) *A History of Invention: From stone axes to silicon chips*, UK: Little Brown and Company.

Winchester, Simon (2008) *Appendix: The man who loved China*, New York: Harper Collins Publishers.

Winchester, Simon (2009) *Atlantic*, New York: Harper Collins Publishers.

Wood, Frances (2002) *The Silk Road: 2000 years in the heart of Asia*, Berkeley CA: University of California Press.

Wood, Michael (2007) Writer and presenter of television series: *The Story of India*.

Wosk, Julie (2001) *Women and the Machine: Representation from the spinning wheel to the electronic age*, Baltimore MD and London: Johns Hopkins University Press.

Yafa, Stephen (2006) *Big Cotton*, New York: Viking Penguin.

Yarwood, Doreen (1988) *Illustrated Encyclopedia of World Costume*, London: B T Batsford.

Zhou, Xun and Hunming, Gao (1984) *5000 Years of Chinese Costumes*, Hong Kong: Commercial Press, p. 76.

Electronic references

A Brief History of Heating and Cooling America's Homes, posted: October 26, 2007, *http://sunhomedesign.wordpress.com/2007/10/26/a-brief-history-of-heating-and-cooling-americas-homes/* [accessed: March 15, 2014]

BBC Sport Olympics Fina extends Swimsuit Regulations, *http://news.bbc.co.uk/sport2/hi/olympic_games/7944084.stm* Page last updated at 11:40 GMT, Thursday, March 19, 2009 [accessed: September 31, 2013]

Carlson, I Marc (1995) Footwear of the Middle Ages, November 11, 1995 (Electronic Version 8.3 *www.personal.utulsa.edu/~marc-carlson/shoe/SHOEHOME.HTM* posted: October 26, 2001 [accessed: January 17, 2014]

Cultural China *http://kaleidoscope.cultural-china.com/en/10Kaleidoscope2918.html* The
   Drawloom, ©2007–2011, *cultural-china.com*. All rights reserved [accessed: March
   14, 2014]
Diliberto, Gioia (2009) Flights of Fashion: How Amelia Earhart became America's First
   Celebrity Designer, *http://www.huffingtonpost.com/users/becomeFan.php?of=hp_
   blogger_Gioia Diliberto http://www.huffingtonpost.com/author/index.
   php?author=gioia-diliberto http://www.huffingtonpost.com/users/login/* posted:
   October 23, 2009, 8:08 am [accessed March 13, 2014]
Greenspun, Phillip (1999) History of Photography Timeline, June 1999 (updated January
   2007) *http://photo.net/learn/history/timeline* [accessed: March 14, 2014]
Harris, Richard (2011) These Vintage Threads are 30,000 years Old. *http://www.npr.org/
   templates/story/story.php?storyId=112728804* [accessed: February 25, 2011]
Harwood, Anne (2008) Male Garments in Mughal-Era India c. 1574 for the Scholars of St
   Thomas Aquinas, 2008 *http://www.aharwood.ca/personae/costuming.htm*
   [accessed: January 26, 2014]
Hawks, Chuck (2013) Tips for the Motorcycle Passenger (Or How To Get Invited To Go
   Riding Again), *networking http://www.internetsociety.org/internet/what-internet/
   history-internet/brief-history-internet* [accessed: December 31, 2013] *http://www.
   chuckhawks.com/motorcycle_passenger_tips.htm* [accessed: November 26, 2014]
History: The Schiffli Lace and Embroidery Manufacturers *www.schiffli.org/history.htm*
   [accessed: February 9, 2014]
*http://americacomesalive.com/newsletter-archive/early-air-travel-the-friendly-skies-
   november-2009/* [accessed: November 26, 2014]
http://www.departures.com/travel/travel/high-style-flight-attendant-uniforms Schumaker,
   Erin. High Style Flight Attendant Uniforms [accessed: November 26, 2014]
http://www.coldesi.com/learning-center/learn-about-embroidery/history-of- [accessed:
   March 14, 2014]
http://humanorigins.si.edu by the Smithsonian's Human Origins Program [accessed:
   March 14, 2014]
http://www.trendytennis.com/2011/02/gaultier-tennis-collection-spring.html [accessed:
   September 30, 2013]
NASA, Aerogel from Space to Fashion *http://spinoff.nasa.gov/Spinoff2010/cg_2.html*
   [accessed: November 26, 2104]
Otzi-Museum, The Ice Man. South Tyrol Museum of Archeology, The Ice Man's Clothing
   and equipment *http://www.iceman.it/en/clothing-equipment* [accessed: January 18,
   2014]
Parry, Karima, Plastic Fantastic Specializing in Bakelite, Celluloid, Lucite, and other
   vintage plastic costume jewelry from the 1920s to the 1960s (*http://www.
   plasticfantastic.com/about.html*) [accessed: March 14, 2014]
Sedivy, Mr, The Clothing of the Ice Man, Highlands Ranch High School, Highlands
   Ranch, Colorado, *http://mr_sedivy.tripod.com/iceman4.html an4.html* [accessed:
   January 18, 2014)
The Tennis Racquet, *http://wings.avkids.com/Tennis/Book/racquet-01.html* [accessed:
   January 10, 2012]

INDEX

Numbers in italics indicate images or data located in tables